Foundations of IT Service Management

with ITIL® 2011

Brady Orand

2nd Edition PUBLISHED BY

ITILyaBrady

www.ITILyaBrady.com

Copyright © 2013 by Brady Orand

ISBN 1466231327

EAN-13 978-1466231320

PREFACE

When ITIL® version 3 (now referred to as ITIL® 2007) was released in 2007, millions of people were introduced to the concepts of the service lifecycle. This latest version, ITIL® 2011, released in August of 2011, further expands our knowledge of the service lifecycle as we learned more about service management. ITIL® itself espouses the concept of continual improvement for services and the processes that support the services. ITIL® itself is another component of our services to be continually improved as it is the source of knowledge that provides us with the guidance in which to manage our services, develop our processes, and build the capabilities that we need to truly add value to the business.

This latest edition of "Foundations of IT Service Management with ITIL® 2011" is based on the improvements made in ITIL® 2011. This book follows the latest syllabus to provide you, the reader, with the latest information to help you in your service management endeavors. This book, however, is not intended to replace the ITIL® core volumes as these volumes contain a wealth of knowledge over five volumes and thousands of pages. That much information cannot be condensed into a book of this size. It is the intent of this book to bring you the basic, foundation-level knowledge of the concepts of IT service management contained within ITIL® 2011.

One of the questions people often ask about ITIL® 2011 is "What's new in the new version of ITIL?" Interestingly enough, there's not a whole lot that is new in ITIL® 2011. The new version of ITIL® adds clarity to the previous version as well as formalizes familiar concepts and guidance present in ITIL® 2007.

One big improvement is the volume on service strategy. Service strategy has been almost totally rewritten in order to make it more fluid, allowing it to be read much easier. This gives readers the opportunity to really understand many of the complexities of developing a strategy for services as well as for us, the instructors, the ability to teach these concepts much more readily. Also included in service strategy is the introduction of a new process, business relationship management. While this is a new process for ITIL, the concept of business relationship management is not new.

Another new process that is been added is design coordination in service design. While design coordination is not necessarily a new concept, it has been given the focus it deserves by formalizing the process. Other improvements to the core volumes include adding more detail to many of the other processes. This guidance helps us to improve our understanding of the processes based on the experiences others have learned through the adoption of these processes.

Writing a book, even if it is "just" an update, is a significant undertaking. We've gone to great lengths to make sure that we provide the most current and most accurate information within these pages. However there's bound to be an error or two. If you find errors or would like to share your critique, please feel free to contact me as it is the feedback that I get from readers that helps me improve over time.

This edition of the book is the result of such feedback. As the author, I take this feedback seriously and strive to improve the book over time. I would like to thank Ala Halaseh, Lee Rider, Dan Ciorciari, Paul Fenstermacher, and Frank Van Alstine for their feedback. In particular, I appreciate the work of Etienne Thilliez for going through the book line by line and offering suggestions. This was no small undertaking on his part.

Brady Orand
Brady@ITILyaBrady.com
April 18, 2013

ABOUT THIS BOOK

This book was written to prepare you for your ITIL® Foundation exam. Through the chapters of this book, you will be introduced to the service lifecycle and the processes described within each of the service lifecycle stages. More importantly, you will learn how these processes work together to provide IT services.

In addition to this book, there are many resources available online to assist you with your exam preparation. Some of the resources you may find valuable can be found on my website at www.ITILyaBrady.com. At the time of this writing, there are study guides, audio reviews, sample exam questions and study material checklists.

Chapters in this book are organized around the major topics present in the syllabus provided by APM Group (APMG), the organization responsible for the ITIL® certification syllabi. This syllabus is also available on the website.

Even though this book is designed around the syllabus published by APMG, my desire through this course is not only to prepare you for the ITIL® Foundations certification exam, but also to provide insight into how ITIL® may improve your IT organization. While many courses and books exist to convey material to you simply to help you pass the exam, I want to ensure that you improve and change the way you look at IT.

However, I also understand that the primary desire of the reader is probably to pass the ITIL® Foundations exam. While almost everything in this course is candidate for exam questions, there are certain key things that are far more likely to be on the exam. These items are focused on in the chapter review sections at the end of each chapter.

ABOUT THE AUTHOR

I have been an ITIL® instructor since 2005. Even though I had worked in the IT field for close to two and a half decades, I did not truly understand IT until my first exposure to ITIL® three years earlier through my ITIL® Foundations course. Ever since then, I have been pursuing my ITIL® education to be the best instructor that I can possibly be. Along this path, I have obtained many of the ITIL® v2 certifications, including the Service Manager certification as well as all the certifications for ITIL® v3 (and now ITIL® 2011)

I started my corporate career as an intern at a microchip company you may have heard of, called Intel®. My job there was to develop parts of a software product for Novell® networks. Even though this was the early 1990s, I still run across some people who continue use the products that I helped create.

I then went on to a company that focuses solely on software, BMC Software®, where I was responsible for a line of integration products that integrated BMC's products with other vendor products. This is where I really started learning the complexities of managing the IT infrastructure. This is also where I started my consulting and training career.

After BMC, my career led to a big-five consulting firm where I learned what "big projects" really are. As part of a 1,000-person project, I had the opportunity to learn more about the operational aspects of IT and how critical effective processes are to the success of such a large organization. I often look back on this experience and think about how we did things that were right, how we did things that were wrong and how both of these are addressed by ITIL®.

My first true teaching opportunity came when I then joined a smaller consulting company based outside of Chicago. As the ITIL® Practice Manager, my job was to create offerings around the concepts of IT service management. The majority of my time was spent building training offerings and delivering this training. This is where I found that I truly enjoyed delivering training. However, the travel wasn't as much fun as it used to be.

I now work independently as a trainer, training course provider and consultant. I deliver training on behalf several companies, but the travel is much more tolerable. This also gives me the opportunity to pursue many of my own interests, such as study guides, exam preparation material, white papers, and other pursuits.

In my courses, I combine the book learning with practical experience from the many varied roles that I have had in my career. In this book, I have attempted to reflect this style on paper.

Contents

1

GETTING STARTED

INTRODUCTION

This book introduces you to the concepts of IT service management based on ITIL®. In my many years of providing ITIL® training, the one thing that remains constant is that every individual has a different learning style. Some people prefer reading, while others prefer live or video presentations. In all cases, however, I have found that almost everyone responds well to analogies.

Through these analogies, this book is intended for all types of readers. Whether you are in a live class with an instructor, an online class with presentations, or learning on your own, this "Foundations of IT service management" is for you. This book includes many tips to remember for the exam as well as a set of questions at the end of every section. Also included is a set of comprehension questions to help you internalize the material and get the fullest comprehension possible. My sample answers to these comprehension questions are on my web site www.ITILyaBrady.com. Please make use of any resources on the site to assist you in your IT service management endeavors.

In this book, the restaurant business is used as analogy through the introduction of a fictitious entrepreneur, Geppetto Garcia, and his company. Geppetto's restaurant can teach us a lot about the concepts of service. After all, restaurants with poor service don't last long. After exploring Geppetto's startup problems and the lessons he learned from them, we will explore how Geppetto Garcia's integrated the concepts of service into the corporation's IT department.

Through this exploration, the concepts of IT service management are explored and applied to Geppetto Garcia's through a case study. I hope you find this exploration useful and that it assists with your retention of the information in the following pages.

GEPPETTO GARCIA'S

Geppetto Garcia, a multi-cultural, American-born son of second-generation immigrants, grew up working in his cousin's restaurant for years. Geppetto's desire to cook was immense. His dream was always to have a restaurant of his own. He longed for a restaurant that would cater to every customer's desires and to serve meals to please any appetite.

At the age of 28 and after investing all of his life savings, Geppetto opened his first restaurant, named Geppetto Garcia's. Geppetto's 25-table restaurant opened in a prime location to serve both the lunchtime business crowd, as well as the before- and after-theater diners. Geppetto's restaurant employed a kitchen staff of three full-time employees, four wait staff, and four part-time helpers to bus tables and wash dishes.

Opening day was slow. Geppetto wanted to see how the walk-in traffic was before he started advertising. His first customer, a lone businessman at lunch, walked in between meetings. Geppetto met the gentleman at the door and promptly seated him.

"What can I get you?" asked Geppetto.

"What do you have?" asked the businessman.

"Whatever your heart desires, I'll make it for you!" Geppetto's responded.

"Hmmm," said the businessman. "I've been thinking about my Czech grandmother's goulash lately. She used to make it for me when I was a kid."

"You got it!" replied Geppetto.

Geppetto promptly entered the kitchen to make his first customer the finest Czech goulash he could. However, Geppetto had never made goulash before, and he had to look it up in his recipe book. Unfortunately, he did not have a recipe book that had goulash in it. Turning to the Internet, he quickly looked up "Czech Goulash" and found the following recipe:

Czech Goulash

¼ cup shortening

2 cloves garlic, minced

1 ½ pounds cubed beef

1 medium onion, chopped

¼ teaspoon sweet paprika

½ teaspoon caraway seeds

Salt and pepper to taste

2 cups water

2 tablespoons flour

In a cast iron Dutch oven, sauté onion in shortening. Add garlic and sauté until translucent. Add meat, onion, paprika, caraway seeds, salt and pepper. Brown well.

Add ½ cup of the water and simmer, covered, until meat is tender, about 1 hour.

Sprinkle flour over drippings in the pan and stir until brown. Add remaining water. Simmer 10 to 20 minutes.

Serve over cooked egg noodles.

Serves 6-8[1]

1   Source: Recipe Gold Mine at www.recipegoldmine.com

Geppetto was excited. He had all of these ingredients except the sweet paprika. All he had was regular paprika, but the recipe called for sweet paprika. Geppetto left the recipe for his kitchen staff to start and went to the gourmet grocer to procure some sweet paprika.

Thirty minutes later when Geppetto returned, the goulash was ready for the paprika. Once the ¼ teaspoon of sweet paprika was added, Geppetto went to the dining room to check on his customer.

Noticing that the businessman was drumming his fingers impatiently, Geppetto approached the gentleman.

"Your goulash is being prepared," said Geppetto.

"Sounds great, but I have a meeting in 30 minutes so I must leave very soon," said the gentleman.

"I'll see what I can do to speed it up!" responded Geppetto.

Geppetto then returned to the kitchen.

"Cook faster!" he yelled at the kitchen staff.

Geppetto then turned up the heat (both literally and figuratively) to get the goulash to cook faster.

Just over an hour later, the goulash was ready. Geppetto spooned the goulash on a plate over some egg noodles, garnished it with parsley, and headed to the dining room. Upon entering the dining room, Geppetto walked in only to find an empty table where the businessman had been.

For the next week, Geppetto experienced similar situations over and over again. In his quest to provide whatever meal the customer requested, he could very rarely prepare the dish the customers asked for before they became frustrated and left. Geppetto was left with fully cooked Chateaubriand, Buffalo burgers, grilled duck, and lamb chops. While he and his kitchen staff were preparing fantastic dishes, there was no way they could cook just anything to order.

The first week was miserable for Geppetto. The kitchen staff was threatening to quit trying to please everyone by making so many different dishes. The wait staff was looking for other positions because customers were not leaving tips. But who would? To make things worse, the food that Geppetto was purchasing was going bad because he would buy in bulk to save money only to use a small part of it while the rest went unused. Geppetto was spending a lot of money to pay salaries, rent and debts, not to mention the costs for the food suppliers. He was running his business at a significant loss.

Geppetto quickly realized that he could not be everything to everyone. First, he needed to determine his menu. Ideally, his menu would consist of meals that would minimize the variety of supplies he would require – thus limiting food that would spoil before it was used.

His meal selection would also have to be within the limits of his kitchen staff. The meals should be prepared through a series of well-defined steps, thus simplifying the preparation. This would also result in the meals being predictable and consistent.

Geppetto also realized that he had a lot of talent and creativity in the kitchen staff. He decided that he would involve his kitchen staff in these decisions and take advantage of their capabilities. His kitchen staff also represented diverse backgrounds: Mediterranean, Asian and South American. Together they decided to select recipes from different continents and countries and provide a menu representing meals from around the world.

Therefore, Geppetto developed the following criteria for meals that he would serve:

Meals would be prepared from fresh ingredients

Meals would be prepared from ingredients that could be used in other meals or ingredients with a longer shelf life (such as dried spices, frozen foods and dried staples)

Meals would represent specialties from each culture and country

Meals would be repeatable, consistent and prepared as much as possible prior to the lunch and dinner rush

Meals would be moderately priced for customers, providing a balance between quality, cost, speed and ambiance

Geppetto scoured his recipe books and the Internet for recipes that met these criteria. From the thousands of recipes that Geppetto found, he and his team found many that met these criteria or could be modified to meet these criteria. Geppetto and his team selected 44 recipes that met the criteria and also met the needs of his target customers. These recipes provided everything they needed to prepare entrees and desserts. Geppetto also had his grandmother's Pasta Primavera recipe that he added to the list, making the total number of items that would go on his menu 45.

Geppetto then enlisted the wait staff to help design the menu. When designing the menu, they included a section for entrees and desserts. They quickly realized that appetizers, soups and salads were missing. Using the ingredients included in the previously selected recipes, Geppetto and his team developed appetizers, soups and salads that could be quickly prepared and added these to the menu.

Based on this menu, Geppetto worked with his kitchen staff to prepare these meals by creating processes that could be reused or modified for the specific menu. While his kitchen staff had some issues at first, they quickly learned to create these meals on demand by establishing specific processes and procedures to prepare the meals. Helping to achieve these efficiencies and improved delivery of meals was preparing parts of the meals beforehand. The more the team could get done prior to the lunch and dinner rush, the better prepared they were when the restaurant became busy.

Geppetto also worked with his wait staff to develop processes and procedures for handling customers, including timely seating, taking orders, and handling special requests. Just as his kitchen staff realized, the more they could get done prior to the busy times, the easier it was to provide great service.

Within a very short period, Geppetto Garcia's became very popular with his target market of business professionals at lunch and the theater crowd in the evenings. Once the word got out, Geppetto Garcia's became popular with the weekend brunch and late lunch diners as well.

Over time, Geppetto Garcia owned one of the most popular restaurants in the region and began to expand to other cities. Geppetto realized that the business was bigger than he thought and began opening specialty restaurants that focused on expanded menus of specific regional cuisines. These restaurants include Garcia's Cantina serving Mexican fare, GG's Steak House with a mid-range menu around steaks and chops, GG's Smokehouse focusing on Southern-style barbecue, Geppetto's Italian featuring entrees from the various regions of Italy, and Geppetto's Sports Bar with a full bar and a pub-style menu. A new endeavor for Geppetto Garcia's is GG's American Grill, a high-end dining experience that caters to the most discriminating diner. This restaurant even features the Czech Goulash recipe – the first meal that he prepared for a customer!

Geppetto Garcia's grew so big that a corporate office was established and within six years, the company went public, offering stock that was traded on the NASDAQ with the stock symbol GPTO. This enabled Geppetto to open 212 restaurants throughout the United States with plans to expand to areas outside the United States.

Geppetto learned a lot from his experience running a restaurant. He learned that it is impossible to be able to provide everything that someone could ask for, but instead it's best to focus on things that customers need. This permits focus on specific activities that can be standardized to create consistency. He also realized that communication with customers is critical. This communication is performed in many ways – by greeting customers upon arrival, through menus, asking how their meal is, and ensuring they are satisfied when they leave, and also through e-mail and Web surveys to ensure their needs are being met.

Geppetto's new corporation needed to keep these lessons in mind. Even though running a company is very different than running a single restaurant, most of the basics remain the same. Therefore, Geppetto will ensure that all aspects of the corporation will adopt these basic principles and look for ways to improve services to customers and ensure that these services balance cost and quality with the customers' needs.

THE GROWTH OF GEPPETTO GARCIA'S

Geppetto is a restaurateur at heart. Restaurants are what he knows best. As the business grew, and the corporation evolved, Geppetto hired people with specialized skills and knowledge to handle specific areas of the business. One of these areas was Information Technology (IT). Geppetto could barely send an e-mail, but it didn't stop him from running a successful business. To fill the need for an IT leader, Geppetto found Mark Renner, a man who understood both IT and customer service.

Mark Renner, the new Chief Information Officer, recognized the need for IT to be focused on satisfying the customers of IT. Just like when Geppetto researched recipes, Mark searched for best practices in providing IT services. Mark discovered the IT Infrastructure Library®.

RESTAURANTS AND IT

If the above fictional accounting of Geppetto and his restaurant seems outrageous, it is. No restaurant that I know of would dream of opening its doors without having some form of menu or offering to its customers. Restaurants cannot attempt to provide any requested meal on demand like that. It is impossible to create every possible meal on demand and be able to meet the customer's needs.

Restaurants are often low-margin businesses due to intense competition. They make very little profit from an individual meal. They must therefore make their profit through larger-volume business in order to survive. To provide higher volume, restaurants must be as effective and efficient as possible. This is done by attracting customers to their offerings, as well as developing and establishing processes that are definable, repeatable, consistent, and measurable, so they can be improved.

If restaurants realize this, then why doesn't IT? Many of the IT organizations that I have visited attempt to be everything to everyone. They operate without a menu, have very little defined processes and only communicate with their customers when they have to through ill-defined channels. This is made even more difficult since many of them can't identify who their customers are!

IT can learn a lot from Geppetto and his experience with building a corporation from a single restaurant. In this book, we are going to explore the IT Infrastructure Library® and how Geppetto would approach many of these concepts based on his common-sense approach. This exploration will assist you, the reader, in preparing for your ITIL® Foundation exam, formally known as the Foundation Certificate in IT service management.

GEPPETTO GARCIA'S NEW SERVICES

Emil Delgassi, Geppetto Garcia's Chief Operating Officer, recognized that restaurant customers want to share their enjoyment of the various Geppetto Garcia restaurants with their friends and family. One of the ways in which they want to do this is to introduce gift cards. Gift cards have become very popular over the years and are now sold not only at the business itself, but also at other retail stores, including grocery stores, department stores and drug stores.

Emil's idea involves the creation of gift cards that are customized for each of the restaurant brands. However, not all restaurant brands will choose to have gift cards, so it must first be determined which restaurants will participate in the gift card idea.

Another idea that Emil has seen work with other restaurants is "car-side" service. Car-side service targets those customers who desire a meal from one of the many restaurants in the Geppetto Garcia family but who do not have time to dine inside the restaurant. This take-out service involves customers calling the restaurant or ordering online and then coming to pick up their meal at the time indicated when the order was placed.

During our exploration of ITIL®, we will see how these new services take advantage of the concepts within ITIL® to ensure that they are targeted toward the right customers, designed well, transitioned into operation with a minimum of risk, and can be operated as efficiently and effectively as possible.

OBJECTIVES OF THIS BOOK

This book will help you prepare for the ITIL® Foundations exam. In addition, you should complete this book with a better understanding of ITIL®, the service lifecycle, and the processes within each of the service lifecycle stages.

To help you study for the ITIL® Foundations exam, there is certain information in this course that you should know. ITIL® describes the service lifecycle. The service lifecycle has five distinct stages: service strategy, service design, service transition, service operation, and continual service improvement. Each of these stages has the following:

Inputs and outputs

Describes the relationship between this stage and others

Principles and key concepts

Describes the purpose and approach to the stage of the service lifecycle

Processes and Functions

Describes the processes that are inherent within each stage of the service lifecycle. The processes within continual service improvement are not within the scope of the ITIL® Foundation exam and, subsequently, will not be discussed.

Functions are described in the service operation stage of the service lifecycle.

In addition, each process within the service lifecycle stage has its own goals and objectives, key concepts, activities, key performance indicators (KPIs), critical success factors (CSFs), and challenges. As you will see, some processes require more focus than others while discussing each of these topics. Other processes are not presented in as much detail, but still convey the objectives and key concepts for the process. At a minimum, you should know the purpose of the process, key concepts, and the way the process interacts with other processes. Certain processes require additional knowledge for the exam.

CERTIFICATION REQUIREMENTS

The ITIL® Foundations certification exam is required in order to obtain the Foundations in service management certificate. This certification is the first in a progressively advancing series of certifications available in IT service management.

In order to obtain the Foundations-level certification, you must successfully pass the Foundations certification exam. This exam is a one-hour, 40-question, multiple choice exam, where guesses are not penalized. In other words, don't leave any answers blank.

In order to pass the exam, you must get 26 or more questions correct. This represents a 65% grade on the exam. Numerical exam results are not publicized, only an overall pass or fail result. A 65% is just as good as a 95%; both lead to certification.

There are several routes you can pursue to take the exam. The examination providers that I recommend are Thompson Prometric and Pearson VUE. Both of these providers specialize in conducting on-demand certification exams. I have taken Microsoft® certification exams from them, as well as Project Management (PMI®) certification exams, and the process to take an exam is fairly straightforward.

You can contact Thompson Prometric at www.prometric.com and Pearson VUE at www.vue.com for more information on taking the ITIL® exam.

Skills in Service Management

Delivering service successfully depends on personnel involved in service management having the appropriate education, training, skills and experience. These skills require updating when changes occur within the environment. The specific roles within ITIL® service management all require specific skills, attributes and competencies from the people involved to enable them to work efficiently and effectively. However, whatever the role, it is imperative that the person carrying out that role has the following attributes:

> "Awareness of the business priorities, objectives and business drivers
>
> Awareness of the role IT plays in enabling the business objectives to be met
>
> Customer service skills
>
> Awareness of what IT can deliver to the business, including latest capabilities
>
> The competence, knowledge and information necessary to complete their role
>
> The ability to use, understand and interpret the best practice, policies and procedures to ensure adherence"[2]

Standardizing job titles, functions, roles and responsibilities can simplify service management and Human Resource Management. Many service providers use a common framework of reference for competence and skills to support activities such as skill audits, planning future skill requirements, organizational development programs and resource allocation.

The Skills Framework for the Information Age (SFIA) is an example of a common reference model for the identification of the skills needed to develop effective IT services, information systems and technology. More information on SFIA can be found at www.sfia.org.uk.[3]

---

2   Quoted text is from Service Design © Crown copyright 2011 Reproduced under license from the Cabinet Office

3   The Skills Framework for the Information Age is owned by the SFIA Foundation: www.SFIA.org. uk

QUALIFICATION SCHEME

Upon completion of the ITIL® Foundations certification exam, you are eligible to continue your IT service management education and to pursue further certifications. The ITIL® Foundations certification is a prerequisite for these intermediate courses.

There are two paths through education opportunities: the IT service lifecycle Stream and the IT Service Capability Modules. The service lifecycle Stream addresses each of the service lifecycle stages in five courses. The Capabilities Stream addresses specific concepts within the service lifecycle, regardless of the stage of the service lifecycle involved. These courses show that many of the activities and processes have involvement in more than one discrete service lifecycle stage.

Once the required number of courses is completed successfully in a given path, you have the opportunity to take the Managing Across the Lifecycle course. Successful completion of this course, along with the prerequisite credits, will earn you the ITIL® Expert Certification.

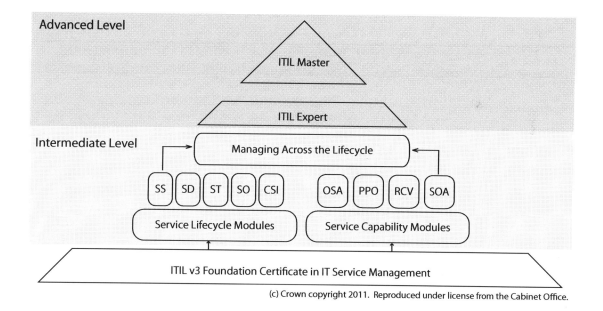

(c) Crown copyright 2011. Reproduced under license from the Cabinet Office.

Figure ITIL® Qualification Scheme

ITIL® SERVICE LIFECYCLE STREAM COURSES

Service Strategy

The service strategy course provides an in-depth understanding of the service strategy stage of the service lifecycle. In the service strategy course, students gain an understanding of the principles of service strategy: defining services and market spaces, conducting strategic assessments as well as defining the processes of Financial Management, Demand Management, and Service Portfolio Management.

- Benefits of establishing a strategic view to services within IT
- Principles of developing market spaces, defining services, and designing a service portfolio
- Determining and managing demand for services
- Conducting strategic assessments
- The specific service strategy processes of
    - Strategy Management for IT Services
    - Service Portfolio Management
    - Financial Management
    - Demand Management
    - Business Relationship Management

Service Design

The service design course provides an in-depth understanding of the service design stage of the service lifecycle. In the service design course, students gain an understanding of the principles of service design, service design activities, concepts, inputs and outputs.

- Benefits of proper design of services and changes to services
- Greater understanding of the activities involved in designing services in accordance with best practices
- Considerations for all aspects of services that must be designed
- The specific processes in service design of
    - Design Coordination
    - Service Level Management
    - Service Catalog Management
    - Capacity Management
    - Availability Management
    - IT Service Continuity Management
    - Information Security Management
    - Supplier Management

Service Transition

The service transition course provides an in-depth understanding of the service transition stage of the service lifecycle. In the service transition course, students gain an understanding of the principles of service transition, management and control of service transition activities, and service transition activities around communications, commitment and organizational change.

- Benefits of transitioning services into production environments
- Establishing control of components that make up services
- Managing and communicating organizational change
- Specific service transition processes of
  - Transition Planning and Support
  - Service Asset and Configuration Management
  - Evaluation
  - Service Validation and Testing
  - Change Management
  - Release and Deployment Management
  - Knowledge Management

Service Operation

The service operation course provides an in-depth understanding of the service operation stage of the service lifecycle. In the service operation course, students gain an understanding of the principles of service operation, its activities, concepts, inputs and outputs, and the functions included.

- Principles of effective and efficient service operation in accordance with best practices
- Organizing service operation
- Roles and responsibilities of the functions within service operation and how they contribute to all stages of the service lifecycle
- The processes within service operation of
  - Event Management
  - Incident Management
  - Request Fulfillment
  - Problem Management
  - Access Management

Continual Service Improvement

The continual service improvement course provides an in-depth understanding of the continual service improvement stage of the service lifecycle. In the continual service improvement course, students gain an understanding of the principles, methods and techniques of continual service improvement.

- How continual service improvement integrates within all service lifecycle stages
- Measurement and reporting of services
- Continual Service Improvement and Service Level Management
- The importance of properly defining metrics and measurements to support the organizational mission
- Return on Investment (ROI) concepts
- Various business questions for continual service improvement
- The 7-Step Improvement process

ITIL® SERVICE CAPABILITY STREAM

Service Offerings and Agreement (SO&A)

The Service Offerings and Agreements course provides the student with a deep understanding of the concepts associated with IT as a Service Provider. Within this course, the student will obtain knowledge relating to establishing and maintaining relationships between IT as a Service Provider and the business as a customer of the Service Provider. Starting with development of a Service Portfolio, the student will understand the structure of the documented services and agreements that record the roles and responsibilities of those who deliver and support services to the customer.

- Documenting services and requirements within the Service Portfolio
- Production and management of the Service Catalog
- The set of agreements that documents the roles and responsibilities of the various parties involved in providing services
- Production and maintenance of Service Level Agreements
- Using Demand Management to identify patterns of business activity
- Specific processes including
  - Service Portfolio Management
  - Service Catalog Management
  - Service Level Management
  - Demand Management
  - Supplier Management
  - Financial Management
  - Business Relationship Management

Operational Support and Analysis (OS&A)

The Operational Support and Analysis intermediate course teaches the student the key principles involved in effective operational support of services within the domain of the IT Service Provider. This course also teaches the roles and responsibilities required to provide efficient and effective operational support of services.

- Understanding of the processes and process activities involved in providing operational support and analysis of services
- Effective structures for organizing roles for operational support and analysis of services
- Operational activities of processes contained within non-operational service lifecycle stages
- Key processes within Operational Support and Analysis
  - Event Management
  - Request Fulfillment
  - Incident Management
  - Problem Management
  - Access Management

Planning, Protection and Optimization (PP&O)

The Planning, Protection and Optimization course immerses the student into the activities involved in planning services and changing services, protecting services and the business from outages and disasters, as well as ensuring the right levels of service availability, capacity, security and continuity are provided in a cost-effective manner. Through this course, students will learn the concepts and activities involved in planning and ensuring the quality of services and changes to those services.

- Elements involved with the practice of planning, protection and optimization of services
- Ensuring the capabilities to realize successful designs of services through managing capacity, availability, IT service continuity and information security
- Understanding the elements involved to support the overall Business Continuity Management efforts of the organization
- Understanding how information security plays a part in the overall corporate governance framework
- The roles and responsibilities involved in planning, protection and optimization of services and changes to services
- Specific processes involved in the planning, protection and optimization of services include:
  - Capacity Management
  - Availability Management
  - IT Service Continuity Management
  - Information Security Management
  - Demand Management

Release, Control and Validation (RCV)

The Release, Control and Validation course teaches students the concepts and activities present in the processes involved in the successful release, control and validation of services and changes to services before entering the production environment. This course is recommended for those who want to ensure successful transition of changes to service and organizational change within their environment.

- Processes across the service lifecycle pertaining to the capability of Release, Control and Validation of services and changes to services
- Ensuring successful service transition through managing and controlling change
- Assuring the integrity and quality of a service transition through proper service validation and testing
- Minimizing risk through periodic evaluation of transition activities and processes
- Assuring committed service level performance through fulfilling requests
- Roles and responsibilities involved in effective release, control and evaluation of transition activities
- Specific processes involved in Release, Control and Validation include:
  - Change Management
  - Release and Deployment Management
  - Service Validation and Testing
  - Service Asset and Configuration Management
  - Knowledge Management
  - Request Fulfillment
  - Service Evaluation

SERVICE MANAGEMENT AS A PRACTICE

OVERVIEW

Managing IT today involves far more than just managing the technology within IT. Businesses are demanding more from IT services. IT service management is a different perspective on managing IT. Instead of managing IT technology, IT service management involves organizing IT as a set of services that are aligned to the business needs.

By changing the way we view IT, from a technology provider to a service provider, we focus on the outcomes that are important to the business. This change in perspective simultaneously changes the culture within IT to become more professional and better aligned with the needs of the business.

ISSUES FACING IT

As IT has evolved over the years, it has become more than the enabling organization that it started to be. Today's IT organization is a critical component to just about every aspect of business. Unfortunately, IT as an organization suffers because managing technology the way it was done in the past is no longer sufficient. The stakes are far too high for the business to tolerate mistakes.

As technology has advanced and business use of technology has grown, IT has struggled to meet these new demands. In my experience, IT organizations struggle to keep the current environment operating to meet existing business needs, resulting in a purely reactive environment. This leaves little time or energy for the constant new requirements that arrive on a daily basis.

As a result, IT is constantly suffering from lack of appreciation for its hard work and efforts. The business fails to see the value that IT provides, and IT has a difficult time communicating this value. At the end of the year, the costs of IT are a focus that leads to budget cuts and head-count reduction, while at the same time, the requirement to provide better service increases.

The key issues for IT are that it is not able to improve because of the lack of time, proper measurements and, frankly, motivation. Projects that are conducted for the business are constantly being interrupted because of operational issues. When the resultant projects are late or deliver less than the required functionality, IT is always to blame. Thus, the existing IT organization suffers from a lack of motivation and under appreciation.

From the business perspective, IT does not provide what the business needs. This is largely due to the issue that the business fails to communicate its needs to IT and fails to involve IT in the planning. Without IT's involvement, the needs of the business are difficult to understand and, therefore, cannot be met.

The constant and continual advancement of technology results in the business wanting more and more from IT to support technology so the business can stay competitive. As IT organizations mature, they become better aligned to the business and begin to consistently meet the needs of the business. These maturing IT organizations help ensure competitiveness of the company as a whole.

EVOLVING ROLE OF IT

While IT started solely to support technology, IT doesn't just support technology any longer. If the business wanted technology, there is nothing that would keep the business from acquiring its own technology. Many computer vendors are available to the business, as well as to IT. In fact, the business could even go to a discount retailer and purchase a perfectly good computer, along with some sodas, maybe a movie and also some dryer sheets!

The fact is the business doesn't want technology. The business wants the service that is enabled by technology. Fortunately for IT, businesses would rather not mess with the technological issues or the costs associated with managing technology. Businesses are fine leaving the technology know-how to IT, as long as they can achieve their business desired outcomes.

SIDEBAR: SERVICES AND THE DRY CLEANER

Most people have been to a dry cleaner. What most people do not realize, though, is everything that is involved in this seemingly simple service. As a process consultant, I am highly prone to probe behind the front counter of a service provider to understand better the steps to providing a service. The dry cleaner by my house is no exception.

When the dry cleaner first opened, I was one of its first customers. They are located in a very convenient place in my neighborhood outside of Houston, Texas, and are priced reasonably. Plus, clothes dropped off before 9:00 AM are ready for pickup after 5:00 PM. That is very convenient if there is an evening event.

After visiting the dry cleaner on numerous occasions, I started to become curious about what actually happens at the dry cleaner after my clothes are dropped off. So, I asked the owner who gladly took me on a tour of his shop and helped me understand what it takes to get clothes cleaned and pressed.

You may think that this in no way relates to IT. However, it does.

Let's start by looking at what a dry cleaner really does. A dry cleaner provides the following services for their customers:

Cleaning and pressing of clothes

The dry cleaner accepts soiled clothes and returns them at a later time, cleaned and pressed. The returned clothes may or may not be starched, according to your request. When returned, the clothes may be on hangers or may be boxed. When you pick up your clothes, you expect that this will be completed to your satisfaction.

Minor alterations

Many dry cleaners perform minor alterations and clothing repair. These alterations may be to take in the waist on a pair of slacks, raise or lower a skirt hem, or fix buttons.

"Big" items

Periodically, we need to get our comforters, sleeping bags, and other very large items cleaned. The dry cleaner will clean these items at a higher cost, of course.

Wedding Dresses

Many dry cleaners, including the one that I frequent, will clean and pack wedding dresses in a box. This is to preserve the appearance of the dress, and it is treated to prevent fading over time. With this service, you can save a wedding dress until you can pass it down to your daughter.

THE DRY CLEANING PROCESS

If you've never been in the back room of a dry cleaner to see what your clothes go through, it can be an interesting trip. Let's look at the process that your clothes go through after we drop them off.

Step 1 – Drop off

When I drop off my clothes at the dry cleaner, I put them on the counter for the clerk to count and calculate the price I pay for them to be cleaned. Once counted, the clerk looks up my name in the computer system and inputs the details of my clothes. I commonly have three pairs of pants and seven shirts to be cleaned. These details go into the system, and a bill is produced, which I have to pay when I drop off the clothes.

Step 2 – Preparation

When the bill is paid and I am given my pickup receipt, they take my clothes and put them in a cloth bag. This bag is then tied, and a tag is put on the bag that identifies my clothes and keeps them separate from everyone else's. This bag is thrown into a pile with other bags until they are processed.

Step 3 – Cleaning

During the cleaning step, many bags full of clothes are placed into a washer. This washer contains a chemical that, during the wash cycle, removes the dirt and soil from the clothes. Once the clean cycle has been completed, the chemical is drained and another chemical is introduced to get rid of the first chemical. This is similar to the rinse cycle on our washing machines.

Step 4 – Drying

Once the clothes have completed the cleaning step, they are taken out of the chemical washer and placed into a dryer. The dryer then dries the chemical out of the clothes, much like conventional dryers remove water out of our home laundry.

Step 5 – Sorting and Pressing

The clothes are now clean. However, they must be sorted according to customer and pressed. After the drying step, the bags of clothes are removed and placed into a bin. Individually, the bags are opened and the tag on the bag retained to identify which clothes belong to which customer.

The clothes from a bag are removed and placed on the press. At this time, starch may be added according to your specifications to stiffen the cloth in the shirts. Each item of clothing is then individually pressed and placed on a hanger. Once a certain number of items have been hung, they are covered in plastic and tagged to identify them with an individual customer. This continues until all clothes in the bag have been pressed and hung.

Step 6 – Storing

When a bag of clothes has been processed, the bundle of clothes on hangers is then placed on the clothes rack. The location of the bundle is input into the system identified by the tag number, which is linked to the customer information, and the location on the rack where the clothes are stored. You may have many bundles of clothes, depending on how many items you delivered to be cleaned. These bundles are individually stored, but are referenced in the system for easy retrieval.

Step 7 – Delivery

When you pick up your clothes at the dry cleaners, you produce a pickup receipt. This receipt identifies you as the customer and includes a list of all of the items that you dropped off. The clerk will look up your information in the system to locate your clothes on the rack. Once they get a list of all your clothing bundles, they retrieve them from the rack and deliver them to you at the front counter.

I often check to make sure that I have received all of the items that I dropped off by checking the pickup receipt to ensure that the right number of items has been returned. I also look to verify that the clothes that have been returned are actually mine. Even though other people might have better clothes than mine, I want to make sure that they fit. I've never had an issue here because their process seems to work very well, but it's always a good idea to verify that the service you receive meets your expectations.

The sidebar example describes the process that my dry cleaner goes through to clean my clothes. This should be fairly representative of most dry cleaners, as the process of cleaning clothes shouldn't change much from one dry cleaner to another.

However, this isn't all that the dry cleaner does to provide cleaning services for customers. Other things they do include the following:

Changing filters on the washer

Changing filters on the dryer

Disposing of chemical waste in a safe manner

Ordering hangers, chemicals, printer paper, plastic clothes wrap, etc.

Sweeping the floors and ensuring cleanliness of the facility

Negotiating maintenance agreements for the washers and dryers

Paying salaries

Paying utility bills, such as electricity, water and gas

Finding lost clothes

Completing income taxes

Complying with Environmental Protection Agency (EPA) and Occupational Health and Safety Administration (OSHA) guidelines

Learning the latest dry cleaning techniques and applying those to the business

Many, many other things

All of these additional activities are paramount to ensuring that dry cleaners provide the best possible service they can. Without these activities being performed, the likelihood of the quality of service declining is quite high (particularly if the electricity hasn't been paid).

But, do we, as customers, care about these activities? Think about this for a bit.

Not really. Our main desire is to get our clothes cleaned at a reasonable price. We evaluate the performance of the dry cleaner based on many factors that have very little to do with these additional activities. We base our evaluation of the dry cleaner on customer service, cleanliness of clothes, reliability, timeliness, convenience and of, course, price.

While these additional activities are important, we do not pay for them to be performed. If these activities were not performed, it would have a negative effect on the quality of the service that customers receive. This quality of service is evaluated by how clean the clothes are, whether or not we get what we pay for, whether or not our clothes have missing buttons, and other factors that have no direct relationship on these extra activities.

> ### Key Point
>
> We pay for the output of a service, not the activities used to provide this service

The key point to be made from this exercise is that *we pay for the output of this service, not the activities used to provide this service.* This output represents our desired outcomes.

Now that we have explored the dry cleaner, let's turn our attention to IT. When the question of "what does IT do?" is asked of people within IT, I often get the following types of responses:

Application development

Application administration

Network administration

Patch management

Server management

Vendor management

Service Desk support

Computer and network security

Change management

Desktop support

Release management

Software distribution

Quality testing

Quality assurance

Metrics reporting

Customer service management

Project management

Data backup, archiving and retrieval

IT strategy and architecture

And many, many other things as well

This list of activities and responsibilities is common to almost all IT organizations with a few exceptions. Each of the items in this list is vitally important and must be performed. However, consider the following question:

As a customer, would you pay for these activities to be performed?

Absolutely not - with a few exceptions. Even though each of the items on this list is important, they do not focus on the output of a service. If any of these activities were not performed, or not performed well, the quality of the services suffers. However, these activities do not constitute a service.

The point of this story is that we judge a service and pay for a service by how the service meets our desired outcomes. The business is no different. The business would have no desire for technology if there were no business desired outcomes tied to the technology. Since business must move faster and more efficiently, there are not many options other than to utilize technology to support the desired outcomes of the business.

Instead, business wants services. The services that business wants must be aligned to their business desired outcomes in order to have any perceived value to the business. Services are focused on the value provided to the cus-

> **Key Point**
>
> IT exists to provide services, not technology.

tomer. Services include the ability to achieve the business desired outcomes but also the activities and processes that the business doesn't see that support a service. These processes include the design processes, transition processes, operational processes and improvement processes to support that service.

For example, business does not really want e-mail. While every organization makes considerable use of e-mail, e-mail is not a service, just an application. The ability to communicate within the organization, as well as external to the organization, is the service the business wants. Today, we just happen to provide this service through e-mail. Tomorrow, we may provide this service through some completely different mechanism (such as telepathy)!

WHAT ARE SERVICES?

> **Key Point**
>
> A service is defined as a means of delivering value to customers by facilitating outcomes customers want to achieve without the ownership of specific costs and risks.

A service is defined as *"a means of delivering value to customers by facilitating outcomes customers want to achieve without the ownership of specific costs and risks."*[4]

Services have specific characteristics:

Services create value

Services create value of some form for the customer. If the service has no associated value, there will be no customers. The easiest way to understand this concept is to think about the services that you utilize: cable television, cell phone service, or Internet services are all examples of services that create some value for you. If there were no value, you would not need the service.

Services remove the risk of ownership from customers

Customers want to achieve some outcome without being forced to own the technology, knowledge, or other underlying components that make up that service. For example, a customer wants an inventory control system in order to manage inventory. What they desire is a way to track inventory without having to understand the inventory application, installation or configuration and without managing the server it resides on or the network the application uses to communicate. IT provides this service, assumes ownership of these costs, and maintains the required knowledge. This allows IT to share these costs among multiple customers, thus lowering individual customer costs and allowing the customer to focus on key competencies.

Services facilitate outcomes that customers want to achieve

---

4   Quoted text is from Service Strategy © Crown copyright 2011 Reproduced under license from the Cabinet Office

Services are provided to facilitate some outcome that the business desires. This business-desired outcome must be well understood to ensure that the service is constructed in a way that ensures the business desired outcome is met.

Services reduce the effect of constraints

Providing services reduces the effects of constraints that may be imposed other ways. Costs, knowledge, and abilities are only a few constraints that can be reduced through the delivery of shared services.

With or without services, customers will find a way to achieve their outcomes using whatever resources they have available. Many times, these resources are constricted by performance or constraints. Services should improve a customer's resources by improving performance or removing or reducing constraints.

For example, suppose a company sells farming supplies in rural areas in the country. The sales reps regularly visit medium to large scale farms to present new products and help farmers reorder products. They do this by filling out an order form using pen and paper and then input that order into the ordering system when they get back to their office.

The IT Service Provider can provide value by increasing the performance of the customer asset – the sales rep. We can do this by providing a mobile ordering service where the sales rep can take the order (or point the end-customer to a web site) on the spot instead of being constrained by having to travel back to the office.

In short, constraints can refer to anything that may limit the customer's assets. It may refer to constraints in time, constraints in how many customers they can handle or even how many students can be in a single class. It is our job as service providers to understand the constraints that limit customers and find innovative ways to reduce or eliminate these constraints.

By doing so, we can help our customers break through any performance barriers to remain competitive.

SERVICE MANAGEMENT

Services are inherently different from other deliverables in that services have different influencers. While services come in a wide variety of forms, they all share the same characteristics of being intangible, associated with customer outcomes, and highly perishable. If services are not used, they lose their

---

Key Point

Characteristics of services include:

Services create value

Services remove the risk of ownership from customers

Services facilitate outcomes that customers want to achieve

Services reduce the effects of constraints

---

value.

Coffee beans, for example, are picked during harvest time. The beans are then processed and stored in a manner conducive to later use. Even though coffee beans are ultimately perishable, they have a shelf life, so excess beans can be stored until needed.

Services, on the other hand, are immediately perishable. If services are not consumed at the moment they are delivered, they are wasted. Excess service cannot be stored, and high demand for services may result in the inability to meet that demand.

Because of the difference between services and other deliverables, services must be managed differently. IT service management (ITSM) is a collection of shared responsibilities, plus interrelated disciplines and processes, that enable an organization to measure, control, and ultimately manage the IT infrastructure to deliver high-quality, cost-effective services to meet both short- and long-term business requirements. This can involve supporting one or more business areas – ranging from single-application access to a complex set of facilities spread across a number of differing platforms.

> **Key Point**
>
> Service Management is defined as a set of specialized organizational capabilities for providing value to customers in the form of services.

Service Management is defined as a *"set of specialized organizational capabilities for providing value to customers in the form of services."*[5] service management is the result of focusing an organization's capabilities and resources to produce value in the form of services. This desired outcome should meet the business needs. If appropriately focused and executed, value is created for the business.

In order to better meet the needs of the business, IT must embrace the concepts of service management. By doing so, IT becomes a Service Provider instead of a technology provider.

> **Key Point**
>
> A Service Provider is an organization that provides services to internal or external customers.

GEPPETTO GARCIA'S GIFT CARD SERVICE

Back to the restaurant analogy, Emil Delgassi, recognizing that he needed help to realize the new gift card service that he wanted to bring to Geppetto Garcia's, went to Mark Renner, the CIO. Mark's initial impression of the idea was great. He thought that gift cards would be very well received by customers.

However, in order to ensure that both Mark and Emil were on the same page when it came to the gift cards, Mark sat down with Emil to identify what

---

5   Quoted text is from Service Strategy © Crown copyright 2011 Reproduced under license from the Cabinet Office

this service would actually be and what its business desired outcomes would entail.

Emil and Mark determined that the basic business desired outcome is to increase revenues and profits for individual restaurant brands by developing a new channel to reach out to customers. For the end customer, their desired outcome is to give the gift of the Geppetto Garcia dining experience.

Both Emil and Mark recognized that they would need some assistance with this project as neither of them knew exactly how the gift card service would work from a technical perspective. However, developing the definition of the service and identifying the business desired outcomes is the first step. From this definition, the guidelines are established for the rest of the work involved in establishing this service.

INTRODUCTION TO ITIL®

GOOD PRACTICES

Good practices are practices that are commonly used within an organization. Good practices are often derived from best practices until they are commonly performed and become a commodity. At this point, they become good practice. Good practices are validated across a diverse set of environments and are critiqued in more than just a single organization.

Seat belts in cars are a good example of best practice becoming good practice. Seat belts were not standard equipment in cars until after 1958. Wearing seat belts was a best practice by drivers even after 1958. As we learned more about the advantages of wearing seat belts, the best practice of wearing seat belts became good practice as more and more people began to wear them while driving. Over time, this good practice expanded to passengers in cars, as well, and today, wearing seat belts is compulsory for drivers and passengers.

ITIL® is an example of best practice becoming good practice. While ITIL® started as a library of defined best practices, it has been reviewed, tried and validated across a diverse set of organizations. This use of ITIL® has resulted in its becoming a good practice that IT organizations can adopt. In the future, the practices within ITIL®, just like seat belts, may become required for some organizations. This is starting to come true today with many government contracts requiring competing vendors to be ITIL® compliant. This ITIL® compliance is measured through the adoption of ISO 20000 - a standard focused on ITIL® practices.

ITIL® is the combined result of people around the world, who have been tasked with documenting their best-practice experiences. The contributors to the IT Infrastructure Library have vast experience in a wide variety of industries and organizations.

WHAT IS ITIL®?

I affectionately refer to ITIL® as "documented common sense." It is my contention that any organization with enough vision, forethought, time, need, and desire would come up with almost all of the things that ITIL® documents. The organization may use different words to mean the same things as in ITIL®, but the ideas would be there.

The IT Infrastructure Library® (ITIL®) is simply a set of practices that people just like you have documented because they work well. ITIL® is not prescriptive in that it does not document how to do things. It simply documents what can and should be done. Along with the ITIL® core library is supplemental information that provides more prescriptive guidance, but overall, ITIL® simply shares with us what other people have found to be the best way to approach IT as a service provider.

The Cabinet Office is an office of the British HM Treasury that currently owns the rights to ITIL®. ITIL® was originally developed in the mid-1980s by the Central Computer and Telecommunications Agency (CCTA), in collaboration with subject-matter experts, practitioners, consultants, and trainers to help organizations improve the way we use and manage IT. The CCTA is now incorporated into the Cabinet Office and does not operate as a separate entity.

The Cabinet Office now has the authority for maintenance and improvement of ITIL®, as well as implementing the best practices in commercial activities in the UK's government. The Cabinet Office continues to build on this practice by working with international organizations to develop and share business and practitioner guidance to further enhance this world-class best practice.

ITIL® 2011

The current version, ITIL® 2011, was introduced in July, 20. This version of ITIL® had the involvement of the IT service management Forum (itSMF). The itSMF is a worldwide forum involved in promoting the concepts of IT service management and organizing events and conferences to bring IT service management practitioners together.

The itSMF US chapter can be found on the Web at www.itsmfusa.org. The itSMF also promotes Local Interest Groups (LIGs) for those that want to meet on a regular basis in the cities in which they live or work. LIGs for your area can also be found on the itSMF US Web site.

THE SUCCESS OF ITIL®

ITIL® has been utilized since the mid-1980s and quickly became the de facto standard in service management. There are many reasons ITIL® is successful. First, it is vendor-neutral. ITIL® focuses on processes, not specific tools, so ITIL® will work for any organization that provides internal, external, or shared IT services.

Second, ITIL® is non-prescriptive. It is adaptable to meet the needs of any organization with any type of customer. It is not something that needs to be followed precisely, but can be modified to fit the needs of any organization.

The third, and perhaps the most important, reason is that ITIL® represents the experiences and thought leadership of the world's best-in-class service providers. ITIL® has been developed over many years by people with experience in the industry. Their learning experiences have been put to paper to allow others to learn from these experiences and to be able to grow beyond what ITIL® has documented.

ITIL® is adopted by organizations to allow service providers to be able to deliver value for customers through the services they provide. It also allows service providers to integrate the strategy for services with the business strategy and customer needs. Additionally, ITIL® provides guidance to measure, monitor, and optimize IT services and performance by providing services that value to the business at the right cost.

Organizations that have adopted ITIL® inherently experience a change in their culture. This culture change evolves an organization from being a technology provider to being a service provider. This focus on offering service enhances IT's ability to manage its capabilities and resources, manage risk and ensure that services value to the business.

ITIL® AND OTHER STANDARDS

ITIL® is not an exclusive framework. ITIL® documents "what" a mature IT organization should do, not "how" it should do it. Other standards still play a very important part in maturing an IT organization. In particular, ISO 20000 is the ISO/IEC certification for organizations around IT service management.

ITIL® has been around since the 1980's when the first version was introduced. Over the past 20+ years, ITIL® has evolved as the de facto standard in IT service management. ITIL® v3, was delivered in 2007 (now referred to as ITIL® 2007) and introduced the service lifecycle. This latest version, ITIL® 2011 expands on what we learned in ITIL® 2007.

THE ITIL® CORE

A service, much like an application, has a lifecycle with defined stages during the life of the service. The service lifecycle defines five key stages within this lifecycle: service strategy, service design, service transition, service operation and continual service improvement. These service lifecycle stages work together to provide a complete service from conception through retirement of the service.

The ITIL® 2011 core volumes were published in July, 2011. ITIL® is supplemented with complementary guidance that documents specific best practices by industry and by organization. Additional publications are being made available through the continued effort of people around the world as they document various aspects of ITIL®. These additional publications are available through the ITIL® Web site at www.best-management-practice. com.

> ### *Key Point*
>
> ISO/IEC 20000 is an industry standard based on ITIL˙.

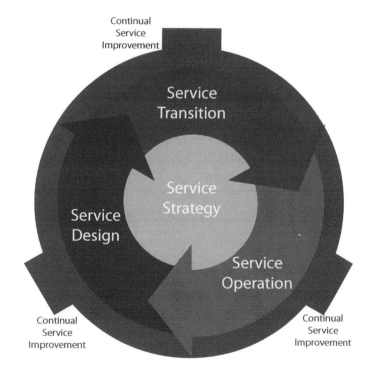

©Crown copyright 2011 Reproduced under license from the Cabinet Office

Figure - Service lifecycle

SERVICE LIFECYCLE

ITIL® approaches the practice of service management through a framework called the service lifecycle. The service lifecycle represents the stages that a service goes through during its life.

ITIL® documents the stages of the service lifecycle based on the input from people all over the world in various industries. This library provides guidance for the practice of IT service management.

5 CORE VOLUMES

> **Key Point**
>
> ITIL® includes five core volumes:
>
> Service Strategy
>
> Service Design
>
> Service Transition
>
> Service Operation
>
> Continual Service Improvement

The ITIL® core is a set of books that provides guidance for each of the stages of the service lifecycle. These core volumes follow each stage of the service lifecycle by documenting the lifecycle stage objectives, concepts and the processes within each stage of the service lifecycle.

DETAILED SERVICE LIFECYCLE MODEL

While the service lifecycle diagram provides a view of the stages of the service lifecycle, it doesn't really provide the whole picture. The service lifecycle Detail diagram is a more detailed model of the service lifecycle that I share in my ITIL Foundations classes.

Starting at the top of the diagram, service providers support the business processes. It is important to remember that IT exists solely for the purpose of supporting the business. IT supports the business through delivery of services that provide value to customers by facilitating outcomes customers want to achieve without the ownership of specific costs and risks.

The concept of managing these services is, of course, service management. Service management is a set of specialized organizational capabilities for providing value to customers in the form of services.

These specialized organizational capabilities are provided in the form of processes and functions. This is where the service lifecycle comes in. The service lifecycle includes the processes and functions of the service provider and is a representation of the service provider's specialized organizational capabilities.

Within each stage of the service lifecycle is a set of activities, concepts, and models to achieve the goals and aims of each stage. Some of these stages contain definitions of processes, while others contain definitions of processes and functions. A brief overview of the service lifecycle stages and the relevant processes follows:

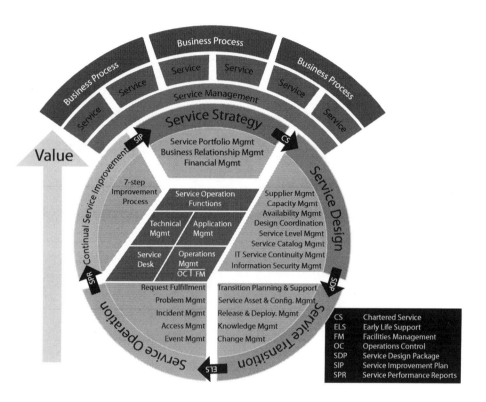

Service Strategy

The service strategy volume provides guidance in developing an overall strategy for IT service management. This involves understanding your markets, your customers, your capabilities and resources, and the financial constraints under which these services must be defined, delivered and supported. Service strategy also includes the ongoing processes of strategy management for IT services, service portfolio management, financial management, demand management and business relationship management.

The overall purpose of service strategy is to develop a strategy for our specific markets (customers) based on services that result in the IT organization being non-optional. The IT organization should be the best option as a "vendor" of services that understands the requirements of the business and delivers services that are superior to any other vendor.

Processes documented within service strategy include:

Strategy Management for IT Services[6]

Strategy management for IT services is the process of defining and maintaining strategies with regard to services as well as the management of those services. It articulates how a service provider enables an organization to meet its business desired outcomes.

Service Portfolio Management

Service portfolio management is the process of maximizing the return on investment while managing risk. Through this dynamic method for governing investments, service portfolio management maximizes the value being delivered to the business by the service provider.

Financial Management for IT Services

The financial management for IT services process works throughout the service lifecycle to provide financial input to other processes. From a service strategy perspective, financial management for IT services evaluates investments in services to assist with strategic decision-making.

Demand Management[7]

The demand management process works closely with the business to identify and understand patterns of business demand. From this pattern of demand, demand management strives to balance the cost, quality, and capacity of services and define service packages that meet customer expectations.

Business Relationship Management

The business relationship management process works throughout the service lifecycle to be the link between the service provider and the customer at the strategic and tactical levels.

Service Design

The service design volume provides guidance on the principles of balancing

---

6   This process is beyond the scope of Foundation-level knowledge and is not covered in this text.

7   This process is beyond the scope of Foundation-level knowledge and is not covered in this text.

design against a diverse set of constraints. It also discusses how to design a service that meets the business needs, is financially justifiable, and can be supported as an ongoing concern. Service design incorporates these requirements into a set of design documents upon which a service, or modification to a service, can be developed.

Service design promotes a service to service transition through the service design package (SDP). The SDP contains everything necessary for the build, test, deployment, and operation of a service.

Together, the following processes in service design ensure that the utility and warranty needed to support the business are designed.

Service Catalog Management

The service catalog management process ensures that consistent information about what services are available in operation is widely available.

Supplier Management

Supplier management is the process of managing suppliers and contracts to ensure value for money is obtained.

Service Level Management

Service level management is the process that works closely with the business to ensure that the needs of the business are well understood and the capabilities of the service provider are properly represented to the business.

Availability Management

Availability management not only designs the proper availability into the services but also tests availability mechanisms, responds to availability issues, and strives to improve availability according to the needs of the business.

Capacity Management

Much like availability management, capacity management also works through the service lifecycle, but from a capacity perspective. Capacity management designs the appropriate capacity and performance into the services, as well as evaluates effects of changes on capacity and performance, responds to capacity-related issues, and improves capacity.

IT Service Continuity Management

IT service continuity management works closely with the business continuity plan to ensure that the appropriate IT technical and service facilities can be resumed within required and agreed business timescales.

Information Security Management

Information security management is the process of ensuring that the security of data and information is considered throughout the service lifecycle.

Design Coordination

The design coordination process ensures that individual designs are well-coordinated to ensure that comprehensive and appropriate designs are created that meet the needs of the business.

Service Transition

The service transition volume provides guidance on the transitioning of a service into operation. Service transition considers all elements required for a service. These elements include all aspects of a service, both technical and non-technical. This holistic view of a service helps to ensure that the service is transitioned in a way that it can be supported as an ongoing concern as effectively and efficiently as possible.

Service transition is a critical stage of the service lifecycle that takes the SDP from service design to build, test, and deploy a service or change to a service into operation. Service transition ensures that the requirements of the business are met through the deployed services while minimizing risk to the business. Once a service has been deployed, service transition supports this service through early life support (ELS). Early life support ensures that the service is properly managed until service operation can support that service on its own.

The processes within service transition include the following:

Transition Planning and Support

The transition planning and support process ensures that transitions are well-supported through the transition stage of the service lifecycle. In addition, transition planning and support strives to improve the transition stage of the service lifecycle ensuring efficiency and effectiveness.

Service Asset and Configuration Management

Service asset and configuration management is the record-keeping process for service management. Service asset and configuration management controls the integrity of the IT infrastructure through the creation of a logical model of services. This logical model identifies the configuration items (CIs) and their relationships to each other and how they work together to support a service.

Change Management

The change management process manages changes to minimize risk to the business for all changes throughout the service lifecycle. Change management ensures that standardized methods and procedures are used for efficient and prompt handling of all changes.

Release and Deployment Management

Release and deployment management is the process of ensuring that only the right components are packaged in a release and deployed into the live environment while minimizing risk to the business. Release and deployment management also ensures that the business is prepared to accept the release.

Knowledge Management

Knowledge management is the process of maintaining the knowledge of the services and infrastructure throughout the service lifecycle. Knowledge management ensures that knowledge is maintained and can be delivered to the right person at the right time to enable better decision making.

Service Validation and Testing[8]

Service validation and testing is the process in service transition to ensure that a service if fit for purpose and fit for use. Not only does service validation and testing test the functionality of a service, but also validates the service against its requirements.

Change Evaluation[9]

The change evaluation process is a process that evaluates the intended and unintended effects of a change to determine the risk that is present with a change. Change evaluation strives to understand the risks and interface with change management to mitigate those risks.

Service Operation

The service operation volume provides guidance on the effective and efficient operation of the service. Service operation is where the value of the service is

---

8   This process is beyond the scope of Foundation-level knowledge and is not covered in this text.

9   This process is beyond the scope of Foundation-level knowledge and is not covered in this text.

realized and the strategy of the organization is executed. Service operation is important to continual service improvement, as the service operation stage is where the services are monitored and improvements are identified through the service performance reports.

The processes documented within service operation include:

Event Management

Event management is the process of detecting events, making sense of them, and determining the appropriate control action.

Incident Management

Incident management is the process of responding to issues with services. In the case of an issue with a service, incident management restores the service as quickly as possible to minimize the adverse impact to the business.

Problem Management

Problem management supports incident management by resolving underlying problems in the environment. Problem management prevents incidents from occurring as well as minimizing the impact of incidents that cannot be prevented.

Request Fulfillment

Users, at times, require IT to perform some action to support them. These types of requests are not incidents, but service requests. The request fulfillment process deals with these requests from users through the standardization of common requests for prompt and efficient handling.

Access Management

Access management is the operational process to provide access to services contained within the service catalog to users who are entitled to access those services while restricting access to services from users that are not entitled to access those services.

Continual Service Improvement

The continual service improvement (CSI) volume provides guidance that ensures improvements to a service are diligently executed. Continual service improvement is defined in such a way that it should be integrated into all of the other lifecycle stages. The CSI volume describes improvement as a continual activity and not just an afterthought.

Based on the service performance reports from service operation, CSI strives to identify improvements and document recommended improvements in the service improvement plan (SIP) for consideration within service strategy.

The process documented within continual service improvement is:

7-step Improvement Process

The 7-step improvement process provides a disciplined approach to correlating data from a wide variety of measurements within a process or service.

PROCESSES, FUNCTIONS AND ROLES

OVERVIEW

IT service management is made possible through a combination of functions and processes. A process is defined as "*a structured set of activities designed to accomplish a specific set of objectives*"[10] while a function is defined as "*units of organizations specialized to perform certain types of work and responsible for specific outcomes*".[11] Processes are performed by functions providing coordination across the functions.

PROCESSES

Geppetto Garcia quickly realized that in order to serve his customers well, he needed to develop processes to prepare meals for his customers. The kitchen staff worked with Geppetto to develop processes to support meal preparation. For Chicken Parmigiana, for example, the process consists of a number of steps with defined procedures.

The basic process for preparing Chicken Parmigiana consists of the following steps:

1. Bread chicken
2. Cook chicken
3. Spoon marinara sauce onto plate
4. Place cooked chicken on plate
5. Place Parmesan cheese on chicken
6. Place plate in oven to melt cheese

---

10   Quoted text is from Service Strategy © Crown copyright 2011 Reproduced under license from the Cabinet Office

11   Quoted text is from Service Strategy © Crown copyright 2011 Reproduced under license from the Cabinet Office.

7. Add spaghetti noodles to plate

8. Spoon sauce over spaghetti noodles

A process consists of a set of activities that build upon each other until a specific outcome is achieved. Each specific outcome is individually countable. In the above case, the specific outcome is a Chicken Parmigiana dish. By counting the specific outcomes, the number of Chicken Parmigiana dishes prepared can be counted.

Each specific outcome is delivered to a customer of the process. The customer of the process does not have to be the end consumer of the output of the process. Oftentimes, the outputs of the process are inputs into another process. In this case, the customer of the Chicken Parmigiana process is the server. The server, through process, will then deliver the meal to the customer.

The process does not start until a triggering event occurs to initiate the process activities. In our case, a meal is ordered and an order is sent to the kitchen. This specific event (an order) begins the process of creating a Chicken Parmigiana meal.

Processes are also measurable. Because they are measurable, they are performance driven. With a process, we can tell how long it takes to perform the process and even how long it takes to perform the individual activities within the process. In our example, the time it takes to prepare a Chicken Parmigiana meal should be well known, so if a table of diners orders different meals, each of the meals can be started at a time when they can all be completed at the same time to be delivered to the process customer (the server) together.

Processes have no staff or defined organization; they are simply sets of activities. They act on a defined triggering event (input) to provide some defined output. Processes have roles, responsibilities, and tools and require management control to ensure that the output is delivered reliably. Processes also define policies, standards, guidelines, activities and work instructions that govern them. Lastly, processes are closed-loop systems that provide feedback for corrective action to be applied.

For the exam, remember that processes must be measurable, have a specific output, deliver value to a customer, and respond to a trigger. The term MaSsaCRe may help remember this.

M – Measurable

S – Specific output

C – Customer

R – Respond to a trigger

> ### Key Point
>
> Processes are measurable, provide a specific outcome, deliver outcomes to customers and respond to a trigger.

Process Control

When designing a process, it's not wise to focus on designing a perfect process, but a process with built-in improvement mechanisms for long-term improvement. This is accomplished through process control that measures, evaluates, and continually improves the process. Process Control is defined as *"the process of planning and regulating, with the objective of performing a process in an effective, efficient and objective manner."*[12]

Even though processes do not define organizations or people, many times we will refer to processes as if they were actual organizations or individuals. For example, incident management passes information to problem management. This example appears as if different people are involved in this hand-off of information. In fact, the opposite is true – processes have no organization or staff. In this example, when information passes from incident management to problem management, it is likely that the information will be passed by a single individual without realizing the change from one process to another. This is done through the effective implementation of procedures to support the processes.

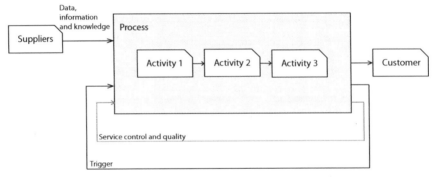

©Crown copyright 2007 - Reproduced under license from the Commerce Office

Figure - Basic Closed Loop Process

---

12   Quoted text is from Service Strategy © Crown copyright 2011 Reproduced under license from the Cabinet Office

FUNCTIONS

Functions are defined as *"units of organizations specialized to perform certain types of work and responsible for specific outcomes."*[13] In Geppetto Garcia's restaurant, the kitchen staff is an example of a function. The kitchen staff is an organization trained to perform specialized types of work (cook). They are also responsible for specific outcomes (the individual meals).

In your organization, you also have functions of many types. Examples of functions include the service desk or help desk staff, the technical management teams, the application management teams, and the IT operations management teams. These specific functions are addressed in the service operation functions chapter.

Functions have the characteristics of organizations that are self-contained, have specific resources and capabilities, provide performance and outcomes, have their own body of knowledge (usually procedures), provide structure and stability to an organization, and have defined roles and associated authority.

In the coming pages of the book, specific processes and their activities will be explored. It is common to wonder who performs all of these activities. It is the functions that perform these activities within the processes. The processes provide a mechanism for the functions to work together to provide a service. By using processes for cross-functional coordination, functions can be very powerful.

> **Key Point**
>
> A function is defined as units of organizations specialized to perform certain types of work and responsible for specific outcomes.

ROLES

Within many of the processes that we will explore, roles are documented. These roles define the responsibilities that this role performs.

For example, Geppetto Garcia is a restaurateur. He is also a friend and a son. On his days off, he enjoys playing chess in the park. Geppetto Garcia has many roles (restaurateur, friend, son, chess player), but he is only one person. You, the reader, may also have many roles. You are an employee, a friend, or a son or daughter, and you may also be a mom or a dad. From this, you can see that each one of us has multiple roles.

Therefore, a role does not define an individual. A role is defined as *"a set of responsibilities, activities and authorities granted to a person or team."*[14] A role

---

13   Quoted text is from Service Strategy © Crown copyright 2011 Reproduced under license from the Cabinet Office

14   Quoted text is from Service Strategy © Crown copyright 2011 Reproduced under license from the Cabinet Office

> **Key Point**
>
> Roles are defined as a set of responsibilities, activities and authorities granted to a person or team.

> **Key Point**
>
> The Process Owner is defined as the role accountable for ensuring that a process is fit for purpose.

> **Key Point**
>
> The Process Manager is defined as the role accountable for the operational management of a process.

> **Key Point**
>
> The Process Practitioner is defined as the role responsible for carrying out one or more process activities.

is simply a set of responsibilities that are performed. A role may be combined with other roles, so one person can assume multiple roles. Also, a role may be shared, so more than one person can assume a particular role.

In the following chapters, you will learn about specific roles for some of the processes within the service lifecycle. However, there are some generic roles described by ITIL. These roles are generic, and more specific descriptions may be provided later.

Every process should have a process owner and a process manager. The process owner is defined as *"the role accountable for ensuring that a process is fit for purpose."*[15] The process owner is also responsible for the sponsorship of the process, defining process key performance indicators (KPIs), ensuring the process is designed, and is also responsible for identifying opportunities for improvement.

The process manager is defined as *"the role responsible for the operational management of a process."*[16] The process manager ensures that a process operates as expected and identifies areas of potential improvements to effectiveness and efficiency. The process manager also plans and coordinates the activities of the process and is responsible for the monitoring and reporting of a process.

The activities in a process are performed by process practitioners. The process practitioner role is defined as *"the role responsible for carrying out one or more process activities."*[17] Depending on the organization and the process itself, the process practitioner and process manager roles may be performed by a single individual.

Services also have owner roles. The service owner is defined as *"the role responsible to the customer for the initiation, transition and ongoing maintenance and support of a particular service."*[18] The service owner is the main role for a specific service to ensure that the service is meeting its objectives for the customer. The service owner also establishes and maintains relationships with process owners and process managers throughout the service lifecycle to ensure the service is well designed, meets the strategy, is transitioned well, is effectively and efficiently operated, and is continually improved to meet the business needs.

---

15   Quoted text is from Service Strategy © Crown copyright 2011 Reproduced under license from the Cabinet Office.

16   Quoted text is from Service Strategy © Crown copyright 2011 Reproduced under license from the Cabinet Office.

17   Quoted text is from Service Strategy © Crown copyright 2011 Reproduced under license from the Cabinet Office.

18   Quoted text is from Service Strategy © Crown copyright 2011 Reproduced under license from the Cabinet Office.

Larger organizations may have several process managers for one process. This is particularly true for distributed organizations that have one process manager per region. However, there is only one process owner per process. Smaller organizations may combine the roles of process manager and process owner so one person assumes both roles.

Two other roles that are defined are customers and users. A customer is defined as *"the person or group who defines and agrees to the service level targets"*[19] and is the person who represents the business interests. The customer is the person who "pays" for the service or negotiates the service on behalf of the business and the users. Users are the people who use the service on a day-to-day basis.

> **Key Point**
>
> The Service Owner is defined as the role responsible to the customer for the initiation, transition and ongoing maintenance and support of a particular service.

RACI MODEL

Identification of specific roles and responsibilities is made easier through the development of a RACI Model. A RACI Model identifies those who are responsible, accountable, consulted and informed (RACI) for the specific activities in a process.

> **Key Point**
>
> A RACI model is used to define roles and responsibilities in a process.

Responsible

Responsibility refers to the resource that carries out a task to completion. Responsibility may be shared among multiple people.

Accountable

Accountability refers the person that is ultimately responsible for the success or failure of the task. This role has decision-making power regarding the activity. There can be only one person accountable for a specific task. If there is more than one person accountable for a task, when the task fails, finger-pointing occurs and, as a result, no one is accountable. I can think of many examples of this throughout my career and I'm sure you can probably think of examples, as well.

Consulted

Consulted refers to the resources that must be conferred with about a task or activity. Being consulted involves a two-way communication with those conferred. For example, if a change must be made to a service, the Change

---

19   Quoted text is from Service Strategy © Crown copyright 2011 Reproduced under license from the Cabinet Office

Manager may want to consult with the business customers of that service to determine when the change can be made.

Informed

Informed refers to communicating one-way. Informing is simply communicating that something is taking place, with no expectation of a response. For example, once the change manager determines when a change can be made, the change manager may inform the users of that service that the change is being made and when.

A RACI model is developed by listing the activities along the left column of a table and the roles across the top. A matrix is then developed to identify which roles are responsible, accountable, consulted and informed within the process. A RACI model ensures that end-to-end accountability is identified for the process activities and ensures that gaps are identified and can be corrected.

	Change Requestor	Change Manager	Change Approver	Change Implementor	Change Tester
Request a Change	R	A			
Filter the Change		R/A		C	
Approve the Change		A	R		
Build the Change		A		R	I
Implement the Change		A		R	C
Test the Change		A		C	R
Review the Change	C	R/A		C	C
Close the Change	I	R/A	I	I	I

R - Responsible
A - Accountable
C - Consulted
I - Informed

RACI MODEL POTENTIAL PITFALLS

A RACI model has potential problems that should be understood. Within the RACI model, a process activity can only have one person accountable. Sharing accountability can result in finger pointing, resulting in no accountability. The RACI model should also ensure that the responsibilities for closely related processes are properly identified to ensure that the process relationships remain intact.

Processes, in general, have the issue that responsibility may be delegated, but this delegation results in no authority to make decisions. Also, individual agendas or goals may get in the way of satisfying the overall goals of the process. Process interrelationships must also be considered so that there is defined interaction and, perhaps, shared responsibility between activities of highly related processes.

TERMS & DEFINITIONS

Service

Service management

Service provider

Process

Process control

Function

Role

Process owner

Service owner

Process manager

Process practitioner

IMPORTANT POINTS

ITIL® consists of 5 core volumes

> Service strategy
>
> Service design
>
> Service transition
>
> Service operation
>
> Continual service improvement

ITIL® is supported by complementary guidance to improve the effectiveness and efficiency for specific industries and sectors

Services create value

A process is a set of activities that accomplish a specific outcome

Characteristics of a process:

> Measurable
>
> Specific result
>
> Customers
>
> Responds to a trigger or event

Functions are units of organization that perform the activities of one or more processes

RACI Model

> Responsible
>
> Accountable
>
> Consulted
>
> Informed

SECTION REVIEW

1. _____ create value, remove risk of ownership from customers, facilitate outcomes customers want to achieve, and reduce the effects of constraints

   A. Resources

   B. Services

   C. Systems

   D. Processes

2. _____ is a set of specialized organizational capabilities for providing value to customers in the form of services

   A. Service management

   B. Information technology

   C. Technology management

   D. Service

3. Why might an organization want to use ITIL®?

   A. ITIL® is published good practice

   B. ITIL® is a validated framework

   C. ITIL® provides a basis on which to improve

   D. All of the above

4. ITIL® is a stand-alone, totally inclusive framework that eliminates the need to consider any other standard.

   A. True

   B. False

5. The ITIL® core volumes include service strategy, service design, continual service improvement, and what other volumes?

   1. Service optimization

   2. Service operation

   3. Service release

   4. Service transition

   A. 1 and 3

   B. 2 and 4

   C. 1 and 4

   D. 4 only

6. There are times when it is feasible to have more than one person accountable for an activity within a process.

   A. True

   B. False

7. Which of the following is NOT a characteristic of a process?

   A. It responds to a specific event (trigger)

   B. It is timely

   C. It is measurable and therefore performance driven

   D. It provides a specific output to a customer

8. What is the term defined by "units of organization specialized to perform certain types of work and responsible for specific outcomes?"

   A. Processes

   B. Functions

   C. Services

   D. Service management

9. The RACI Model is NOT used to identify which of the following roles?

   A. Who is responsible

   B. Who is accountable

   C. Who is consulted

   D. Who is charged

10. What is the term defined by "structured set of activities designed to accomplish a specific set of objectives?"

    A. Function

    B. Service

    C. Process

    D. Resource

COMPREHENSION

1. Describe the roles of the service owner and process owner.

2. Discuss briefly why an organization could benefit from the concepts of service management instead of technology management.

2

SERVICE STRATEGY OVERVIEW

OVERVIEW

In this chapter, the concepts of service strategy are described. The service strategy volume is largely intended for IT executives. However, it is still important that while learning about IT service management, you understand the basics of service strategy. It is important for everyone to understand why and how decisions are made. A common issue with a job of any type, not just IT, is understanding the big picture. The service strategy volume provides the big picture and describes how each of us is involved in providing services to customers.

Upon completing this chapter, you will understand the basics of service strategy as part of the service lifecycle. You will also have an understanding of value creation through services, as well as concepts in designing services.

GEPPETTO GARCIA'S

Geppetto Garcia's began expanding across the United States. During their expansion, they recognized the need to develop standards that would drive consistency across their restaurants, regardless of the location or specific cuisine of the restaurant. To achieve this consistency, Geppetto developed a strategy that would centralize the provisioning of his restaurants, including maintaining quality standards, inventory control, human resources, accounting, maintaining suppliers, and providing IT services.

The restaurant business, just like almost any other business of reasonable size, requires the use of IT. Geppetto Garcia hired Mark Renner to be the Chief Information Officer (CIO) of Geppetto Garcia, Inc.

Mark realized that in order to meet Geppetto's high quality and consistency standards, he would need to develop standard and consistent IT services that could be provisioned for each restaurant. These IT services would address the areas of inventory control, the restaurant ordering and payment systems, and employee time scheduling. Centralized services for the corporate facilities would involve email services, human resources, finance, sales and marketing, and overall operations.

Mark realized that he had two major markets to focus on – the individual restaurants and as his corporate services. These markets are two distinct markets with differing needs. His first focus is on ensuring the overall business revenue can be maintained. Therefore, he focused on the restaurant market first.

To identify the needs of the services, the customer of that service must first be identified. The restaurants are under the direction of the Chief Operating Officer, Emil Delgassi. Emil's staff includes the vice president in charge of restaurant operations, Genevieve Boswell. Mark contacted Genevieve to discuss the specific needs of the services that her restaurants would require from corporate IT in order to function effectively.

Mark documented these requirements in a service portfolio. The service portfolio matches the individual business requirements to services identified in the service portfolio. From this list of requirements, Mark defined specific services that meet these requirements. These services include specific services for inventory control, employee time scheduling, and ordering and payment services.

Based on the specific services that Mark would offer to the restaurants, he then went to work building the resources and capabilities that he would need to provide these services, including hardware and software, people, tools to measure and maintain the services, and processes to ensure that these services would operate effectively and efficiently and be readily maintained. These resources and capabilities are called service assets.

Mark next developed a plan to prepare for execution of these services. To do this, he evaluated internal and external factors, developed a plan for specific actions, developed policies and procedures to support his plan, and then enacted his plan. His plan involved ensuring that the specific services supplied would be of high enough quality to meet the demand for the services, as well as be financially viable. His overall goal was not to provide the highest quality services, but to provide the right level of service at the right cost.

The services that Mark identified that needed to be developed included inventory control, employee time scheduling, and ordering and payment services. He also understood that each of these services must have an identified customer and someone who "owns" the service and can represent IT's capabilities to the customer, as well as represent the business requirements to IT. This role is called a service owner. From his IT and business analyst staff, he identified three individuals to become the service owners for each of these services.

Mark developed the following table that specified the service, the primary customer and service owner.

Service	Description	Service owner	Customer
Inventory Control	Ensures materials and supplies are delivered to individual restaurants based on consumption rates of stocked materials and supplies	Dina Williams	Genevieve Boswell – VP, Operations
Employee Time Scheduling	Supports scheduling of restaurant employees to maintain the proper level of staffing matched to anticipated demand	Robin Jackson	Brenda Fuller – Director, Time Management (HR)
Ordering and Payment Services	Automates the ordering of meals from diners and prioritizes workflow within the kitchen. Provides diner checks for payment	Russ Diamond	Alan Hamilton – VP, Finance

PURPOSE OF SERVICE STRATEGY

In order to operate and grow successfully in the long term, service providers must have the ability to think and act in a strategic manner. Service strategy describes the strategic decisions that are made regarding services and IT service management. Through these strategic decisions, IT can drive value to the business through its effective application of capabilities and resources.

The purpose of service strategy is to "*define the perspective, position, plans and patterns that a service provider needs to be able to execute to meet an organization's business outcomes.*"[1]

IT organizations were originally established to provide technical services to the business. Today, with the complexity of IT and the dependency of business on technology, IT has, or should, evolve to a service provider. In order to become a service provider, IT must understand the business aspects of providing service. By doing this, IT will become more competitive, more focused, and the preferred "vendor" of IT services to the business.

More than just technical expertise is required to achieve this level. It involves a multi-disciplinary approach that utilizes knowledge in the areas of organizational management, marketing, sales, systems dynamics, and many other areas. These areas are usually not taught to IT people. However, they are critical to IT service providers.

> ### Key Point
> The purpose of service strategy is to "define the perspective, position, plans and patterns that a service provider needs to be able to execute to meet an organization's business outcomes."

---

1   Quoted text is from Service Strategy © Crown copyright 2011 Reproduced under license from the Cabinet Office

The major output of service strategy is the service level package (SLP). The SLP documents the business requirements for a service along with guiding constraints, process requirements and other requirements for the service. The SLP serves as an input to the service design stage of the service lifecycle.

Key Point

The major output of service strategy is the service level package (SLP).

CREATING VALUE THROUGH SERVICES

As discussed earlier, services create value for the customer. This value is created through the effective use of service assets. A service asset is defined as *"any capability or resource of a service provider."*[2]

Key Point

A service asset is defined as any capability or resource of a service provider.

Capabilities consist of the "soft assets" of an organization including:

Management

Organization

Processes

Knowledge

People

Capabilities are the things we know and how we do things in order to accomplish a goal.

Key Point

Capabilities are the things we know and how we do things in order to accomplish a goal. Capabilities are intangible.

Resources are the "hard assets" of the organization including:

Financial capital

Infrastructure

Applications

Information

People

Key Point

Resources are investments we make and the "components" that we use to get things done. Resources are tangible.

Resources are investments we make and the "components" that we use to get things done. Note that people are both capabilities and resources of a service asset. The way we get things done is through people, and we make an investment in people.

If value is created, the result will be that there are no other options for the business than the IT organization. This makes the IT organization as a service provider non-optional and builds IT as a capability within the organization.

---

2   Quoted text is from Service Strategy © Crown copyright 2011 Reproduced under license from the Cabinet Office

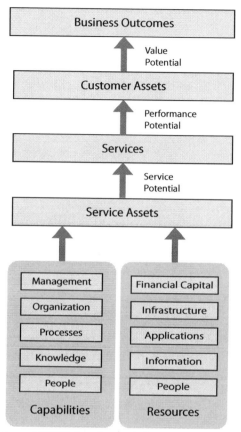

Figure - Creating Value

There is nothing that you can put your hands on and say, "This is the service that we provide." Service is a human concept that is made up of the four Ps – people, processes, partners (vendors) and products (technology). The products are the last and the least important of these four Ps. If all the business wanted was technology (products), it could easily purchase it. However, the business desires a service to help it meet its business-desired objectives.

Defining a service requires understanding the business-desired outcomes of customers. It is these business-desired outcomes that the service is designed to satisfy. Without this understanding, the service's value to the customer is minimized. Understanding the business-desired outcomes requires knowledge other than engineering or technical. It requires the ability to communicate with the customer in terms that the business understands, which means we must have knowledge of not only the business but also sales, marketing, economics and other business-oriented disciplines.

SIDEBAR - SHAREPOINT® PROLIFERATION

One of my pharmaceutical clients related a story to me about SharePoint® servers. When SharePoint® first came out, the IT department was trying them out for its own purposes. One of IT's customers observed an IT staff member working on a SharePoint® server and inquired about it. Once the customer realized some of the things he could do with SharePoint®, he asked for a SharePoint® server.

The IT staff member, anxious to show off his knowledge of the inner workings of technology, fulfilled that request and set up a SharePoint® server for the customer. Soon after that, other customers were asking for SharePoint® servers as well. This caused the proliferation of SharePoint® servers throughout the organization. This, by itself is not a bad thing. Technology is there to help people be more productive. These SharePoint® servers were playing their part in the productivity of the business.

One afternoon, one of the SharePoint® servers suffered a catastrophic failure. This server crashed in a manner, in which no data was recoverable, and the entire server was scrapped. A new SharePoint® server was set up for the business as a result of the failure.

However, the business wasn't satisfied with the new server. They wanted their data back. IT could not provide this request because the data was gone. The business had stored all of their project-related documents, research and design documents, and patent applications on this SharePoint® server. All of that work had to be re-created.

This was a big blow to IT in terms of perceived value. While IT provided exactly what the business asked for, it failed to understand the business desired outcomes and reasons for requesting a SharePoint® server. Had IT taken the time to really understand the customer need for a collaboration environment instead of a SharePoint® server, it would have provided the entire service, including backup and restore, to meet this legitimate need.

If we describe a service in terms of technology (the traditional view of IT), we lose our ability to communicate with the business and thus reduce the value of IT. In short, the business doesn't care about the technology, only about your ability to meet their business-desired outcomes.

The other side effect of being too focused on technology is communications. IT most often solves problems in terms of technology. Therefore, the communication is often technology related. Because of this focus on technology, the business is forced to communicate with IT in terms of technology – terms that IT understands – instead of the business-desired outcomes. Often, this leads to engineering solutions for the business that fail to meet the business-desired outcomes.

The story in the sidebar reveals some interesting things about how IT should approach its solutions to the business. Even though the business request would have probably been provided through the use of a SharePoint® server, the business perspective of IT would have increased dramatically if IT would have taken the time to provide a true service instead of technology. Service strategy assists with this communication by asking "why" we do things before "how" we do them.

Service strategy strives to help IT understand the business perspective of IT in order for IT to be more successful in providing value to its customers. This change of perspective is paramount for IT to advance beyond a technology provider. In the future, companies with IT organizations that have this perspective will be the most successful.

VALUE OF SERVICES

Value can be considered as the level to which a product or service meets the customer needs and is often measured by the price that a customer pays for the product or service. Services, unlike products, have little intrinsic value and the measure of the value of the service is largely based on the return that customers get from utilizing the service.

CHARACTERISTICS OF VALUE

Because of this, the value of a service is not often objective. Determining the value of services must consider the following:

Value is defined by customers

Value of services cannot be determined by the service provider, but rests on the perceptions of the customer. The ultimate value of a service is always determined by the customer and whether or not the service meets their needs.

Affordable mix of features

Regardless of the perception of the service provider, the customer will always pick the service with the best mix of features that is at a price they are willing to pay.

Achievement of objectives

A service has little value to customers if it does not contribute to their ability to achieve their objectives. These objectives are not always revenue based, as in the objective of making money, but may be other non-revenue objectives such as serving the public, complying with legislation, etc.

Value changes over time and circumstances

Value is never constant. As the needs of the business change, the perception of value will change as well. Service providers must continue to re-evaluate the value of a service to their customers to anticipate and address these changes over time.

UNDERSTANDING THE VALUE OF SERVICES

Services have value to an organization only when the value is perceived to be higher than the cost of a service. Understanding the value of a service requires three things:

What service(s) did IT provide?

Simply delivering servers and applications is not enough for the business. IT must be able to link the delivery of a service to the business activities.

What did the service(s) achieve?

This allows the customer to better understand what the service enabled the customer to do.

How much did the service(s) cost?

Customers will compare the cost or level of effort to perform the service themselves against the cost of the service. Additionally, services that have high unanticipated costs (such as services that are difficult to use or access requiring more effort) will have less perceived value.

CREATING VALUE

While services provide and communicate value, value can be a subjective thing. Depending on the person, an old table may be a piece of junk, or it may be a priceless antique. Value is determined by the customer's perception, preferences, and business outcomes. Understanding how value perspective is determined is critical to providing that value.

This perspective is defined, in part, by perception. Customers' perception is influenced by their experiences, what competitors are doing, and their own self image. For example, a customer may be a risk taker or risk adverse. Risk-taking customers may be open to using new technologies and services that are cutting edge. Risk-adverse customers may want to use technologies and services that are very stable and not cutting edge. Understanding what drives the customer's perception is important because the service that is provided may not be perceived as adding value – due entirely to the customer's perception.

Customers also have preferences. These preferences may be driven by past experiences or impressions, among other things. We all have preferences. These preferences may have no basis, other than they are our preferences. If we all had the same preferences, we would all be driving the same model and color car.

Business outcomes also drive value perspective. A service must enable business outcomes to be achieved, or no value will be delivered to the customer.

> ### Key Point
>
> Value is determined by the customer's perception, preferences, and business outcomes.

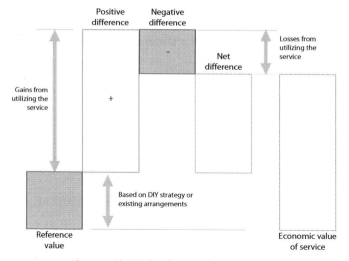

Figure - Economic Value of Service

DEFINING A SERVICE

Customers do not buy services for the sake of the service. They buy the ability to achieve their business-desired outcome.

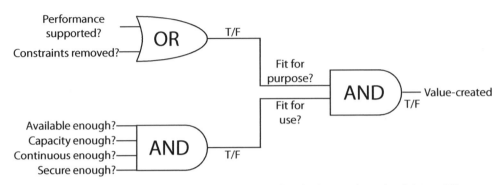

Figure - Utility and Warranty

> **Key Point**
>
> Services are described in terms of utility and warranty.

Services are described in terms of utility and warranty. Utility is defined as *"the functionality offered of a product or service to meet a particular need"*[3] (what it does or fit for purpose). Warranty is defined as a *"promise or guarantee that a product or service will meet its requirements"*[4] (how well it does it or fit for use).

> **Key Point**
>
> Utility is defined as the functionality offered of a product or service to meet a particular need (what it does or fit for purpose).

The utility of a service supports performance of a customer and removes constraints from customers. The warranty of a service refers to the availability, capacity, continuity, and security of a service.

QUESTIONS IN SERVICE STRATEGY

> **Key Point**
>
> Warranty is defined as a promise or guarantee that a product or service will meet its requirements (how well it does it or fit for use).

When defining services in service strategy, the following questions should strive to be answered:

What is our business?

Who is our customer?

---

3   Quoted text is from Service Strategy © Crown copyright 2011 Reproduced under license from the Cabinet Office

4   Quoted text is from Service Strategy © Crown copyright 2011 Reproduced under license from the Cabinet Office.

What does the customer value?

Who depends on our services?

How do they use our services?

Why are these services valuable to them?

These questions are answered by service strategy. During the chapter on the shared service strategy activities, you will find that these shared activities are focused precisely on these questions and how to satisfy the requirements of the customer.

TYPES OF SERVICES

When considering services, there are different types. Some services directly support the business desired outcomes of the customer. These services are called core services. Other services do not directly provide the business desired outcomes of the customer, but support the services that do. These types of services are called supporting services. These supporting services either enable or enhance a core service. Combinations of core services and supporting services are called service packages.

For example, when you visit an ATM machine, your basic desire is to obtain cash. Suppose on your trip to the ATM, the machine is not able to print a receipt but can still dispense cash. You will probably still use the ATM machine because your desired outcome is to walk away with cash in your pocket. The ability to dispense cash is the core service. Printing the receipt is a supporting service, as it enhances the overall service. The ATM machine, with the ability to dispense cash and print a receipt, is the service package.

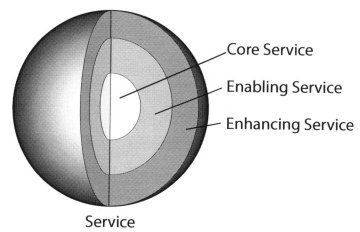

Figure Core, Enabling and Enhancing Services

Supporting services both enable and enhance. Enhancement is adding value to a service above and beyond the core service, such as printing a receipt at an ATM machine. Enabling services are usually services that the customer does not see, such as the communications service. Without the communications service, the ATM does not function. However, the customer rarely knows that this service exists.

Other enabling services for the ATM machine include the network services for communication, the electricity to power the ATM machine, and security services, such as lighting and cameras. Supporting enhancing services for an ATM may be the ability to sell postage stamps, paying bills, or making deposits.

A Service Package is defined as *a "detailed description of an IT service that is available to be delivered to customers."*[5]

The core service is defined as *"a service that delivers basic outcomes desired by one or more customers."*[6]

The supporting service is defined as *"a service that enables or enhances a core service."*[7]

> ### Key Point
>
> A Service Package is defined as a detailed description of an IT service that is available to be delivered to customers.

> ### Key Point
>
> The core service is defined as a service that delivers basic outcomes desired by one or more customers.

> ### Key Point
>
> The supporting service is defined as a service that enables or enhances a core service.

---

5   Quoted text is from Service Strategy © Crown copyright 2011 Reproduced under license from the Cabinet Office

6   Quoted text is from Service Strategy © Crown copyright 2011 Reproduced under license from the Cabinet Office.

7   Quoted text is from Service Strategy © Crown copyright 2011 Reproduced under license from the Cabinet Office..

DEVELOPING A STRATEGY

OVERVIEW

The service strategy stage of the service lifecycle includes the process of strategy management for IT services that guide the overall direction of IT. This process focuses on identifying the market that IT is in, identifying IT's customers, and developing a strategy for execution.

While the details of the strategy management for IT services process are beyond foundation-level knowledge, it is important to understand how strategies around IT services are developed. The basic activities of this process are presented here.

GEPPETTO GARCIA'S

Mark Renner, CIO of Geppetto Garcia's, has recognized that he has two markets to serve. These markets include the internal corporate market and the restaurant market. Within the restaurant market, Mark identified three key services: inventory control service, employee time scheduling service, and the ordering and payment service.

These services have been identified and documented at a high level in the service portfolio. The service portfolio documents all services that the service provider has made any commitment to provide, including any service that has been thought of, but not yet developed. The service portfolio records the business requirements of the service.

Mark and his service owners developed service assets for these identified services. These service assets include ensuring that the right components, people, organization, and knowledge are in place to design, transition, and support these services. One of the services, for example, is the ordering and payment service. This service requires hardware and software components to operate. It also requires network services within each restaurant, as well as a link back to the corporate office. To ensure that this service provides value, the service must be well supported. Mark ensures that this service can be supported by training his staff on how to support it, develop processes to support it, and ensure that the knowledge of the service, including end-user training, is provided for this service.

ACTIVITIES

There are four major activities in strategy management for IT services that assist with development of the service level package that serves as input to service design. These activities are defining the market, developing the offerings, developing strategic assets, and preparing for execution.

DEFINE THE MARKET

This activity is focused on understanding who IT's customers are and identifying customer assets. This activity is critical in ensuring that the proper services are developed, to meet the needs of the business.

Once the customer is identified, this activity continues by identifying the customer's assets. Customers' assets are those things that customers value that enable them to achieve their business-desired outcomes. For example, customer assets can include capital equipment, intellectual property, or processes.

Defining the market starts with understanding the major market drivers. These market drivers provide an overview for the IT strategy.

There are two perspectives when defining a market strategy. The first is to develop a strategy for specific services, such as creating a strategy to capitalize on a specific capability in online services. Popular online shopping, auction, and reservations businesses are good examples. These companies built strategies around their ability to develop Web-based capabilities.

The second perspective is to develop services that align to the strategy. An organization may decide to enter a particular market for a particular customer segment. Services are then created to support that strategy. The emergence of online banking is an example. These companies, forced to respond to customer needs and demands, developed an online strategy, then developed their service assets to support this strategy.

Identifying customers is a top priority. Without understanding the customer, it is difficult to understand the market being served. In order to succeed in their business, customers either develop or purchase assets. Assets can be in the form of equipment, knowledge, and business processes, among others. We must understand these assets in order to assist the business in capitalizing on its assets.

For example, a popular company that specializes in online auctioning relies on linking buyers and sellers so that they can conduct commerce. The company has recognized the importance of this "online community." This online community is one of their assets that distinguishes them from their competitors. The company then decided to provide a mechanism for potential buyers to announce the items they want to buy, thus increasing the potential to link buyers and sellers. A service was developed to enable this mechanism to capitalize on this customer asset.

A customer's goal is to achieve its business-desired outcomes. IT's goal is to provide services that facilitate achieving these business goals. Through analysis of these business-desired outcomes, it can be determined which desired outcomes are served and which are not well-served. The desired outcomes that are not well-served become opportunities to explore for new or updated services.

> **Key Point**
>
> The activities of strategy management for IT services are:
>
> Define the market
>
> Develop the offerings
>
> Develop strategic assets
>
> Prepare for execution

DEVELOP THE OFFERINGS

The 'develop the offerings' activity documents the required service in the service portfolio ensuring that the service description is aligned with the customer's assets and business-desired outcomes. This activity also identifies the capabilities and resources (service assets) that can be leveraged to provide this identified service.

The service portfolio represents commitments made to customers. The service portfolio documents all services, including the services being considered, developed, provided, and retired. The service portfolio documents services in terms of business value and is supported by a business case. This ensures that the business-desired outcomes are not overlooked or ignored.

DEVELOP STRATEGIC ASSETS

This activity focuses on developing the resources and capabilities to support the services that meet business requirements.

Beginning with a focus on customer assets, IT can develop its own strategic assets utilizing its capabilities and resources to develop services. Some customers may not entrust their strategic assets to a provider right away. It may require gaining trust over time by starting out with a small service to enable their business-desired outcomes until the value has been shown and proven.

PREPARE FOR EXECUTION

Preparing for execution identifies the IT strategy based on both internal and external strategic assessments. This activity then defines the requirements and procedures for the remaining service lifecycle stages. These requirements and procedures are documented in the service level package (SLP).

Preparing for service execution is a continual activity. When a service is first planned, the external and internal factors are assessed to establish the objectives. From these objectives, a strategy that outlines the vision, policies, plans, and actions required of that service is generated. A major output of the strategy is to determine the requirements for the remaining stages, particularly around measurement and evaluation of the service. This major output is the service level package, in which these requirements are documented.

Strategic assessments strive to answer questions regarding our services. These questions include:

Which of our services or service varieties are the most distinctive?

What can customers not substitute?

Which of our services or service varieties are most profitable?

Include monetary, profit, social, health, or other major benefits, depending on your business-desired outcomes.

Which of our customers and stakeholders are the most satisfied?

Must understand first how customers determine satisfaction

Which customers, channels, or purchase occasions are the most profitable?

Where are we recovering the most money from our services?

Which of our activities in the value chain are most effective?

What are we doing right?

The answers to these questions reveal patterns regarding services.

Setting objectives involves identifying the actions required in order to realize a strategy. These actions should be well thought out and formulated in a way that focuses all activities toward the defined strategy. The key benefit to setting objectives is that ambiguity is removed from the organization's activities and aligned to the overall strategy.

The objectives and resulting actions should align IT's service assets (comprised of capabilities and resources) to the customer's business-desired outcomes. Focusing on the business-desired outcomes helps the IT organization set priorities for its limited resources, including focus, time, people, and funding.

The defined service should include the elements that are required for success. These critical success factors (CSFs) assist in determining the underlying requirements for a service to help ensure the success of that service.

CSFs, combined with a competitive analysis, identify areas where the IT organization's services can be differentiated from other competitors. Performing this analysis readily identifies areas where further investment should be made and areas where the IT organization provides comparatively little differential value. If it costs more to provide the service ourselves when there are more effective alternatives, these alternatives should be considered, allowing the organization to focus on the services that add differential value.

Every IT organization has limited resources. These resources are in the form of time, money, people, knowledge, and capabilities. Investments in services must be prioritized to areas that have the highest impact on the customer's business in a balanced and cost-justifiable manner. To prioritize, the underserved customers must be identified to understand why the needs are not being properly met. To meet these needs usually involves greater performance or a more innovative approach to the service.

A SWOT analysis (strengths, weaknesses, opportunities, threats) is an analysis technique to identify which market spaces to expand and which should be avoided. Market spaces to avoid can be served by vendors or suppliers as needed. The SWOT analysis assists with decision making with regard to understanding market spaces, the services to offer, the customers to serve, the application of service models to existing or considered services, and the service catalog.

TERMS & DEFINITIONS

Utility

Warranty

Service asset

Capability

Resource

Business case

Service package

Core service

Supporting service

IMPORTANT POINTS

The purpose of service strategy is to provide the ability to think and act in a strategic manner.

The service strategy major output is the service level package.

Value is derived from both utility and warranty.

Services are described in terms of utility and warranty.

Utility refers to fit for purpose by supporting performance or removing constraints.

Warranty refers to fit for use by assuring certain levels of availability, capacity, continuity, and security.

Value is subjective and is influenced by customer perceptions, preferences, and attributes of the service.

Service assets consist of capabilities and resources. Capabilities are intangible and consist of management, organization, processes, knowledge, people, and skills. Resources are tangible and consist of financial capital, infrastructure, applications, information, and people.

The service portfolio represents all commitments we have made in the form of value to the customer.

SECTION REVIEW

1. What is the major output of service strategy?

   A. Service lists

   B. Service level package (SLP)

   C. Service level agreement (SLA)

   D. Operational services

2. What is the purpose of service strategy?

   A. To provide the ability to think and act in a strategic manner

   B. To determine how to pay for services

   C. To justify ITIL® throughout the organization

   D. To ensure accountability of actions to an organization's shareholders

3. Service assets can best be described as what?

   A. The organization's capital purchases

   B. The ability to provide service to external customers

   C. A set of organizational capabilities for providing value to customers in the form of services

   D. Any capability or resources of a service provider.

4. Which of the following statements about value is most correct?

   A. The service provider determines the value of services

   B. The value of a service is determined by the customer

   C. Value of a service cannot be determined

   D. The customer's view of value is irrelevant

5. Service assets consist of what?

   A. Processes and functions

   B. Utility and warranty

   C. Capabilities and resources

   D. Financial capital, infrastructure, applications and information.

6. Which of the following statements is correct?

   A. Capabilities are intangible and resources are tangible.

   B. Capabilities are tangible and resources are intangible.

   C. Capabilities and resources are both tangible.

   D. Capabilities and resources are both intangible.

7. The value of a service is described in terms of what?

   A. Form and function

   B. Capabilities and resources

   C. Utility and warranty

   D. Applications and systems

8. Utility is best described as what?

   A. A promise or guarantee that a product or service will meet its requirements

   B. The functionality offered of a product or service.

   C. The added value that a service delivers to customers.

   D. None of the above.

SECTION REVIEW

9. A service works exactly as described but fails often due to lack of capacity. This is an example of what?

   A. High utility and high warranty

   B. High utility and low warranty

   C. Low utility and high warranty

   D. Low utility and low warranty

10. A service that delivers the basic outcomes desired by one or more customers is what?

   A. Supporting service

   B. Enabling service

   C. Enhancing service

   D. Core service

Comprehension

1. List the types and examples of service assets. Which are tangible and which are intangible?

2. Most households subscribe to cable or satellite television. What are the core and supporting services for this service? Which are enabling services and which are enhancing services?

3

SERVICE STRATEGY PROCESSES

OVERVIEW

This chapter introduces the service strategy processes: service portfolio Management, demand management, financial management for IT services and business relationship management. These processes in particular overlap with other service lifecycle stages. While they are presented in service strategy and play an important part in development of the IT strategy, these processes should be kept in mind when learning the other service lifecycle stages and their processes.

Service portfolio management is responsible for making decisions regarding services and the allocation of service assets to those services. Demand management analyzes the sources of demand for service to identify underlying patterns in an effort to anticipate or influence the demand. Financial management for IT services is the process responsible for managing the funding of services and ensuring the proper stewardship of funds. Business relationship management is the process that enables business relationship managers (BRMs) to provide links between the service provider and customers at the strategic and tactical levels.

These processes commonly share decision-making regarding services. Through these processes, decisions are made to determine which services are viable and which are not and ensure that the services have the appropriate financial commitment.

SERVICE PORTFOLIO MANAGEMENT

GEPPETTO GARCIA'S

Mark Renner, CIO of Geppetto Garcia's, recognizes the need to create a portfolio of services. Mark understands that without having a consistent, documented portfolio of services, it is difficult to represent to the business what IT is providing or planning to provide to support the business desired outcomes. If Mark cannot communicate the services and how they align to the desired outcomes of the business, it is difficult to communicate the value that IT provides and even more difficult to justify funding for resources to support the business.

Mark's service portfolio documents all services that have been conceived, are in operation, or have been retired. These services are documented in terms of the value that they provide to the business. Using the services defined in the service portfolio, Mark can better evaluate the relative importance of each service to ensure that the greatest focus of resources is directed to the services that provide the most value. This helps Mark control the risk within IT and the effects of that risk to the business.

OVERVIEW

Key Point

Service portfolio management (SPM) is responsible for maximizing the return on investment while managing risk.

Service portfolio management (SPM) is responsible for maximizing the return on investment while managing risk. Service portfolio management does this by describing services in terms of business value and articulating the provider's response to the needs of the business.

Service portfolio management is a dynamic method for governing investments in service management across the enterprise and managing them for value. The main concept in service portfolio management is the Service Portfolio. The service portfolio assists this governance by documenting all services under consideration, being developed, being transitioned, operational, or retired.

The service portfolio helps to answer the following questions regarding service:

> Why should a customer buy these services?

> Why should a customer buy these services from us?

> What are the pricing or chargeback models?

> What are our strengths and weaknesses, priorities, and risks?

> How should our resources and capabilities be allocated?

> **Key Point**
>
> Service portfolio management is a dynamic method for governing investments in service management across the enterprise and managing them for value.

KEY POINTS

SERVICE PORTFOLIO

The service portfolio represents the complete set of services managed by the service provider. The service portfolio includes three parts: the service pipeline, the service catalog and retired services. The service portfolio documents all services being considered, being designed, transitioning to operation, in operation, or retired from service.

> **Key Point**
>
> The service portfolio represents the complete set of services managed by the service provider.

©Crown copyright 2011 - Reproduced under license from the Cabinet Office

Figure - Service portfolio

The service portfolio diagram shows the service portfolio and its various components. The service portfolio draws on a common pool of resources (IT staff) to evaluate, design, transition, operate, and continually improve services. The service portfolio assists in the prioritization of where these resources should focus to ensure that the highest priority services receive the attention they require.

The service portfolio consists of the service pipeline, the service catalog, and retired services.

Service Pipeline

The service pipeline is where requirements for services are collected to evaluate these requirements to determine if investment in a service is warranted and how resources should be allocated. The service pipeline draws upon the information collected in service strategy about customers and market spaces.

Service Catalog

The service catalog is a catalog of services that are available to customers and users of IT's services. The service catalog contains descriptions of all services that are operational and should include any third-party services that IT leverages. An example of a third-party service is mobile phones. IT itself does not supply the mobile phones but relies on vendors for the phones. IT adds value to this service by supporting the phone service, managing payments to the vendor, and selecting the vendor.

Retired Services

Retired services are those services that are no longer in operation. These services are documented in the service portfolio to retain the information for later use. Once a service is retired, the information about that service may be useful if the service needs to be offered again or a new service is developed based on some of the characteristics of the retired service.

BUSINESS CASE

Business cases are used to justify proposed business actions. As a decision support and planning tool, business cases are important to document proposed business actions in order to logically present what the expected outcomes are, the financial and business implications of the proposed business action, and the risks that are expected.

Every service should have a business case associated with it. This business case justifies the resources spent in supporting the service. When the service is reviewed, the business case should also be reviewed to ensure that the basis for providing the service is still valid and determine if the reasons for providing the service have changed.

A business case may have the following contents within it:

> Introduction
> Methods and assumptions
> Business impacts
> Risks and contingencies
> Recommendations

> **Key Point**
>
> A business case is a decision support and planning tool to justify significant expenditures.

MANAGING RISK

Service portfolio management controls the risks associated with services. Risk management is a technique to determine these risks and manage these risks. A risk is defined as *"a possible event that could cause harm or loss."*[1] There are many formal risk management frameworks. One of these is Management of Risk® (MoR®).

> **Key Point**
>
> A risk is defined as a possible event that could cause harm or loss.

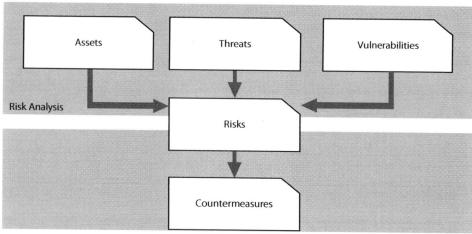

Figure - Managing Risk

---

1   Quoted text is from Service Strategy © Crown copyright 2011 Reproduced under license from the Cabinet Office

ACTIVITIES

When determining which services should be supported, service portfolio management activities evaluate services to promote services to be designed based on the relative value of the service. These activities include defining, analyzing, approving, and chartering the service.

This approach to which services should be considered for the service portfolio is to list all services with no constraints on resources, funding or time. In other words, list all services that could be provided if there were no limits to time, money, or resources. Constraints are then applied to these services and evaluated to determine which services should be provided and then prioritized. Once prioritized, the services that provide the most value and can be performed within the constraints are approved. These approved services are then assigned resources and chartered. Once chartered, the service level package for this service is promoted to service design.

This process should occur regularly and include all services, not just those that are new. This regular review of services provides the opportunity for IT to determine where to apply resources and constraints. This regular review also ensures that the right services are being offered to provide the right level of value to the business.

Define

The 'define' activity develops business cases for all of the services that would be offered if the organization had unlimited resources. This provides an overview of the needs of the business to achieve its business-desired outcomes. This method is triggered by changes to the business that require defining new services or changes to existing services.

When defining a service, the definition of the service should be documented in terms of the value to the business. By focusing on business value, services are more likely to align to that value instead of "morphing" into some service that fails to align to the true customer needs.

Analyze

Since no organization has unlimited resources, the 'analyze' activity prioritizes the services into a set of services that can be offered through an acceptable use of resources. This maximizes the value of the service portfolio by offering high-value services to customers and either discontinuing or finding other ways to provide the lower-value services. Over time, some services become commodities, so it is possible to find alternate sources for these services other than IT. These services are candidates for outsourcing.

Approve

When a service is approved, it is finalized in the service portfolio. This authorizes the service and authorizes the allocation of resources required for the service. When a service is not approved, it must be deliberately disapproved so there is no misconception regarding the service.

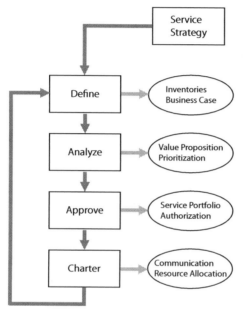

©Crown copyright 2011 - Reproduced under license from the Cabinet Office

Figure - Service Portfolio Management Activities

Charter

Chartering a service involves ensuring the decision for the service is clear and unambiguous. This communication triggers other activities, such as inclusion of the service in the financial forecasts and triggering the processes in service design to design the service. Changes to services are also communicated through the charter method. Services identified for retirement trigger the service being discontinued through service transition.

> **Key Point**
>
> The activities in service portfolio management include define, analyze, approve, and charter.

DEMAND MANAGEMENT

OVERVIEW

Since services are perishable, delivery of services must match the demand for services, or the services are wasted. Failure to anticipate increased demand can result in the inability to meet the demand and decrease the perception of value of customers. For example, with Geppetto Garcia's Inventory Control service, changes in product sales influence the demand for services. Therefore, if a change in sales is anticipated, a change in the service demand also can be anticipated.

DEMAND OF THE GIFT CARD SERVICE

Mark Renner, CIO of Geppetto Garcia's, has been reading articles in the newspaper and industry magazines about the failures that have occurred in other businesses. One of the articles that he reads involves an airline that left passengers stranded for several days due to the failure of one of its computer systems.[2]

Based on this information, Mark decides that he needs to determine when the demand of IT services fluctuates to ensure that the necessary resources are available to meet the demand. Mark uses concepts in the demand management process to determine that the year-end holiday season is when the gift-card service will reach its highest demand. Mark has also identified other peaks in demand around Mother's Day and, for Geppetto's Sports Bar, there is another peak of gift-card usage on Superbowl Sunday.

Based on these peak demand periods, Mark engages the service manager to determine if the gift-card service will operate as expected during these high-demand periods. The service manager will use this information to ensure that the design of the service takes into account these peak demand periods and that the availability and capacity designs of the service are adequate.

2   Comair computer crash could hurt the struggling airline. Charleston Gazette. December 29, 2004

The service manager also ensures that these peak demand periods are documented in the service level agreements by working closely with the service level manager. These high priority periods are communicated throughout IT to ensure that the appropriate levels of support are anticipated.

KEY CONCEPTS

Demand management is a collection of activities that strives to understand and influence customer demand for services and the provision of capacity to meet these demands. There are two aspects of demand management: tactical and strategic.

> **Key Point**
>
> Demand management is a collection of activities that strives to understand and influence customer demand for services and the provision of capacity to meet these demands.

TACTICAL DEMAND MANAGEMENT

Tactical demand management involves influencing demand. One technique to influence demand is differential charging. Differential charging is a technique that charges more or less for a service in an effort to balance demand or lessen peak demand. Cell phone companies, for example, provide reduced-cost calling in the evenings or on weekends. This technique is used to lower the demand during the daytime peak and transfer some of this demand, such as personal calls, to periods when there is excess capacity.

> **Key Point**
>
> Tactical demand management involves influencing demand.

STRATEGIC DEMAND MANAGEMENT

Strategic demand management involves analyzing patterns of business activity (PBAs) to develop user profiles (UPs) to anticipate demand for services. Both internal and external factors are reviewed to understand these patterns. To do this, the sources of demand are determined. Some of these sources include people, processes, and applications. However, just about anything can be a source of demand. Inclement weather, for example, can be a source of demand for cell-phone providers as the call volumes increase during periods of inclement weather.

> **Key Point**
>
> Strategic demand management involves analyzing patterns of business activity (PBAs)

These patterns then assist in determining cyclical changes in demand. Florists, for example, anticipate increased seasonal demand during Mother's Day and Valentine's Day and prepare for increased manufacturing, sales, and shipping during these times.

Once the sources of demand are determined, PBAs that document patterns of demand are developed. The PBAs consider the frequency, volume, location, and duration of that demand. Once documented, these PBAs are under change control.

User profiles (UPs) are then developed to document sources of demand and their individual patterns. These UPs combine one or more PBAs to determine overall patterns. For example, if we know that one user uses 5% of a server's CPU on Friday mornings between 8:00 AM and 10:00 AM, we can better determine how many servers are required for 100 users. Demand management works closely with capacity management to ensure that appropriate capacity is available to meet the anticipated demand.

DEMAND MANAGEMENT THROUGH THE LIFECYCLE

While it is documented in service strategy, demand management is prevalent in the other service lifecycle stages as well. In service strategy, demand management assists with the evaluation of the service portfolio to analyze service and forecast additional resources for services. Demand management also works with financial management to influence demand through differential charging for services.

In service design, the design for services relies on the demand forecasts to optimize the design of the service. Proper design should anticipate the demand for the service to ensure that the service is "the right size" and not over- or under-engineered.

In service design's service catalog management process, the demand for the service is mapped in the service catalog. Lastly, service operation is affected by changes in demand and adjusts the operation of a service through resource scheduling and workload balancing of the service.

FINANCIAL MANAGEMENT FOR IT SERVICES

OVERVIEW

Financial management for IT services is the process that provides financial input and output to other processes. The purpose of financial management for IT services is to "secure the appropriate level of funding to design, develop and deliver services that meet the strategy of the organization."[3] This is done by identifying, documenting, and agreeing on the value of services being received by the customer.

> **Key Point**
>
> The purpose of financial management for IT services is to secure the appropriate level of funding to design, develop and deliver services that meet the strategy of the organization.

FINANCIAL MANAGEMENT AT GEPPETTO GARCIA'S

Services are expensive to provide. In order to ensure that the right services are provided at the right cost, Mark Renner enlists the help of Susan Brockman, a financial analyst, to establish a financial management for IT services process within IT. Susan's new role comes with the responsibility to help IT and the business make better decisions with regard to the services that are provided by IT and the money spent on them.

In order to be effective, Susan must be able to account for all of the expenditures for each service and ensure that all expenditures are allocated appropriately to the correct service. This accounting provides the basis for further evaluation of the investments within a service. Using this information, Susan is better able to analyze the expenditures for a service and communicate these costs to the business.

Susan's desire, under Mark's direction, is to establish a charging system so that the business pays for the services that they utilize or ask for. Through

3   Quoted text is from Service Strategy © Crown copyright 2011 Reproduced under license from the Cabinet Office

a charging system, business becomes more responsible for its decisions and the costs associated with those decisions. Value is also easier to communicate to the business because, once a charging system is in place, IT can communicate in the native language of the business - money. By communicating in this way, it is the desire of Mark Renner to be viewed in the eyes of the business as a service provider and increase the value that IT provides to the business.

Financial management for IT services works in concert with the organization's financial management practice. Following the corporate policies, financial management for IT services acts as an extension of corporate finance for IT-specific financial concerns.

The scope of financial management for IT services includes activities that span the service lifecycle. These activities fall into the categories of accounting, budgeting and charging.

Accounting involves tracking the money spent to provide services throughout the service lifecycle. Accounting ensures that the money spent is assigned to the appropriate cost centers according to the organization's financial management policies.

Budgeting activities strive to determine the financial requirement to provide services during the next fiscal cycle (generally each year). Budgeting identifies the various costs to determine the funding requirement, as well as the timeliness of the funding, to ensure services can be provided as an ongoing concern.

Charging is an optional set of activities, but are a sign of a highly mature organization. The charging activities recover costs of services from customers when those services are rendered. Through proper charging, a service provider can help the customer become more responsible for their consumption of services and help them be more financially responsible for their consumption.

BUSINESS VALUE

Financial management for IT services communicates the value of services to the business. Without understanding the value of the service, it is difficult to make proper decisions regarding these services.

Other values to the business include:

"Improved decision making

Quicker and better evaluated change

Improved service portfolio management

Improved financial compliance and control

Improved operational control

Communication of value capture and creation"[4]

KEY CONCEPTS

COST CLASSIFICATIONS

When accounting for services, the costs are categorized according to cost type. Cost types include labor costs, hardware costs, software costs, travel costs, etc. Costs are also categorized by cost classification. These cost classifications include:

Direct versus Indirect

Direct costs are those that can be allocated entirely to a single customer or service. Direct costs support only that particular customer or service. Examples of direct costs are servers that only support one service, dedicated people to support a single service, or other components that are dedicated to a single service.

Indirect costs, also known as "shared costs," support multiple services or customers. These shared costs should be allocated proportionally to the consumer of that service. For example, if a server is equally allocated to two services, the cost of the server should be allocated equally to each service. Other examples of indirect costs include the network infrastructure, utilities, and the costs of the Service Desk.

Fixed versus Variable

Fixed costs are those costs which are paid regardless of use. These are costs that we must pay even if we do not use the product or service. Examples of fixed costs are servers, buildings, and salaries. These costs must be paid regardless of whether or not we use the server, occupy the building, or engage the people whose salaries we pay.

> **Key Point**
>
> The financial management for IT services cost classifications are:
>
> Direct vs. Indirect
>
> Fixed vs. Variable
>
> Capital vs. Operational

---

4 Quoted text is from Service Strategy © Crown copyright 2011 Reproduced under license from the Cabinet Office

Variable costs vary depending on the use of that service. Utilities are a common example of variable costs. Our utility costs vary depending on how much we use. Other examples include training costs, overtime costs, and travel costs.

Capital versus Operational

Capital costs are for an asset that are above some monetary value. Capital costs are often amortized from income taxes through the life of the asset. Examples of capital costs include buildings, vehicles, and large servers.

Operational costs are incurred for day-to-day operation of the service. These costs include salaries, printer-consumable items, and utilities.

These cost classifications are not mutually exclusive in that a particular cost could be direct, variable, and operational. Using the above classifications, utilities, such as electricity, would include indirect, variable, and operational costs. An expensive tape silo system to back up the entire infrastructure would be an indirect, fixed, and capital cost.

ACTIVITIES

The activities in financial management for IT services interact with processes in all other service lifecycle stages, even though they have been defined in service strategy. Briefly, the financial management for IT services activities include:

Service Valuation

Service valuation strives to produce a value for services that is fair in order to obtain funding to support the service as an ongoing concern. This activity quantifies the funding of services expected from the business.

Demand Modeling

Demand modeling quantifies the funding variations based on demand cycles and models demand behaviors. Demand modeling works closely with demand management and capacity management to determine these demand cycles and costs associated with meeting demand.

Service Portfolio Management

Financial management for IT services works closely with service portfolio management to identify cost structures of services, as well as the costs of services.

Service Provisioning Optimization (SPO)

Service provisioning optimization (SPO) identifies costs and improves competitiveness of services through optimization of those costs.

Accounting

Accounting is the activity that records the consumption of service. Accounting also shows which consumer utilized the service and assigns associated costs to the consumer.

Service Investment Analysis (SIA)

Service investment analysis improves investment decisions by analyzing the costs of a service. Service investment analysis also provides input to help to make decisions regarding which services should be offered.

Compliance

Compliance demonstrates that proper and consistent accounting methods are being deployed. Legislation around Sarbanes-Oxley in the U.S. requires companies to conform to certain accounting practices or face penalties.

Variable Cost Dynamics (VCD)

Variable cost dynamics (VCD) determines the variable sensitivity of services by analyzing the variables that impact the costs of services. The price of oil, for example, is a variable cost in many products and services that we buy in our everyday lives. Variable cost dynamics would be interested in determining the sensitivity of these products and services on the price of oil.

Planning Confidence

Planning confidence is achieved by ensuring that the forecasts and other financial practices are correct within a significant margin of error. Through confidence in planning, assurances for the proper funding are available for the delivery of services.

BUSINESS RELATIONSHIP MANAGEMENT

OVERVIEW

As organizations have recognized the need to establish the role of a business relationship manager (BRM), many have realized that business relationship management is a process in itself and not just a role. The business relationship management process works throughout the service lifecycle to be the link between the service provider and the customer at the strategic and tactical levels.

This improved interaction between the service provider and customer through the business relationship management process ensures that the customer requirements are well understood on a strategic and tactical level. It also ensures that the service provider can respond to those needs with appropriate services.

The purpose of business relationship management has two parts. First, "business relationship management establishes and maintains a business relationship between the service provider and the customer based on understanding the customers and their business needs."[5] This ensures the customer's needs and desires are well understood, as well as identifies potential opportunities to better serve the customer.

Second, business relationship management "identifies customer needs and ensures that the service provider is able to meet these needs as business needs change over time and circumstances."[6] Better understanding these needs and how the needs can be met helps establish business expectations of the service provider at a price the business is willing to pay.

The objectives of business relationship management include:

---

5   Quoted text is from Service Strategy © Crown copyright 2011 Reproduced under license from the Cabinet Office

6   Quoted text is from Service Strategy © Crown copyright 2011 Reproduced under license from the Cabinet Office.

"Ensuring that the service provider understands the customer's perspective of service and is therefore able to prioritize its services and service assets appropriately

Ensuring high levels of customer satisfaction

Establishing and maintaining a constructive relationship between the service provider and the customer

Identifying changes to the customer environment or technology trends that could potentially impact the type, level, or utilization of service provided

Establishing and articulating business requirements for new and changed services

Ensuring that the service provider is meeting the business needs of the customer

Working with customers to ensure that services and service levels deliver value

Mediating cases in which there are conflicting requirements for services from different business units

Establishing formal complaint and escalation processes for the customer"[7]

SCOPE

Business relationship management works throughout the service lifecycle to understand how services meet customer requirements. This means that the process must understand the business outcomes, the services that are currently offered, technology trends, levels of customer satisfaction, and the customers' perceptions of the service provider.

This understanding cannot be obtained solely by business relationship management but also through other processes throughout the service lifecycle. As such, business relationship management works closely with other processes to articulate the capabilities of these processes through the services delivered, as well as relate concerns of the business to these processes where appropriate.

While working closely with customers, business relationship management will establish a process or procedure for also addressing customer complaints and relaying compliments.

7   Quoted text is from Service Strategy © Crown copyright 2011 Reproduced under license from the Cabinet Office

Business Relationship Management and Service Level Management

Both business relationship management and service level management involve significant interfacing with the customer, but the focus of each process is different. Service level management is focused on providing a specific level of service for identified services, while business relationship management's scope is broader in understanding requirements and building relationships at the strategic and tactical level. These differences are identified in the table below.

Differences between business relationship management and service level management

	Business relationship management	**Service level management**
Purpose	To establish and maintain a business relationship between the service provider and the customer based on understanding the customer and their business needs To identify customer needs (utility and warranty) and ensure that the service provider is able to meet these needs	To negotiate service level agreements (warranty terms) with customers and ensure that all service management processes, operational level agreements, and underpinning contracts are appropriate for the agreed service level targets
Focus	Strategic and tactical - the focus is on the overall relationship between the service provider and its customer and which services the service provider will deliver to meet customer needs	Tactical and operational - the focus is on reaching agreement on the level of service that will be delivered for new and existing services and whether the service provider was able to meet those agreements
Primary measure	Customer satisfaction, also an improvement in the customer's intention to better use and pay for the service. Another metric is whether customers are willing to recommend the service to other (potential) customers	Achieving agreed levels of service (which leads to customer satisfaction)

Source: ITIL® Service Strategy

TERMS & DEFINITIONS

Service portfolio

Service pipeline

Service catalog

Retired services

Business case

Risk

Tactical demand management

Strategic demand management

Patterns of business activity (PBAs)

IMPORTANT POINTS

The service strategy processes are:

> Service portfolio management
>
> Demand management
>
> Financial management for IT services
>
> Business relationship management

Service portfolio management is a dynamic method for governing investments in service management across the enterprise and managing them for value.

The service portfolio consists of the service pipeline, the service catalog, and retired services.

Demand management is a collection of activities that strives to understand and influence customer demand for services and the provision of capacity to meet these demands.

The purpose of financial management for IT services is to ensure proper funding of the delivery of IT services.

Business relationship management is the process that enables business relationship managers to provide links between the service provider and the customer at the strategic and tactical levels.

Business relationship management differs from service level management as the business relationship management process focuses on the strategic and tactical levels, while service level management focuses on the tactical and operational levels.

Business relationship management establishes a process for handling complaints and compliments from customers.

SECTION REVIEW

1. Which of the following is NOT a process within Service strategy?

   A. Service portfolio management

   B. Service catalog management

   C. Demand management

   D. Financial management for IT services

2. What is the purpose of service portfolio management?

   A. Manage the service portfolio

   B. Maximize return at an acceptable risk

   C. Ensure proper governance of IT resources

   D. Match IT capabilities with demand for services

3. Which of the following is NOT a question answered by the service portfolio?

   A. How should our resources and capabilities be allocated?

   B. What is the availability of these services?

   C. What are the pricing or charge back models?

   D. Why should a customer buy these services?

4. The service pipeline is what?

   A. The list of services being considered as well as those in operation

   B. The list of services being considered before they go into operation

   C. The pipeline of requirements that should be considered for a new service

   D. The demand for application development resources

5. Which of the following is NOT a part of the service portfolio?

   A. Service specifications

   B. Service pipeline

   C. Service catalog

   D. Retired services

6. Which demand management focus involves the use of patterns of business activity and user profiles?

   A. Current

   B. Tactical

   C. Strategic

   D. Operational

7. Which demand management focus involves the use of differential charging to encourage customers to use IT services at less busy times?

   A. Tactical

   B. Strategic

   C. Current

   D. Operational

8. What are some possible sources of demand?

   A. People

   B. Processes

   C. Applications

   D. All of the above

9. The service portfolio documents services in terms of what?

   A. Outcomes

   B. Demand

   C. Value

   D. Capabilities

10. Which service strategy process has determining PBAs as an activity?

   A. Demand management

   B. Financial management for IT services

   C. Strategy management

   D. Service portfolio management

Comprehension

1. List and provide a brief overview of the processes within the service strategy stage of the service lifecycle.

2. In your organization, how does financial management for IT services play a role? Additionally, how could financial management for IT services support the processes throughout the service lifecycle?

4

SERVICE DESIGN OVERVIEW

OVERVIEW

This chapter provides an overview of the service design stage of the service lifecycle. In this chapter, you will learn the purpose, objectives, and value to business of service design, as well as the key concepts of the value of design, the 4 Ps of service design, and the service design package.

Service design takes the requirements contained within the service charter as input from service strategy. Based on the service charter, service design designs a service or a change to a service to meet the requirements. When designing a service, service design takes into account all of the elements of that service, not just the technical solution. The design of that service also includes the design of knowledge, processes, measurements, and service management tools and processes. This design is included in the major output of service design, the service design Package (SDP).

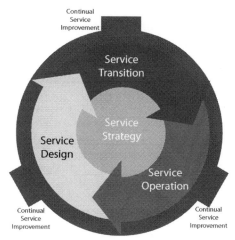

(c) Crown copyright 2007 - Reproduced under license from OGC

Figure - Service Lifecycle

GEPPETTO GARCIA'S GIFT CARD SERVICE

In order to design a service for the ability to process gift cards, Mark Renner recognizes that the IT systems, in particular the retail systems, must change in order to facilitate this new service. However, the technology is only part of the considerations in the design. For this service to provide the most value possible to the restaurants and to the diners, all aspects of this service must be designed.

Mark again met with Emil Delgassi, the Chief Operating Officer for Geppetto Garcia's. Together, they determined all of the aspects of this service that need to be considered as part of the design.

First, they needed to determine what options they had for procurement of the gift cards. They listed the possibilities that they could produce the gift cards themselves or purchase them from a company that specializes in gift cards. When the consideration of involving an outside organization came up, they determined that they needed to inquire about additional services that a company that specializes in gift cards might provide. An external company may better understand how to market, distribute, and manage the selling of gift cards because they may have established channels into the market already.

Another aspect of their design was the processes that need to be developed or changed to support gift cards. The retail systems need to be modified to accept and sell gift cards. However, other processes need to be addressed as well, such as training on how to accept a gift card from a customer and the accounting processes needed to address this new source of purchasing from diners. Therefore, training was added to part of the design of the service.

While reviewing their definition of the business-desired outcome, to increase revenue and profits for the restaurants, Emil and Mark discuss how to ensure that their business-desired outcomes are being achieved. They determine that they need a way to measure gift card sales and redemptions to ensure that the business-desired objectives were being met. Therefore, they added metrics and measurements of the service to be part of the design.

Gift cards, just like any other form of electronic fund transfer, require technology to support it. Mark, being responsible for the Information Technology organization, agrees to address the technology requirements that would be involved in supporting a gift card service. Technology requirements were added to the design.

Also, since Mark was becoming familiar with the concepts of IT service management, he determines that he needs to address any of the service management tools and technology to see if any modifications need to be made to support this new service. Some of the service management tools and technology that he identified right away included the service portfolio, service catalog, configuration management system, service desk tools, and the service knowledge management system. However, he knew that there would be other tools that would need to be considered through the design of this new service.

Together, Emil and Mark created the beginnings of a design document that addressed the service as a holistic service, instead of only as a new technology. Since starting to employ service management concepts, Mark discovered that the traditional view of IT is very short-sighted and that all aspects of a service must be considered when designing a new or changed service. Mark discovered that all aspects of this new service could not be provided by IT only, but IT and the business could provide all aspects of this service by working more closely together to meet the business-desired outcomes.

PURPOSE

The purpose of service design is to "design IT services, together with the governing IT practices, processes and policies, to realize the service provider's strategy and to facilitate the introduction of these services into supported environments ensuring quality service delivery, customer satisfaction and cost-effective service provision."[1] This means that service design must take a holistic approach to design that includes designing:

Service Solution

The solution itself and its supporting components

Tools and Technologies

The tools and techniques required to manage the service

Architectures

Ensuring that the design of the service is consistent with existing services and architectures

Measurements and Metrics

Measurements and metrics to ensure that the service meets its requirements and is being properly managed

Processes

Processes required to design, transition, and operate this service

> ### Key Point
>
> The purpose of service design is to "design IT services, together with the governing IT practices, processes and policies, to realize the service provider's strategy and to facilitate the introduction of these services into supported environments ensuring quality service delivery, customer satisfaction and cost-effective service provision.

---

1   Quoted text is from Service Design © Crown copyright 2011 Reproduced under license from the Cabinet Office

The objective of service design is to "design IT services so effectively that minimal improvement during their lifecycle will be required."[2] Personally, I take exception to this objective because anytime we design a service, improvements can always be made. Additionally, as the business requirements change, the service will require changes to address the new business requirements. I believe the objective should be to design IT services such that they are flexible in order to accommodate not only the current needs, but can be adapted to meet future needs as well.

Value to Business

Good design ensures that the service meets its business-desired outcomes while conforming to the requirements and constraints of service strategy. It is important that the service is designed based on these business needs and continual verification that the service meets these needs is performed.

The value to business of service design includes:

Reduced total cost of ownership (TCO)

Improved quality of service

Improved consistency of service

Improved implementation of new or changed services

Alignment of services to the business

Improved service performance

Improved IT Governance

Effective service management and ITSM processes

Improved decision-making based on higher quality information

Key Concepts

Service design requires inputs from service strategy. These inputs include the service portfolio and service charter, where requirements are gathered and recorded and the strategies and constraints that services must meet are documented.

The resulting solution from service design is more than just the technology but also the service management system and tools, standard architectures, processes and measurements, and metrics. All of these parts of the solution support the transition, operation, and improvement of the service.

---

2   Quoted text is from Service Design © Crown copyright 2011 Reproduced under license from the Cabinet Office

These design components are documented in a service design package (SDP) used by service transition to develop the service and transition it into operation.

All developers, project managers, and others who design services know that good design is invaluable to the business. Good design anticipates and resolves issues that often arise in the development stage or later. However, design is frequently the first thing to be eliminated when the pressures of time start to impact a service.

The value of design includes the following:

Agreed service levels ensuring critical business processes have the proper focus

This involves understanding which business processes are critical and designing services to support those critical business processes.

Measuring IT quality in business or user terms that are better understood

This involves understanding the business-desired outcomes and designing measurements and metrics that map to these business-desired outcomes, thus improving the communication with the business and increasing the perception of value.

Mapping business processes to the IT infrastructure

Mapping business processes to the IT infrastructure defines how the IT technology supports the business processes and relates to the business processes.

Measuring services in relation to business processes

Measuring services in relation to business processes provides the ability to measure how services meet the needs of the business processes.

Mapping infrastructure resources to services

Mapping infrastructure resources to services involves understanding and mapping technology to services and storing this information in the configuration management system (CMS). We will explore the CMS in the service transition section.

Providing end-to-end performance monitoring

End-to-end performance monitoring reveals how the elements of the service impact performance and being able to measure them throughout the entire service. This helps us understand the end-user's perception of the performance of a service, rather than just the IT perception of the service.

Good and proper design resulting in a solution that satisfies the business requirements is easier to operate and support and lowers the total cost of ownership (TCO) of the service. A properly designed service that includes all components of the service is far easier to transition and operate than a poorly designed service or one that does not include all of the necessary components.

Service design ensures:

"Services are business- and customer-oriented, focused and driven

Services are cost-effective and secure

Services are flexible and adaptable, yet fit for purpose at the point of delivery

Services can absorb an ever-increasing demand in the volume and speed of change

Services meet increasing business demands for continuous operation

Services are managed and operated to an acceptable level of risk

Services are responsive, with appropriate availability matched to business needs"[3]

4 PS OF SERVICE DESIGN

There is nothing you can put your hands on in your environment and say "This is the service we offer." A service is a human concept that includes four specific things. When providing a service, people are needed to design, transition, support and improve a service. Processes are required to effectively design, transition, operate and improve a service. Every service requires support from partners (vendors) to design, operate, and support the service. And, lastly, a service requires products (underlying technology) to design, transition, operate, and improve a service.

> **Key Point**
>
> The 4 Ps of service design are the people, processes, partners, and products involved to deliver a service.

A service requires people, processes, partners (vendors), and products (technology). These are the 4 Ps of service design. Without any one of these four elements, the service cannot be provided effectively and efficiently.

FIVE ASPECTS OF DESIGN

Considering the five aspects of design when designing a service helps to ensure that the entire service can be implemented, transitioned, and operated efficiently and effectively. These five aspects include:

---

3   Quoted text is from Service Design © Crown copyright 2011 Reproduced under license from the Cabinet Office

Service Solution

The solution itself and its supporting components

Tools and Technologies

The tools and techniques required to manage the service

Architectures

Ensuring that the design of the service is consistent with existing services and architectures

Measurement systems and metrics

Measurements and metrics to ensure that the service meets its requirements and is being properly managed

Processes

Processes required to design, transition, and operate this service

These five aspects of design are documented in the service design Package (SDP) that is output from service design. An easy way to remember these five aspects is to remember "service design's S.T.A.M.P. of approval".

> **Key Point**
>
> The Five Aspects of Design are:
>
> Service solution
>
> Tools and technologies
>
> Architectures
>
> Measurement systems and metrics
>
> Processes

SERVICE DESIGN PACKAGE

These design of a service is documented in a service design package (SDP) used by service transition to develop the service and transition it into operation. A service design package refers to a set of documents defining all aspects of an IT service and its requirements through each stage of its lifecycle. A service design package is produced for each new IT service, major change, or service retirement.

In addition to specifying the five aspects of design, the service design package contains:

> **Key Point**
>
> A service design package refers to a set of documents defining all aspects of an IT service and its requirements through each stage of its lifecycle.

Service functional requirements

Service level requirements

Service and operational management requirements

Service design and topology

TERMS & DEFINITIONS

Service design package (SDP)

4 Ps of service design

Five aspects of design

IMPORTANT POINTS

The major input to service design is the service charter from service strategy.

The major output of service design is the service design package (SDP) to service transition.

The purpose of service design is the design of new or changed services for introduction into the live environment.

The 4 Ps of service design are people, processes, partners (vendors) and products (technology).

The five aspects of design include:

> Service solution itself
>
> Tools and technologies
>
> Architectures
>
> Measurement systems and metrics
>
> Processes

SECTION REVIEW

1. What is the major input to service design?

   A. Service design package (SDP)

   B. Service transition package (STP)

   C. Service level package (SLP)

   D. Service package (SP)

2. What is the major output from service design to service transition?

   A. Service design package (SDP)

   B. Service transition package (STP)

   C. Service level package (SLP)

   D. Service package (SP)

3. The purpose of service design is best described as what?

   A. To ensure value through the proper implementation of the functionality of a service

   B. The design of new or changed services for introduction into the live environment

   C. To ensure that cost-justifiable availability and capacity exist for current and future services

   D. To provide a logical model of the IT infrastructure and the relationships between components, applications, systems, and services

4. The 4 Ps of service design include people, products, partners and what other item?

   A. Vendors

   B. Positions

   C. Technology

   D. Processes

5. Ensuring that an entire service can be implemented, transitioned, and operated efficiently and effectively describes what?

   A. Five aspects of design

   B. 4 Ps of service design

   C. Functional specifications

   D. None of the above

6. The five aspects of design include which of the following?

   1. People

   2. Service solution

   3. Service management systems and tools

   4. Processes

   5. Technology and architectures

   6. Requirements and specifications

   7. Measurements and metrics

   A. 1, 3, 4, 5, 6

   B. 2, 3, 4, 5, 6

   C. 1, 3, 4, 6, 7

   D. 2, 3, 4, 5, 7

7. The service design package (SDP) is best described as what?

   A. A description of the 4 Ps of service design

   B. A set of documents defining all aspects of an IT service and its requirements through each stage of its lifecycle

   C. Everything necessary for the build, test, implementation, and deployment of a service

   D. The business requirements for a new or changed service

SECTION REVIEW

8. The service design package includes the service functional requirements, service design and topology, and what else?

    A. Service level requirements

    B. Service and operational management requirements

    C. Both A and B

    D. Neither A nor B

9. As an aspect of design, service management systems and tools might include what?

    A. Service portfolio

    B. Management requirements

    C. Processes

    D. People

Comprehension

1. The service design package (SDP) is an important output of service design. What are some of the examples of what the service design package includes?

5

SERVICE DESIGN PROCESSES

OVERVIEW

The service design processes design services in a holistic manner based on the requirements, standards, and constraints in the service charter from service strategy.

The processes in service design are:

Design coordination

Service level management

Service catalog management

Availability management

Capacity management

Information security management

Supplier management

IT service continuity management

Together, these processes consider all aspects of a service to ensure that the service is designed in a manner in which it can be transitioned to operation as effectively and efficiently as possible.

DESIGN COORDINATION

OVERVIEW

Very rarely does a service provider address only one design project at a time but are often inundated with multiple designs at once. The design coordination process ensures that individual designs are well-coordinated to ensure that comprehensive and appropriate designs are created that meet the needs of the business. Additionally, design coordination ensures proper coordination between individual design efforts within the overall service design stage of the service lifecycle.

PURPOSE AND OBJECTIVES

> **Key Point**
>
> The purpose of design coordination is to ensure the goals and objectives of the service design stage are met by providing and maintaining a single point of coordination and control for all activities and processes within the service design stage of the service lifecycle.

The purpose of design coordination is to "ensure the goals and objectives of the service design stage are met by providing and maintaining a single point of coordination and control for all activities and processes within the this stage of the service lifecycle."[1]

The objectives of the design coordination process are to:

"Ensure the consistent design of appropriate services, service management information systems, architectures, technology, processes, information, and metrics to meet current and evolving needs of the business

Coordinate all design activities across projects; changes; suppliers and support teams; and manage schedules, resources, and conflicts where required

Plan and coordinate the resources and capabilities required to design new or changed services

Produce service design packages (SDPs) based on service charters and change requests

---

1 Quoted text is from Service Design © Crown copyright 2011 Reproduced under license from the Cabinet Office

Ensure that appropriate service designs and/or SDPs are produced and that they are handed over to Service Transition as agreed

Manage the quality requirements and hand over points between the service design stage and service strategy and service transition

Ensure that all service models and service solution designs conform to strategic, architectural, governance, and other corporate requirements

Improve the effectiveness and efficiency of service design activities and processes

Ensure that all parties adopt a common framework of standard, reusable design practices in the form of activities, processes, and supporting systems

Monitor and improve the performance of the service design lifecycle stage"[2]

> **Key Point**
>
> The design coordination process is responsible for handing off the service design package (SDP) to service transition.

ACTIVITIES

The scope of design coordination includes all design activities for new or changed services being designed for transition into or out of the live environment. Individual designs vary as some will be extensive and complex and some will be simple and swift. Many of the complex design activities may be done as part of an overall project.

The following activities are part of the service design stage and should be coordinated by the design coordination process:

"Requirements collection, analysis, and engineering to ensure that business requirements, as well as service provider and technical requirements, are clearly documented, agreed, and aligned

Design of appropriate service solutions, technology, processes, information, and metrics to meet business requirements

Review and revision of the design of all processes and the maintenance of processes and process documents involved in service design

Production and maintenance of IT policies and design documents, including designs, plans, architectures, and policies

Review and revision of all design documents for completeness and adherence to standards

Planning for the deployment and implementation of IT strategies

> **Key Point**
>
> The design coordination activities support the overall service design stage of the service lifecycle, as well as support individual designs.

through road maps, programs, and project plans

Risk assessment and management of all design processes and deliverables

Ensuring alignment of designs with all corporate and IT strategies and policies

Production of service designs and/or SDPs for new or changed services"[3]

The service design activities themselves fall with two categories - activities that support the overall service design stage of the service lifecycle and activities that support individual designs.

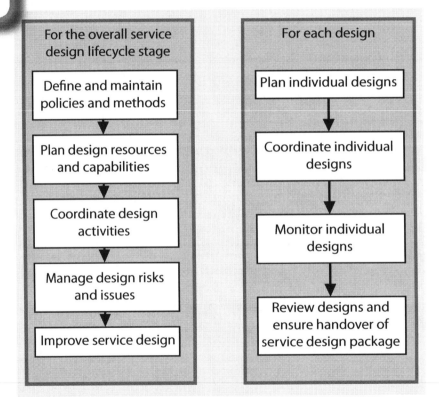

©Crown copyright 2011 - Reproduced under license from the Cabinet Office

Figure - Design Coordination activities

---

3   Quoted text is from Service Design © Crown copyright 2011 Reproduced under license from the Cabinet Office

The activities that support the overall service design stage include the development, deployment, and continual improvement of appropriate service design practices, as well as the coordination of actual design activity across projects and changes. The activities that support the overall service design stage include:

> "Defining and maintaining policies and methods
>
> Planning design resources and capabilities
>
> Coordinating design activities
>
> Managing design risks and issues
>
> Improving service designs"[4]

The activities that support each individual design focus on ensuring that each individual design effort and SDP conforms with defined practices and that they produce a design that will support the required business outcomes. These activities include:

> "Planning individual designs
>
> Coordinating individual designs
>
> Monitoring the progress of individual designs
>
> Reviewing designs and ensuring hand over of the service design Package to service transition"[5]

---

[4]   Quoted text is from Service Strategy © Crown copyright 2011 Reproduced under license from the Cabinet Office

[5]   Quoted text is from Service Strategy © Crown copyright 2011 Reproduced under license from the Cabinet Office.

SERVICE CATALOG MANAGEMENT

OVERVIEW

Service catalog management is responsible for managing the service catalog. This is done by ensuring that: services within the service catalog are consistent with those in the service portfolio; the service catalog is accurate; and it is adequately protected and backed up.

The service catalog is one of the most important concepts in the effective and efficient operation of services. Just as no restaurant (or any other business for that matter) would be able to sell products and services without a menu of services, IT cannot either. One of the big issues with IT that the service catalog resolves is consistency. In most organizations, if the business requires something from IT, what it gets is largely determined by whom it asks and when it asks it. Without a consistent catalog of services, the business and its users have no consistent view of what IT does. This dramatically lowers the perception of the value of IT.

The service catalog provides a source of consistent information regarding services that are available from IT. This consistency assists the business with understanding what services it can rely on in order to achieve its business-desired outcomes. The other benefit of the service catalog is that it assists IT staff in focusing on the services they provide. It also tells IT why IT exists – to provide services and what those services are. Without a service catalog, the information regarding services is not reliable, consistent, or agreed upon.

PURPOSE

Service Catalog Management's purpose is to "provide and maintain a single source of consistent information on all operational services and those being prepared to be run operationally, and to ensure that it is widely available to those who are authorized to access it"[6]. The way that service catalog manage-

---

6   Quoted text is from Service Design © Crown copyright 2011 Reproduced under license from the Cabinet Office

ment provides this single source of consistent information is through the service catalog.

The objectives of the service catalogue management process are to:

> "Manage the information contained within the service catalog
>
> Ensure that the service catalog is accurate and reflects the current details, status, interfaces and dependencies of all services that are being run, or being prepared to run, in the live environment, according to the defined policies
>
> Ensure that the service catalog is made available to those approved to access it in a manner that supports their effective and efficient use of service catalog information
>
> Ensure that the service catalog supports the evolving needs of all other service management processes for service catalog information, including all interface and dependency information"[7]

> **Key Point**
>
> Service catalog management's purpose is to provide and maintain a single source of consistent information on all operational services and those being prepared to be run operationally, and to ensure that it is widely available to those who are authorized to access it.

KEY CONCEPTS

The service catalog contains the details of all operational services being provided or those being prepared for transition into the live environment. The services in the service catalog may be documented in a text document or a spreadsheet or maintained on a Web site, or a fully-actionable service catalog can be created similar to an online shopping experience.

There is no "right" way to produce a service catalog, as different service providers may have different needs based on the types of customers they support and whether customers are internal or external to the organization. A service provider may decide to display different views of the service catalog based on the needs of its customers.

> **Key Point**
>
> The service catalog contains the details of all operational services being provided or those being prepared for transition.

TWO-VIEW SERVICE CATALOG

One typical construction of a service catalog for an internal or shared service provider is a two-view service catalog that documents the business services that the customers can view as well as the technical services that underpin the business services.

---

7   Quoted text is from Service Design © Crown copyright 2011 Reproduced under license from the Cabinet Office.

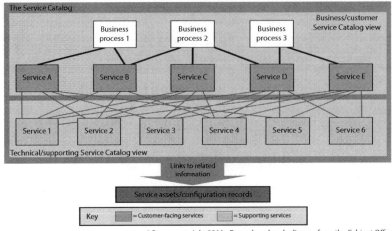

©Crown copyright 2011 - Reproduced under license from the Cabinet Office

Figure - Two-view Service Catalog

The business service catalog is the user view into the service catalog and provides information regarding the services that users and customers can request from IT. The technical service catalog is the IT view of the services that are delivered to the customer, together with the supporting services and shared services. This is also referred to as the IT-to-IT service catalog.

The service catalog also serves to relate the services provided, business service and technical services, to the underlying service assets that are used to provide the services. This enables the service provider to be able to track how service assets are linked to services and, in turn, linked to the business outcomes they support.

THREE-VIEW SERVICE CATALOG

Another way to construct the service catalog is by providing multiple views based on the types of customers the service provider supports. An example of this is a three-view service catalog that contains a view of wholesale services available to wholesale customers, as well as retail services available to retail customers. In this example, the service provider delivers services to external customers.

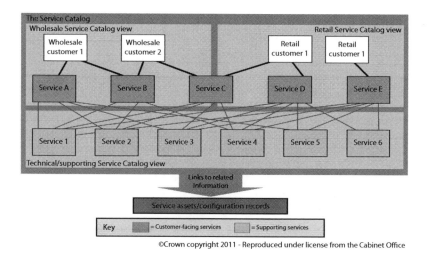

Figure - Three-view Service Catalog

The technical services are also maintained within a three-view service catalog that, just like the two-view service catalog, contains the details of the technical services or supporting services that underpin both the wholesale and retail services.

There may be many other views into a service catalog depending on the needs of the service provider, as well as the types of customers the service provider supports. When providing services to a number of internal customers, the service provider may choose to provide specific views relevant to each customer within the service catalog. These views into the service catalog may duplicate services that are used by more than one customer.

ROLES

The service catalog manager is responsible for the production and maintenance of the service catalog. This includes ensuring that all operational services and transitioning services are recorded in the service catalog and the service catalog is consistent with the information in the service portfolio. The service catalog manager reviews the service catalog periodically, particularly prior to the release of a service into service operation, to ensure that the service catalog is accurate. The service catalog manager also ensures that the service catalog is adequately protected from unauthorized viewing and backed up.

SERVICE LEVEL MANAGEMENT

GEPPETTO GARCIA'S

Mark Renner recognizes the importance of the IT services to meet the needs of the business. Without the business and its ability to operate effectively, IT would have no reason to exist. To ensure that the services are operating properly, Mark appoints a service level manager, John Lawson.

It is John's job to ensure that the service requirements are well understood and document the levels of service required in service level agreements (SLAs). John, as service level manager, must negotiate the levels of service with the business. Once negotiated, the service is monitored in operation, and the monitoring reports are reviewed periodically with the business.

When a service is not operating according to the needs of the business, the recognized improvements are made part of a service improvement program (SIP). The service improvement program is a formal program to improve a service. Any recognized improvement opportunities are recorded in the SIP for further action.

Overall, John Lawson is the central point of contact between the IT service provider and the business customer regarding operational issues. John is the point of contact to communicate with the business through all stages of the service lifecycle related to the level of service required. John also ensures the SLAs are properly documented and reviews occur with the business on a regular basis.

OVERVIEW

The service level management (SLM) process is the conduit between IT and the business to represent the operational capabilities of IT to the business. SLM also strives to understand the levels of services the business needs and communicate these needs so that services can be delivered to meet these specific business needs.

PURPOSE

The purpose of service level management is to "ensure that all current and planned IT services are delivered to agreed achievable targets."[8] This is accomplished through a constant cycle to define, document, agree, monitor, measure, report, and review the level of IT services provided with the representatives of the business.

SLM is similar to an account management role with our service providers. For example, your organization's computer supplier has a designated account manager to ensure that your organization is satisfied with their computers. The account manager helps to resolve issues, as well as look for other areas where their products and services can add value to the organization.

When the requirements for new services, changes to service, or improvements to service are provided, SLM defines the new or changed service. Once defined, the service is negotiated with the business to obtain agreement to the level of service to be provided to meet the requirements.

> **Key Point**
>
> The purpose of service level management is to ensure that all current and planned IT services are delivered to agreed achievable targets.

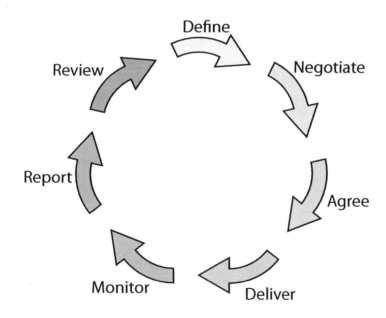

Figure - Service Level Management

The agreed service is then delivered. During delivery of the service, the service is monitored to identify gaps and deficiencies in the service. Periodically, this service is reviewed with the business and a new level of service is defined based on the findings in the review.

When a service is first introduced into the environment, the reviews of the service should be more frequent. As the service matures, the review become less frequent but should be conducted at least annually.

OBJECTIVES

Key Point

The main objective of Service Level Management is to define, document, agree, monitor, measure, report, and review the level of IT services provided with the representatives of the business.

Service level management ensures that an agreed level of IT service is provided for all current IT services and that future services are delivered to agreed achievable targets. This is accomplished through the objectives.

The objectives of Service Level Management are to:

"Define, document, agree, monitor, measure, report and review the level of IT services provided and instigate corrective measures whenever appropriate

Provide and improve the relationship and communication with the business and customers in conjunction with business relationship management

Ensure that specific and measurable targets are developed for all IT services

Monitor and improve customer satisfaction with the quality of service delivered

Ensure that IT and the customers have a clear and unambiguous expectation of the level of service to be delivered

Ensure that even when all agreed targets met, the levels of service delivered are subject to proactive, cost-effective continual improvement"[9]

SCOPE

Service level management provides a regular point of contact to the business

---

9   Quoted text is from Service Design © Crown copyright 2011 Reproduced under license from the Cabinet Office

by representing IT as a service provider. Through service level management, the business has a consistent point of contact to communicate their needs. SLM also manages the SLAs and provides reviews and negotiations for services to the business.

SLM also represents the needs of the business to IT in coordination with business relationship management. SLM produces service level requirements (SLRs) that represent the business interests and requirements for IT to satisfy through levels of service.

The scope of service level management is to provide a service for the customer and improve that service based on customer needs. To do this, SLM must establish a relationship with the business and ensure that relationship is maintained. SLM is a document-intensive process and ensures that service level agreements, service level requirements, operational level agreements, and underpinning contracts are established to support the service in accordance with business needs.

Working with the customer, service level management strives to ensure that services meet the needs of the customer. It does this through providing high-quality services, proactively preventing service failures, reviewing SLAs and SLA breaches, investigating failures to services, and coordinating a service improvement program (SIP).

If SLM seems like it has a lot of responsibility, it does. However, SLM does not do all of these things alone. SLM works with other processes such as business relationship management, supplier management, capacity management, and availability management. SLM works with all other processes to ensure quality services.

Business Relationship Management and Service Level Management

While service level management and business relationship management are both focused on communications and building relationships between the service provider and the customer, business relationship management is focused on a more strategic perspective of identifying the customer needs and ensuring that the service provider is able to meet the customer's needs. Service level management focuses on the operational relationship between the service provider and customer, working to deliver the level of service required by the business.

KEY CONCEPTS

Service level management is a document-intensive process. The documents produced and managed by SLM include those described below.

SERVICE LEVEL AGREEMENTS

A service level agreement (SLA) is a written agreement between an IT service provider and the IT customer to define the key service targets and responsibilities of both parties. SLAs should be clear and concise, and emphasize agreement between IT and the business. While SLAs must be adhered to, they should not be used as a way to hold either party ransom for failure to meet the agreement, but be focused on enhancing the performance of the business.

Service level agreements document the agreements for service between IT and the business. Many organizations approach these agreements generically as a "one-size-fits-all" agreement. By approaching SLAs in this manner, they fail to recognize the individual needs of the business unit, and SLAs are viewed as guidelines instead of agreements.

SLAs can be tailored to meet the specific needs of the business. They can be constructed by customer, by service, or as a combination of customer and service. IT service management strives to understand the needs of the business and to meet those needs. SLAs document these needs and the provider's response to these needs.

Service-based SLAs

Service-based SLAs cover the relevant issues of a specific service for all customers of that service. For example, all users may use the Internet service. A service-based SLA for the Internet service would apply to all customers of that service.

Customer-based SLAs

Customer-based SLAs address all services for a single customer. For example, the finance group may have a customer-based SLA for all services that the finance group uses.

Multi-level SLAs

SLAs can be multi-leveled. Multi-level SLA structures may be developed to customize a level of service for customers while still retaining reusability and consistency. A sample multi-level SLA structure could include a corporate-level SLA covering all of the generic issues appropriate to every customer throughout the organization; a customer-level SLA covering all issues specific to a single customer; and a service-level SLA covering all issues relevant to a specific service for a particular customer group.

SERVICE LEVEL REQUIREMENT

A service level requirement (SLR) is a customer requirement for an aspect of an IT service. SLRs are based on business objectives and are used to negotiate agreed service level targets. SLRs are provided to IT to communicate the requirements that must be met through services.

SERVICE LEVEL TARGET

A service level target (SLT) is a commitment to a specific level of service derived from service level requirements. Service level targets identify objective, measurable targets that IT uses to verify whether or not the specific service level requirement is being met. An SLA documents one or more service level targets.

OPERATIONAL LEVEL AGREEMENTS

An operational level agreement (OLA) is an agreement between internal parts of the same organization to support services. OLAs document the responsibilities of the various groups in IT that are responsible for support and maintenance of the services. These agreements define how internal IT organizations support each other in order to provide a specific level of service to the business. Through OLAs, the organization understands its objectives, and roles are more clearly defined.

UNDERPINNING CONTRACTS

An underpinning contract is an agreement between IT and an external third party. Underpinning contracts help to support (or underpin) the agreements that IT has in place to deliver a service to the business. These contracts may take many forms, such as statements of work, license agreements or out-

> **Key Point**
>
> A Service Level Requirement (SLR) is a customer requirement for an aspect of an IT service.

> **Key Point**
>
> A Service Level Target (SLT) is a commitment to a specific level of service derived from Service Level Requirements.

> **Key Point**
>
> An Operational Level Agreement (OLA) is an agreement between internal parties to support services.

sourcing agreements. While service level management is not responsible for these underpinning contracts, SLM assists supplier management in the review of these contracts to ensure that they are appropriate for, and support, the needs of the business.

ACTIVITIES

SLM is responsible for representing the capabilities of IT to the business as well as representing the requirements of the business to IT. The activities involved include:

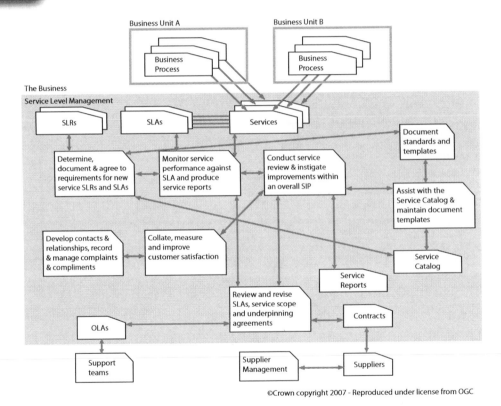

©Crown copyright 2007 - Reproduced under license from OGC

Figure - Service Level Management Activities

"Determining, negotiating, documenting and agreeing requirements for new or changed services in SLRs, and managing and reviewing them through the service lifecycle into SLAs for operational services

Monitoring and measuring service performance achievements of all operational services against targets within SLAs

Producing service reports

Conducting service reviews, identifying improvement opportunities for inclusion in the CSI register, and managing appropriate SIPs

Collating, measuring and improving customer satisfaction, in co-operation with business relationship management

Reviewing and revising SLAs, service scope, and OLAs

Assisting supplier management to review and revise underpinning contracts or agreements

Developing and documenting contacts and relationships with the business, customers and other stakeholders, in cooperation with the business relationship management process

Providing appropriate management information to aid performance management and demonstrating service achievement

Logging and managing complaints and compliments, in cooperation with business relationship management.

Designing SLA frameworks

Developing, maintaining and operating SLM procedures, including procedures for logging, actioning and resolving all complaints, and for logging and distributing compliments

Making available and maintaining up-to-date SLM document templates and standards

Assisting with the design and maintenance of the service catalogue"[10]

SLM does not perform all these activities itself. SLM works closely with other processes to measure service performance. SLM specifically focuses on the communications with the customer and coordinates the activities of other processes to provide the customer reports and improvements to services.

---

10   Quoted text is from Service Design © Crown copyright 2011 Reproduced under license from the Cabinet Office

ROLES

The service level manager is responsible for ensuring that the activities within service level management are being performed. The service level manager may be supported by account managers, business service analysts, or similar roles to ensure that high-quality services are being delivered to customers.

The specific service level manager responsibilities include:

> Ensuring that the current and future service requirements of customers are identified and understood
>
> Ensuring that the current and future service requirements are documented in SLAs and SLRs
>
> Negotiating and agreeing to levels of service
>
> Negotiating and agreeing to OLAs
>
> Assisting with the production of the service portfolio and the service catalog
>
> Ensuring service reports are produced
>
> Developing and maintaining relationships
>
> Measuring, recording, analyzing, and improving customer satisfaction

SERVICE LEVEL MANAGEMENT PROCESS RELATIONSHIPS

Service level management is the process that represents the service to the customer. To properly represent the service, SLM must work with all other processes to understand how a service is operating and what level of service is possible. However, there are specific processes that SLM works most closely with. These notable processes include:

Change Management

> SLM reviews the forward schedule of change (FSC) to communicate with the customer.
>
> SLM assists with the impact assessment for changes - particularly around critical business times - to minimize impact to the business.

Service Asset and Configuration Management

SLM refers to service asset and configuration management to understand the composition of the service.

AVAILABILITY MANAGEMENT

OVERVIEW

Availability management is the process that provides a point of focus and management for all availability-related issues relating to both services and components, ensuring that availability targets in all areas are measured and achieved. Availability of services is extremely visible to customers and users. Therefore, availability management strives to understand the underlying aspects that contribute to availability of services, measure them, and find ways to improve availability.

The overriding principles that guide availability management include:

"Service availability is at the core of customer satisfaction and business success

When (not if) services fail, it is still possible to achieve business, customer, and user satisfaction by responding to the failure in a way that influences perception of service

Improvement can only begin after understanding how services support the business

Service availability is only as good as the weakest link

Availability is not just reactive, but proactive

It is cheaper to design availability than to bolt it on later"[11]

> **Key Point**
>
> The purpose of Availability Management is to ensure that the level of availability delivered in all IT services meets the agreed availability needs and/or service level targets in a cost-effective and timely manner.

PURPOSE

The purpose of availability management is to "ensure that the level of availability delivered in all IT services meets the agreed availability needs and/or service level targets in a cost-effective and timely manner."[12]

---

11   Quoted text is from Service Design © Crown copyright 2011 Reproduced under license from the Cabinet Office

12   Quoted text is from Service Design © Crown copyright 2011 Reproduced under license from the Cabinet Office.

Availability management works closely with service level management to understand these identified needs and also to support SLM reporting requirements.

Objectives

The objectives of availability management to support this purpose are to:

"Produce and maintain an appropriate and up-to-date availability plan that reflects the current and future needs of the business

Provide advice and guidance to all other areas of the business and IT on all availability-related issues

Ensure that service availability achievements meet all their agreed targets by managing services and resources-related availability performance

Assist with the diagnosis and resolution of availability-related incidents and problems

Assess the impact of all changes on the availability plan and the availability of all services and resources

Ensure that proactive measures to improve the availability of services are implemented wherever it is cost-justifiable to do so"[13]

KEY CONCEPTS

Availability

Availability is defined as *"the ability of a service, component, or configuration item (CI) to perform its agreed function when required."*[14] Also known as uptime, availability is calculated by dividing the total available time within a given time period by the agreed availability.

A configuration item (CI) is essentially anything needed to provide a service and is under the control of change management. CIs are discussed in detail in service transition.

> **Key Point**
>
> Availability is defined as the ability of a service, component, or Configuration Item (CI) to perform its agreed function when required.

---

13   Quoted text is from Service Design © Crown copyright 2011 Reproduced under license from the Cabinet Office

14   Quoted text is from Service Design © Crown copyright 2011 Reproduced under license from the Cabinet Office.

For example, suppose the server was down for 8 hours in a given work week. There are 168 hours in a work week. The server was available for 160 hours during the week (168 – 8). Dividing the 160 hours by the 168 total hours in the week results in .952. Multiplying this result by 100 results in calculating the percentage availability of 95.2%.

$$Availability = (168 - 8) / 168 * 100 = 95.2\%$$

Reliability

Reliability refers to how long a component stays operable before a failure and is defined as "*a measure of how long a service, component, or CI can perform its agreed function without interruption.*"[15] Reliability is measured as mean time between service interruptions (MTBSI) by dividing the time the service was available by the number of breaks. This shows the average time the service is running without failure.

Reliability can also be measured by the mean time between failures (MTBF) by subtracting the total downtime from the available time and dividing by the number of breaks. This shows the average time between failures of the service.

Maintainability

Maintainability refers to how quickly a component can be returned to operational status after a failure and is defined as "*a measure of how quickly and effectively a service, component, or CI can be restored to normal working after a failure.*"[16] Maintainability refers to how quickly a failure can be responded to. The speed in which a failure is responded to depends on many things, such as:

> Time to record the failure
>
> Time to respond
>
> Time to resolve
>
> Time to physically repair
>
> Time to recover

Availability management strives to understand and measure these contributory factors to downtime and find ways to reduce or eliminate these factors.

Maintainability is measured as mean time to restore service (MTRS) and

> **Key Point**
>
> Reliability is defined as a measure of how long a service, component, or CI can perform its agreed function without interruption.

> **Key Point**
>
> Maintainability is defined as a measure of how quickly and effectively a service, component, or CI can be restored to normal working after a failure.

---

15   Quoted text is from Service Design © Crown copyright 2011 Reproduced under license from the Cabinet Office

16   Quoted text is from Service Design © Crown copyright 2011 Reproduced under license from the Cabinet Office.

is calculated by dividing the total downtime experienced by the number of outages. This reflects the average time to restore service following a failure.

Serviceability

Serviceability is defined as *"the ability of a third-party supplier to meet the terms of its contract."*[17] Serviceability plays a role in overall maintainability and is also a key component of downtime to measure and control. This refers to the arrangements made with vendors to maintain and fix components that are part of a service.

VITAL BUSINESS FUNCTIONS

Every business organization has vital business functions (VBFs). VBFs are the business-critical elements of the business process that drive the business-desired outcomes. VBFs are the elements of the business process that are more vital than other elements.

For example, the vital business function of an ATM machine is to dispense cash. A less vital function is the ability to produce a receipt. When you go to an ATM machine, your objective is to receive cash. The receipt is important, but not as important. If you can't get cash, the ATM machine shuts down. If you can't get a receipt, the ATM still functions, but in a limited capacity.

VBFs have different characteristics. These characteristics are high availability, fault tolerance, continuous operation, and continuous availability.

> High availability is a characteristic of the IT service that minimizes or masks the effects of IT component failure.

> Fault tolerance is a characteristic of an IT service to continue to operate after one of the components has failed.

> Continuous operation is a characteristic of an IT service to eliminate planned downtime. Continuous operation is provided by ensuring that a service is operable even though individual components may not be operable.

> Continuous availability is a characteristic of an IT service to achieve 100% availability masking planned and unplanned downtime

All IT organizations have limits on their resources, people, time, and money. Therefore, it is critical to work with the business (through service level management) to determine what the vital business functions are. Once the vital

17   Quoted text is from Service Design © Crown copyright 2011 Reproduced under license from the Cabinet Office

Key Point

Serviceability is defined as the ability of a third-party supplier to meet the terms of its contract.

Key Point

Vital business functions (VBFs) are the business-critical elements of the business process that drive the business-desired outcomes.

business functions are understood and documented, IT can prioritize where its limited resources are allocated to ensure that the maximum benefit is derived from these limited resources.

EXPANDED INCIDENT LIFECYCLE

Availability management can be a tenacious process. Tenacity is needed in order to understand the contributing factors of downtime and reduce these factors.

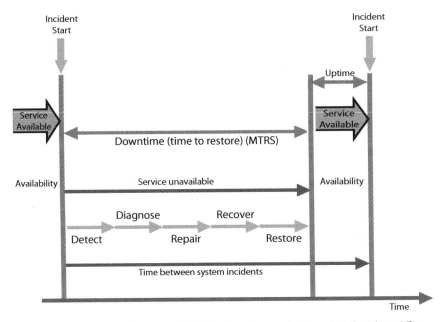

©Crown copyright 2011 - Reproduced under license from the Cabinet Office

Figure - Expanded Incident Lifecycle

The expanded incident lifecycle explores these contributing factors. When an incident occurs, it takes time to detect the incident. Some incidents are detected by monitoring tools, while others are reported by users. In a perfect world, no incidents would be reported by users; they would all be detected before the user was impacted and resolved with no impact. However, since we don't live in a perfect world and have limited resources, the focus should be on the highest-priority services.

Detecting incidents is not the only contributing factor to downtime. It also takes time to diagnose incidents, repair incidents, recover incidents, and restore services from an incidents.

Detection

Detection of an incident occurs when the incident is reported to the service desk. This detection can be through monitoring tools (working with event management) or through a user call to the service desk. Ideally, every incident would be detected automatically. Detecting every single incident automatically would be very laborious and time consuming.

Diagnose

Determining the cause of an incident takes time, as well. Availability management strives to reduce this time by working closely with other processes, such as problem management and knowledge management, to ensure that scripts are developed to assist with the diagnostics, diagnostic tools are available, and the proper knowledge is contained within the service knowledge management system to assist with this diagnostic. Incident-handling staff also need to be trained to better understand how to diagnose an incident using these available tools and scripts.

Availability management also strives to find other ways to minimize this contributing factor to downtime. While diagnostic activities may take a great deal of time, availability management may use resilience and redundancy techniques to ensure the service is still operational even though some part of it may have failed.

Repair

Repairing a service due to an incident involves many different activities that can only be partially defined prior to an incident occurring. Availability management strives to ensure that the appropriate measures are in place to ensure that repair to a service can be performed as quickly as possible. This includes designing response techniques into a service such as fail-over and fault tolerance to ensure that repair components are available and training or specialized personnel are available to repair the service.

Recover

Recovering the service involves bringing the service back to its operational state. This may involve ensuring that all components of the service are operating as expected and that the incident has been resolved.

Restore

Restoration of a service involves bringing a service back to its usable state. After recovery, there are times when data may need to be restored to ensure that users can continue to use the service as they did prior to the incident occurring.

ACTIVITIES

Availability management is a process that has activities through many stages of the service lifecycle. These activities are both proactive and reactive. In the service design stage of the service lifecycle, the proactive activities include understanding the risk to the availability of a service, designing availability into a service, and improving availability through implementing cost-justifiable measures to counter the risk to availability.

In service transition, availability management is responsible for reviewing all new and changed services from an availability standpoint. Availability management is also responsible for testing the availability mechanisms for services.

In service operation, the reactive activities of availability management include monitoring, measuring, analyzing, reporting, and reviewing service and component availability, as well as investigating all service and component unavailability and instigate remedial action.

> **Key Point**
>
> Availability Management activities are both reactive and proactive.

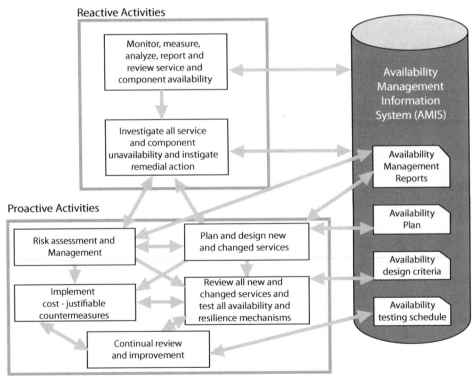

©Crown copyright 2011 - Reproduced under licence from the Cabinet Office

Figure - Availability Management Activities

Good availability management will be oblivious to which stage of the service lifecycle is currently being addressed, but will instead provide a holistic approach to the availability of services, regardless of the stage of the service lifecycle.

Other key availability management activities include:

> "Determining the availability requirements from the business for a new or enhanced IT service and designing availability
>
> Determining the VBFs in conjunction with the business and IT service continuity management (ITSCM)
>
> Determining the impact arising from component failure in conjunction with ITSCM
>
> Providing additional resilience to prevent or minimize impact to the business
>
> Defining targets for availability, reliability, and maintainability
>
> Establishing measures and reporting of availability, reliability, and maintainability
>
> Reviewing IT service and component availability and identifying unacceptable levels
>
> Investigating the underlying reasons for unacceptable availability
>
> Producing and maintaining an availability plan that prioritizes and plans IT availability improvements"[18]

AVAILABILITY MANAGEMENT INFORMATION SYSTEM

The availability management process is supported by the availability management information system (AMIS). The AMIS is a system to store and maintain availability-related information. The information contained and maintained in the AMIS includes availability management reports, availability plans, availability design criteria, and availability testing schedules.

> **Key Point**
>
> The availability management information system (AMIS) is a system to store and maintain availability-related information.

---

18   Quoted text is from Service Design © Crown copyright 2011 Reproduced under license from the Cabinet Office

CAPACITY MANAGEMENT

OVERVIEW

Managing capacity requires balancing costs against resources to make efficient use of cost-justifiable resources. It also requires balancing supply with demand to ensure that the current and future demand can be met.

The capacity management process provides a single focus of management for all capacity- and performance-related issues, relating to services. Capacity management works closely with demand management to understand and influence the demand against available resources.

PURPOSE AND OBJECTIVES

> ### Key Point
>
> The purpose of capacity management is to ensure that the capacity of IT services and the IT infrastructure meets the agreed capacity- and performance-related requirements in a cost-effective and timely manner.

The purpose of Capacity management is to "ensure that the capacity of IT services and the IT infrastructure meets the agreed capacity- and performance-related requirements in a cost-effective and timely manner."[19]

Capacity management achieves this purpose through its objectives to:

"Produce and maintain an appropriate and up-to-date capacity plan, which reflects the current and future needs of the business

Provide advice and guidance to all other areas of the business and IT on all capacity- and performance-related issues

Ensure that service performance achievements meet all of their agreed targets by managing the performance and capacity of both services and resources

Assist with the diagnosis and resolution of performance- and capacity-related incidents and problems

---

19   Quoted text is from Service Design © Crown copyright 2011 Reproduced under license from the Cabinet Office

Assess the impact of all changes on the capacity plan, and the performance and capacity of all services and resources

Ensure that proactive measures to improve the performance of services are implemented wherever it is cost-justifiable to do so"[20]

KEY CONCEPTS

Capacity management involves more than just understanding the current capacity requirements but understanding all aspects of demand for capacity. There are three sub-processes to capacity management that provide insight into these aspects. As shown in the diagram, these sub-processes include business capacity management, service capacity management and component capacity management.

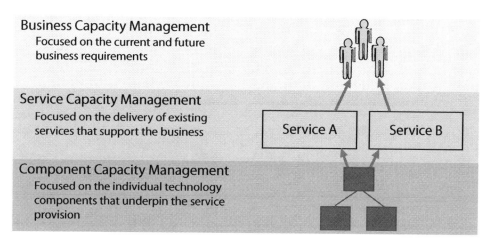

Figure - Capacity Management Sub-processes

Business Capacity Management

Business capacity management is focused on the current and future business requirements for capacity. For example, if the business were to state that it is going to increase sales by 40% over the next year, business capacity management must understand how this change in business would influence capacity requirements for the service and the underlying components.

---

20   Quoted text is from Service Design © Crown copyright 2011 Reproduced under license from the Cabinet Office

Service Capacity Management

Service capacity management is focused on ensuring that the current capacity can be delivered by the service and that changes in demand can be delivered. There are many examples in the news of companies that failed to anticipate demand for services and lost business because of failures in delivering the required capacity. Well-established companies are not immune to this. A popular online auction site, online book retailer, and an airline have made the news in the past because of interruptions in service due to lack of capacity.

Component Capacity Management

Component capacity management is familiar to most organizations because this sub-process monitors individual component capacity. Typical monitoring includes monitoring disk space, CPU usage, and memory usage. Component capacity management is also concerned with understanding the human resources required to meet demand for capacity.

Component capacity management metrics are often combined to reflect the service capacity.

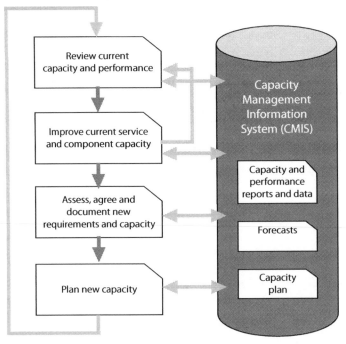

©Crown copyright 2011 - Reproduced under license from the Cabinet Office

Figure - Capacity Management Activities

ACTIVITIES

Capacity management activities include reviewing current capacity and performance; improving current service and component capacity; assessing, agreeing, and documenting new capacity requirements; and planning new capacity. Capacity management is supported by the capacity management information system (CMIS) that stores the forecasts, capacity plan, and capacity and performance reports and data.

> **Key Point**
>
> The capacity management information system (CMIS) stores the forecasts, capacity plan, and capacity and performance reports and data.

CAPACITY PLAN

The capacity plan is used by all areas of the business and IT management and is acted on by the IT service provider and senior management of the organization to plan the capacity of the IT infrastructure. It contains information on the current usage of service and components and plans for the development of IT capacity to meet the needs of new growth of both existing service and any agreed new services. The capacity plan should be actively used as a basis for decision making.

> **Key Point**
>
> The capacity plan contains information on the current usage of service and components and plans for the development of IT capacity to meet the needs of new growth of both existing service and any agreed new services.

Analyzing capacity

Initiating any required tuning

Assessing new technology

Producing capacity reports

Being a focal point for all performance-related issues

INFORMATION SECURITY MANAGEMENT

OVERVIEW

Organizations have become very security conscious with good reason. There have been various stories in the news about companies losing critical customer and employee data. This issue is becoming more exacerbated as we condense more and more information onto smaller devices. DVDs, thumb drives, and other media can store lots of information in a very small space. These devices are also very easy to lose if control measures are not in place.

PURPOSE

The purpose of the information security management process is to "align IT security with business security and ensure that the confidentiality, integrity and availability of the organization's assets, information, data and IT services always matches the agreed needs of the business."[21]

Availability is met when the information is available and usable when required and systems can appropriately resist attacks and prevent and recover from failures.

Confidentiality is met when the information is observed by or disclosed to only those who have a right to know.

Integrity is met when the information is complete, accurate, and protected against unauthorized modification.

Authenticity is met when business transactions, as well as information exchanges between enterprises or with partners, can be trusted.

---

21   Quoted text is from Service Design © Crown copyright 2011 Reproduced under license from the Cabinet Office

KEY CONCEPTS

INFORMATION SECURITY FRAMEWORK

Information security management establishes a security framework to support the process and ensure that security encompasses the entire lifecycle of the service.

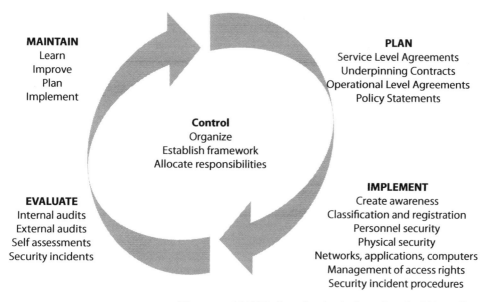

MAINTAIN
Learn
Improve
Plan
Implement

PLAN
Service Level Agreements
Underpinning Contracts
Operational Level Agreements
Policy Statements

Control
Organize
Establish framework
Allocate responsibilities

EVALUATE
Internal audits
External audits
Self assessments
Security incidents

IMPLEMENT
Create awareness
Classification and registration
Personnel security
Physical security
Networks, applications, computers
Management of access rights
Security incident procedures

©Crown copyright 2011 - Reproduced under license from the Cabinet Office

Figure - Security Management Framework

At the core, the information security management framework consists of:

Establishing specific security policies that address the strategy, control and regulation of security

Establishing a set of controls to support the policies

Developing a comprehensive security strategy that is closely linked to business objectives, strategies, and plans

Establishing an effective security organizational structure

This core supports the following components of the framework:

> Managing security risks
>
> Monitoring processes to ensure compliance
>
> Monitoring all IT service management processes to ensure compliance with security requirements
>
> Training and awareness of strategy and plans
>
> Establishing a communications strategy to ensure that security requirements and policies are known and understood

INFORMATION SECURITY MANAGEMENT SYSTEM

All the information required by information security management should be contained within the security management information system (SMIS). The SMIS records all security-related information, including standards, management information, procedures, and guidelines.

POLICIES

Information security management develops an overall information security policy. This policy drives all activities and refers to specific underpinning security policies. The information security policy must have the support of top management to ensure that it can be enforced and promote adherence to the policies.

The information security policy is supported by specific underpinning policies. These specific underlying policies depend on the unique organization, but some of the policies to consider include:

> Use and misuse of IT assets
>
> Access control policy
>
> Password control policy
>
> E-mail policy
>
> Internet policy
>
> Anti-virus policy
>
> Information classification policy
>
> Document classification policy
>
> Remote access policy
>
> Supplier access policy
>
> Asset disposal policy

The information security policy and its underpinning policies must be distributed to everyone within the organization if it is expected to be followed.

ACTIVITIES

As shown in the figure, the security framework involves five key activity groups. These activity groups are control, plan, implement, evaluate, and maintain.

Control

Security control is provided though the development and communication of policies and procedures, understanding security requirements, and implementing an organization that can manage security effectively, and allocating responsibilities for security.

Plan

Planning for security is driven by the requirements contained in the security chapter of the service level agreement (SLA). The SLA contains any security requirements from the business that are above and beyond the standard organizational security.

Planning for security also includes planning and reviewing the underpinning contracts, operational level agreements (OLAs), and policy statements to determine if modifications are necessary to accommodate the security requirements.

Implement

The implementation activities involve creating awareness about security, developing a classification and registration system for security and data, and securing the networks, applications, computer, and other components for a service. Implementation also involves establishing security for personnel and physical security, as well as managing access rights.

Information security management also reviews incidents from incident management to resolve security-related incidents.

Evaluate

The evaluation activities for information security management include internal and external audits and self assessments. Internal audits involve an IT security specialist group to audit the security of the organization. External audits involve hiring an external group to audit the security of the organization. Self assessments involve the organization assessing its own security, usually using checklists provided by information security management.

Security incidents are also evaluated in this activity group to evaluate the actions to take regarding security-related incidents.

Maintain

The maintenance activities involve understanding what was found in the evaluation activities, learning from those findings to improve security, and implementing improvements to the organization.

SUPPLIER MANAGEMENT

OVERVIEW

Supplier management, commonly referred to as vendor management, is responsible for obtaining value for money from suppliers and ensures that suppliers and their contracts are aligned with the needs of the business. Supplier management formally manages the suppliers in a way that provides value to the organization based on the commitments and contracts with the suppliers.

PURPOSE AND OBJECTIVES

The purpose of supplier management is to "obtain value for money from suppliers and to provide seamless quality of IT service to the business by ensuring that all contracts and agreements with suppliers support the needs of the business and that all suppliers meet their contractual commitments."[22]

The objectives of supplier management are to:

> "Obtain value for money from suppliers and contracts
>
> Ensure that contracts with suppliers are aligned to business needs, and support and align with agreed targets in SLRs and SLAs, in conjunction with SLM
>
> Manage relationships with suppliers
>
> Manage supplier performance
>
> Negotiate and agree contracts with suppliers and manage them through their lifecycle
>
> Maintain a supplier policy and a supporting supplier and contract management information system (SCMIS)"[23]

> ### Key Point
>
> The purpose of Supplier Management is to obtain value for money from suppliers and to ensure that suppliers perform to the targets contained within their contracts and agreements while conforming to all of the terms and conditions.

---

22   Quoted text is from Service Design © Crown copyright 2011 Reproduced under license from the Cabinet Office

23   Quoted text is from Service Design © Crown copyright 2011 Reproduced under license from the Cabinet Office.

KEY CONCEPTS

UNDERPINNING CONTRACTS

Underpinning contracts, or contracts, are the agreements between IT and IT's vendors. The underpinning contracts are maintained by supplier management to ensure that value is obtained from suppliers and aligned to the services the contracts support.

While contracts are agreed to in the supplier management process, service level management will be involved in reviewing the contracts to ensure that the contracts provide the appropriate support for the SLAs. Service level management works with the supplier management process but leaves the actual negotiation of the contract to the supplier management process.

> **Key Point**
>
> Underpinning contracts, or contracts, are the agreements between IT and IT's vendors.

SUPPLIER AND CONTRACT MANAGEMENT INFORMATION SYSTEM (SCMIS)

The supplier and contract management information system (SCMIS) contains all the records for suppliers and their associated contracts. The SCMIS also contains the list of all services and/or products supplied by the supplier.

All activities in supplier management reference this database and ensure that the database is accurate and timely. With an accurate SCMIS, important dates are not missed, and suppliers are well managed. If contract deadlines are missed or delayed, it could result in added expense and penalties.

> **Key Point**
>
> The supplier and contract management information system (SCMIS) contains all the records for suppliers and their associated contracts.

SUPPLIER CATEGORIZATION

Categorization of the supplier and the contract reflects the relative importance of the supplier or contract to the organization. This categorization is determined by the risk and impact of the supplier for non-performance and the value and importance of the supplier or contract. Some suppliers are commodity suppliers. Commodity suppliers are those that provide low-value and low-risk services, such as paper and toner for printers. Paper and toner can easily be obtained through other suppliers.

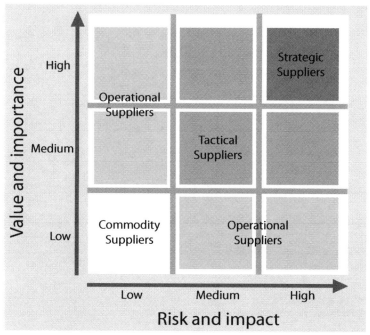

©Crown copyright 2011 - Reproduced under licence from the Cabinet Office

Operational suppliers are those suppliers who have a low impact but medium or high risk to the organization or those that provide medium- or high-value service, but are low risk. Examples of operational suppliers include utility providers of electricity, gas, and water. Tactical suppliers are those suppliers that have higher risk and value to the organization. These suppliers may be contracted to provide short- to medium-term solutions such as contract project work.

The strategic suppliers are those suppliers that provide high value and are high risk if they cannot perform. These suppliers are contracted to provide services that are core to the organization. These strategic suppliers usually have relationships with the higher levels of the organization's executive staff.

The purpose of categorizing suppliers is to ensure that the most important suppliers are provided with the support and attention that they require to be successful. This isn't to say that commodity suppliers should be ignored but that the most attention should be given to where it is most needed.

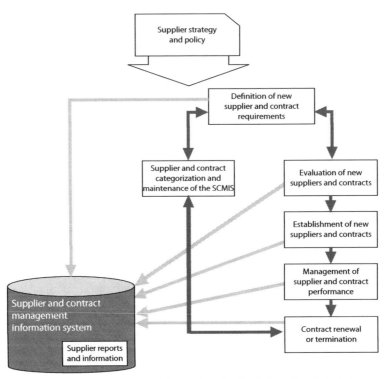

Figure - Supplier Management Activities

ACTIVITIES

Supplier management involves a set of integrated activities to develop strategies, evaluate suppliers, and manage suppliers.

Supplier Strategy and Policy

Supplier management develops strategies and policies with regard to the suppliers. This strategy and policy provides overriding guidelines for the remaining activities.

Evaluation of New Suppliers and Contracts

When new suppliers are considered, supplier management evaluates the new suppliers and the proposed contracts to ensure that both conform to the strategy and policy set forth.

Establish New Suppliers and Contracts

Upon acceptance of new suppliers and contracts, these suppliers and contracts are established in the supplier and contract management information system (SCMIS) to ensure that they can be properly managed.

Supplier and Contract Management and Performance

Periodically, the suppliers and contracts are evaluated to ensure that they are in compliance with the obligations agreed to in the contract. This evaluation also ensures that the organization is conforming to its obligations to the suppliers and contracts, as well.

Contract Renewal and/or Termination

When contracts are scheduled to expire, the contract is reviewed to determine if it should be renewed or terminated. Termination of a contract involves formal procedures to ensure that all terms and obligations of the contract have been satisfied by both the supplier and the organization.

Supplier Categorization and Maintenance of the SCMIS

The supplier and contract management information system (SCMIS) is a location to store all of the records regarding the suppliers and the contracts for the suppliers. When a new supplier and contract have been established, the supplier and/or contract should be categorized in the SCMIS. The SCMIS also requires periodic maintenance to prune or archive old records and ensure that the SCMIS is performing its objectives.

IT SERVICE CONTINUITY MANAGEMENT

OVERVIEW

IT service continuity management (ITSCM) is responsible for maintaining the necessary ongoing recovery capability within the IT services and their supporting components in the event of a disaster. While most organizations have disaster-recovery processes in place, the differentiator between disaster recovery and IT service continuity management is that ITSCM is tightly integrated with the business continuity plan (BCP).

IT service continuity management achieves the recovery capability by introducing risk reduction measures and introducing recovery options. ITSCM requires all members of the organization to support it effectively. ITSCM also must have support from senior management to ensure that plans are in place, resources are allocated, and funds are available to provide the recovery capability.

ITSCM strives to align recovery of the IT technical and services infrastructure based on the priority of business processes. In availability management, the concept of vital business function (VBF) was explored. These VBFs play a major part of ITSCM, as well. ITSCM strives to understand these VBFs to ensure that services are recovered according to business priority.

PURPOSE AND OBJECTIVES

The purpose of IT service continuity management is to "support the overall business continuity management (BCM) process by ensuring that, by managing the risks that could seriously affect IT services, the IT service provider can always provide minimum agreed business continuity-related service levels."[24]

> ### Key Point
>
> The purpose of IT service continuity management is to support the overall business continuity management (BCM) process by ensuring that, by managing the risks that could seriously affect IT services, the IT service provider can always provide minimum agreed business continuity-related service levels.

---

24   Quoted text is from Service Design © Crown copyright 2011 Reproduced under license from the Cabinet Office

ITSCM objectives are to:

"Produce and maintain a set of IT service continuity plans that support the overall business continuity plans of the organization

Complete regular BIA exercises to ensure that all continuity plans are maintained in line with changing business impacts and requirements

Conduct regular risk assessment and management exercises to manage IT services within an agreed level of business risk in conjunction with the business and the availability management and information security management processes

Provide advice and guidance to all other areas of the business and IT on all continuity-related issues

Ensure that appropriate continuity mechanisms are put in place to meet or exceed the agreed business continuity targets

Assess the impact of all changes on the IT service continuity plans and supporting methods and procedures

Ensure that proactive measures to improve the availability of services are implemented wherever it is cost-justifiable to do so

Negotiate and agree contracts with suppliers for the provision of the necessary recovery capability to support all continuity plans in conjunction with the supplier management process"[25]

> **Key Point**
>
> Business continuity management is the business process responsible for managing risks that could seriously impact the business.

ACTIVITIES

ITSCM begins with input from business continuity management (BCM). Business continuity management develops a business continuity strategy and resultant business continuity plans. ITSCM develops its requirements and strategy and implements ITSCM with respect to this business strategy and plan.

As shown in the IT service continuity management diagram, the ITSCM activities are organized around a series of stages. These stages include initiation, requirements and strategy, implementation, and ongoing operation.

Initiation

The initiation stage recognizes the need for IT and the business to determine the scope of the process and develop the supporting process policies. During

---

25   Quoted text is from Service Design © Crown copyright 2011 Reproduced under license from the Cabinet Office

initiation, IT and the business work together to establish a project to develop an ITSCM plan and BCM plan. This stage allocates resources to begin development of the requirements and strategy.

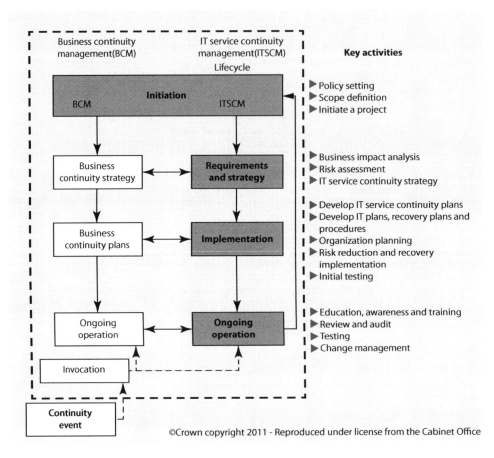

Figure - IT Service Continuity Management Activities

Requirements and Strategy

> **Key Point**
>
> BIA is the activity identifying critical business functions and determining the impact of their interruption.

The requirements and strategy stage works closely with the business continuity management process to perform a business impact analysis (BIA). The BIA considers the business processes and prioritizes these processes by the impact caused when these processes are interrupted.

From this BIA, a risk assessment is conducted to determine the risks to the business. The ITSCM strategy is developed to provide guidance for the remaining stages.

Implementation

The implementation stage is where the work is performed to create an ITSCM plan that is aligned to the business continuity plan and put it into operation. This stage involves developing the ITSCM plans, the IT plans, and recovery plans and procedures to support the ITSCM plan. Organizational planning considers the support requirements from the organization to implement and provide ongoing support of the ITSCM plan. Testing strategy is also developed that involves testing the plan upon initial implementation and then providing ongoing testing of the plan at least annually.

Ongoing Operation

Once the plan has been implemented, it requires ongoing operation for the activities to remain aligned with the needs of the business. Because the ITSCM plan is one that we hope is not ever invoked, it runs the risk of becoming stale and out of date. Ongoing education, awareness, and training are provided to ensure that the plan is current and has organizational awareness.

Through ongoing operation, the plan is periodically reviewed and audited for any changes in business requirements for consideration and updates to the plan. At least annually, the plan is tested to identify any gaps and opportunities for improvement.

Change management has special considerations with ITSCM. Changes have the potential to impact the ITSCM plan. When a change is introduced into the live environment, the change is also duplicated in the recovery or fail over environment to ensure that the environments remain consistent.

Invocation

The Invocation stage is triggered when a major failure or disaster has occurred that warrants invoking the IT Service Continuity plan. When the plan is invoked, the plan is carried out as practiced and tested. During invocation, there should be no major decisions to make, as these decisions have been pre-determined and tested.

IMPORTANT POINTS

The processes in service design are:

> Design coordination
>
> Service level management
>
> Service catalog management
>
> Availability management
>
> Capacity management
>
> Information security management
>
> Supplier management
>
> IT service continuity management

The purpose of service level management is to ensure that all operational services and their performance are measured in a consistent, professional manner throughout the IT organization and the reports produced meet the needs of the business customers.

The goal of service level management is to ensure that an agreed level of IT service is provided for all current IT services and that future services are delivered to agreed targets.

The objective of service level management is to define, document, agree, monitor, measure, report, and review the level of service agreed with the business.

The purpose of service catalog management is to provide a single source of consistent information about all of the agreed upon services and ensure that this information is widely available to those who are approved to access it.

The service catalog includes the business service catalog and the technical service catalog.

The purpose of availability management is to ensure that cost-justifiable IT availability exists to match the current and future identified needs of the business.

Availability management activities are both reactive and proactive.

The purpose of capacity management is to ensure that cost-justifiable IT capacity for all areas of IT always exists and is matched to the current and future agreed needs of the business.

Capacity management sub-processes include business capacity management, service capacity management, and component capacity management.

The purpose of information security management is to align IT security with business security to ensure that information security is effectively managed.

The purpose of supplier management is to obtain value for money from suppliers and ensure that suppliers perform to the targets contained within their contracts while conforming to all of the terms and conditions.

The purpose of IT service continuity management (ITSCM) is to support the overall business continuity management process by ensuring that the required IT technical and service facilities can be resumed within required and agreed business time scales.

The purpose of design coordination is to ensure the goals and objectives of the service design stage are met by providing and maintaining a single point of coordination and control for all activities and processes within this stage of the service lifecycle.

The design coordination activities support the overall service design stage of the service lifecycle, as well as individual designs.

The scope of design coordination includes all design activities for new or changed services being designed for transition into or out of the live environment.

TERMS & DEFINITIONS

Information security policy

Contract

Supplier and contract management information system (SCMIS)

Business continuity management (BCM)

Business impact analysis (BIA)

SECTION REVIEW

1. Service level management (SLM) represents IT as a service provider and

   A. Represents business interests to IT

   B. Manages the service desk

   C. Guarantees delivery of capabilities to the customer

   D. Improves all processes based on a continual improvement focus

2. Service level agreements should be consistent throughout the organization for all customers for all services.

   A. True

   B. False

3. The two views into the service catalog include:

   A. Vendor catalog and user catalog

   B. Business service catalog and technical service catalog

   C. User service catalog and business service catalog

   D. Technical service catalog and vendor catalog

4. Availability efforts are always reactive.

   A. True

   B. False

5. The term given for the business-critical elements of a business process is called what?

   A. Business priority

   B. Critical business activity

   C. Critical business function

   D. Vital business function

6. What is the name given for the system that holds availability management reports, the availability plan, availability design criteria, and the availability testing schedule?

   A. Configuration management system (CMS)

   B. Availability management information system (AMIS)

   C. Capacity management information system (CMIS)

   D. Availability support system

7. What is the term used for the ability of a service, component, or CI to perform its agreed function when required?

   A. Availability

   B. Reliability

   C. Maintainability

   D. Serviceability

8. What process provides a point of focus and management for all capacity- and performance-related issues, relating to both services and resources?

   A. Demand management

   B. Capacity management

   C. Availability management

   D. Service level management

9. What is the name given for the system that holds forecasts, the capacity plan, and capacity and performance reports and data?

    A. Capacity management information system (CMIS)

    B. Configuration management system (CMS)

    C. Availability support system

    D. Availability management information system (AMIS)

10. What is the name of the process that aligns IT security with business security to ensure information security is effectively managed?

    A. Access management

    B. Information security management

    C. Availability management

    D. Network security management

11. What is the name of the process that is responsible for maintaining the ongoing recovery capability within the IT services and their supporting components?

    A. IT service continuity management

    B. IT service risk management

    C. Disaster management

    D. Risk management

COMPREHENSION

1. Which processes within service design include activities that occur in other service lifecycle stages? What are some of the process activities?

2. Before committing to a specific level of service within a service level agreement (SLA), service level management must consider all other service design processes. Why?

6

SERVICE TRANSITION OVERVIEW

OVERVIEW

The service transition stage of the service lifecycle takes as input the service design package (SDP) from service design to build and prepare the service for operation in the live environment. Service transition is responsible for managing the changes and releases to a service, as well as controlling modifications to a service.

In this chapter, the overview of service transition is discussed, including the purpose, objectives and value to business. Other key concepts, including the service knowledge management system (SKMS), are also included.

Service transition accepts the service design package (SDP) from service design to ensure that all aspects of a service, not just the service technical solution, are transitioned into operation. This helps to ensure that the service can be properly supported. The output of service transition is the deployed service through early life support that includes the service, metrics and measurements, service levels, procedures, processes and knowledge of the service. This serves to ensure that the service can be properly supported in Service Operation, that it can be measured to ensure that it meets the needs of the business, and that it can be continually improved.

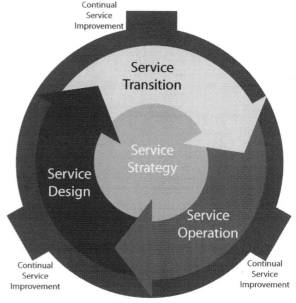

(c) Crown copyright 2007. Reproduced under license from OGC.

Figure - Service Lifecycle

TRANSITIONING THE GIFT CARD SERVICE

Mark Renner recognizes through his study of the concepts of IT service management that transitioning a service into operation is the highest risk for a new service. The transition activities of a new or changed service can cause a great deal of interruption to the existing services and processes that support a service. To minimize the risks from transition of the gift card service into operation, Mark established transition processes based on ITIL®.

These processes that Mark established are to minimize the risk of disruption to the business. They also ensure that expectations are well-established for both IT and the business so that everyone knows what to expect with this new service. Mark also ensured that one of the most commonly overlooked issues with new services, early life support, is considered, and the resources are allocated to support the service when it is released to operation until the operations staff can fully support it. This insures that the service is properly supported upon deployment until service operation staff can fully support this service on their own.

To minimize disruption during the transition, Mark established a well-defined test and evaluation plan. This test and evaluation plan goes far beyond just testing the functionality of the IT portion of the service but also includes all other aspects of the service. These aspects include ensuring that staff is trained on the new service and the support of the service, the roles and responsibilities to transition and support the service are well defined and considered early in the transition, the operational aspects of the service are tested, and that the knowledge gained during the design and transition of the service is conveyed to the operations staff through the service knowledge management system.

PURPOSE AND OBJECTIVES

Service Transition's purpose is to "ensure that new, modified or retired services meet the expectations of the business as documented in the service strategy and service design stages of the lifecycle."[1] This is done primarily through the processes of change management and release and deployment management and controlled through the process of service asset and configuration management.

---

1   Quoted text is from Service Transition © Crown copyright 2011 Reproduced under license from the Cabinet Office

The objectives of Service Transition are to:

"Plan and manage service changes efficiently and effectively

Manage risks relating to new, changed or retired services

Successfully deploy service releases into supported environments

Set correct expectations on the performance and use of new or changed services

Ensure that service changes create the expected business value

Provide good-quality knowledge and information about services and service assets"[2]

BUSINESS VALUE

Business obtains value from service transition through the assurance that the service is well-built and can be supported. Business also depends on service transition to align the new or changed service with the customer's business requirements and operations. Most of the time, a change to a service, including seemingly minor changes, are part of some larger business transition. The business must understand what the change to the service involves in order to prepare its business transition around this change.

Proper service transition also ensures that customers and users can use the new or changed service in a way that maximizes value to business operations. Service transition includes aspects to communicate the change to the service to business and its users so that maximum value can be attained from the service.

Business benefits from service transition through this holistic approach to change and the ability to control change. With proper service transition processes, the business objectives can be more readily met in a predictable manner, reducing the need for re-work and wasted time due to poor transition into operation.

Service transition provides value to:

"Enable projects to estimate the cost, timing, resource requirement and risks associated with the service transition stage more accurately

---

2   Quoted text is from Service Transition © Crown copyright 2011 Reproduced under license from the Cabinet Office

Result in higher volumes of successful change

Be easier for people to adopt and follow

Enable service transition assets to be shared and re-used across projects and services

Reduce delays from unexpected clashes and dependencies – for example, if multiple projects need to use the same test environment at the same time

Reduce the effort spent on managing the service transition test and pilot environments

Improve expectation setting for all stakeholders involved in service transition including customers, users, suppliers, partners and projects

Increase confidence that the new or changed service can be delivered to specification without unexpectedly affecting other services or stakeholders

Ensure that new or changed services will be maintainable and cost-effective

Improve control of service assets and configurations"[3]

KEY CONCEPTS

Service transition is a critical stage between service design and service operation. Far too often, IT organizations deploy services into production by "tossing them over the fence." This results in a poorly deployed service that fails to meet business objectives during a painful deployment process.

Lately, the news has reported many stories specifically targeting the transportation industry. These articles have reported numerous transportation disruptions. The primary cause of these disruptions has been poorly transitioned services. One airline in particular experienced long ticketing delays due to improperly released applications that support their services.

In order to overcome these difficulties, service transition processes formalize the transition of a service, or a change to a service, into operation. Service transition does not end when the service is "operational," but includes sup-

---

3   Quoted text is from Service Transition © Crown copyright 2011 Reproduced under license from the Cabinet Office

port through the service's early life to ensure that the business objectives can be met and the service is well supported. This overlap between service transition and service operation is called early life support.

DEFINITIVE MEDIA LIBRARY

The definitive media library (DML) is a repository for all media in its definitive state. The media assets of an organization traditionally include software. However, in today's environment, other types of media are becoming quite prevalent. These types of media may include banners for Web pages, video clips, movies, flash components, and many other forms of media that are required for a service.

Before software or any media is installed into the production environment, it must first be checked into the DML as an authorized version of that media. The DML has required check-in procedures to ensure that the media is approved, virus free, definitive, and properly prepared for use in the operational environment. The check-in procedures of the media also ensure that the media is of the correct quality to be included as part of a service. Included in the check-in of media are appropriate licenses, contracts, and other relevant documentation.

The DML includes support for both physical media and electronic media. Physical media includes the software and other media that may be delivered to IT in a physical format, such as on CD or DVD. Electronic media includes media that has been developed within IT or delivered through electronic downloads.

These procedures also ensure that services can be properly built, provide better control, promote standardization in the environment, and ensure that only authorized components are in use in the live environment. A service must be built on components of known quality. The DML assists in controlling these assets to ensure that only authorized, quality components are used.

This check-in to the DML is applied to both developed software and purchased software. Any software in the DML is in its definitive, installable state, rather than source code. Source code control is the development team's responsibility, and development should turn over fully completed, installable software, including the installation packages. However, there is an exception. While source code control is primarily the responsibility of development, some source code is included as part of a service. Some examples of source code as part of the definitive version of a service include Java script, PHP source, etc.

> **Key Point**
>
> Early life support is the overlap between service transition and service operation to ensure that a service is adequately supported until service operation can support the service on its own.

> **Key Point**
>
> The definitive media library (DML) is a repository for all media in its definitive state.

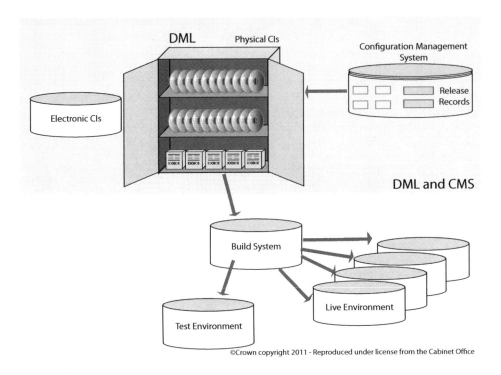

Figure - Definitive Media Library

The Definitive Media Library is the "secure library in which the definitive authorized versions of all media CIs are stored and protected."[4] The DML may also contain associated components such as licenses and documentation regarding the media. The media in the DML is under the control of change management and is recorded in the configuration management system. The DML may be multiple locations, depending on the organization.

When a new release is being prepared, only media contained within the DML are to be used as part of the release. This ensures that the media components of that release are of sufficient quality.

The DML must be kept separate from development, test, and live environments. This prevents contamination of the media in the DML in the event any other environments were to become corrupted.

---

4   Quoted text is from Service Transition © Crown copyright 2011 Reproduced under license from the Cabinet Office

DEFINITIVE SPARES (DS)

Definitive Spares involve providing secure storage areas of definitive hardware spares. These definitive storage areas maintain spare hardware components and assemblies, which are maintained at the same level as comparative systems in the live environment.

The DS ensure ease of implementation when new hardware is required or when components fail and require replacement. All hardware in the DS should be pre-configured to organizational standards to reduce the time it takes to provision this hardware. Implementing a DS helps to ensure standard hardware configurations are used throughout the organization when possible.

> **Key Point**
>
> Definitive spares involve providing secure storage areas of definitive hardware spares.

TERMS & DEFINITIONS

Early life support

Definitive media library (DML)

Definitive spares (DS)

IMPORTANT POINTS

The major input to service transition is the service design package (SDP) from service design.

The major output of service transition is the service transition package (STP) to service operation.

Service transition supports services in their early life through early life support until service operation can support the service on its own.

The purpose of service transition is to manage the transition for a new or changed service into production.

SECTION REVIEW

1. The main input to service transition is what?

   A. Service transition package (STP)

   B. Service level package (SLP)

   C. Service package (SP)

   D. Service design package (SDP)

2. The main output from service transition is what?

   A. Deployed service through early life support (ELS)

   B. Service level package (SLP)

   C. Service package (SP)

   D. Service design package (SDP)

3. The purpose of service transition is what?

   A. To manage the transition for a new, changed or retired service into production

   B. To ensure that all changes follow standardized processes and procedures

   C. To ensure that a new service can be properly supported until service operation can support the service on its own

   D. To ensure that services can be deployed into operation with minimal risk

4. What is described by the overlap between service transition and service operation to ensure that a service is adequately supported until service operation can support the service on its own?

   A. Organizational overlap

   B. Early life support

   C. Deployment

   D. Release considerations

5. What would NOT be stored in the definitive media library (DML)

   A. Definitive versions of electronic media

   B. Master copies of software

   C. Master copies of software documentation

   D. Backups of application data

6. The DML includes which of the following?

   A. A physical store only

   B. An electronic store only

   C. Both a physical and electronic store

   D. Neither a physical nor an electronic store

7. Which of the following is NOT an objective of service transition?

    A. To ensure there is minimal unpredict-able impact on the production services, operations, and support organization

    B. To increase proper use of the services, underlying applications, and technology solutions

    C. Create a logic model of the IT infra-structure relating components, applica-tions, systems, and services

    D. Provide clear and comprehensive plans that enable the customer and business change projects to align their activities with the service transition plans.

Comprehension

1. Describe early life support. Why is early life support important when transitioning a new service into pro-duction?

7

SERVICE TRANSITION PROCESSES

OVERVIEW

The service transition stage of the service lifecycle involves transitioning a service from design to an operational service. The processes involved in this stage are focused on reducing risk during transition, as well as improving ongoing control of the service.

The service transition processes include:

Transition planning and support

Change management

Service asset and configuration management

Release and deployment management

Knowledge management

TRANSITION PLANNING AND SUPPORT

OVERVIEW

Service transition is a crucial stage of the service lifecycle. Many organizations may be working on multiple transition projects at once with each project in a different stage of its transition. Additionally, while these projects are being actively worked on, there may be multiple additional projects that are preparing to leave service design to be transitioned into the live environment.

While each transition project may be well-managed, the entire workflow and pipeline of transitions must be managed to ensure that they are properly staffed and resourced, properly planned, and completed to meet business needs. Transition planning and support provides this overall support for individual transitions as well as planning for future transitions.

> **Key Point**
>
> The Transition Planning and Support purpose is to provide overall planning for service transitions and to coordinate the resources that they require.

PURPOSE

The purpose of transition planning and support is to "provide overall planning for service transitions and to coordinate the resources that they require."[1]

The objectives of transition planning and support are to:

"Plan and coordinate resources to ensure that the requirements of Service Strategy encoded in Service Design are effectively realized in Service Operation

Coordinate activities across projects, suppliers, and service teams

---

1   Quoted text is from Service Transition © Crown copyright 2011 Reproduced under license from the Cabinet Office

Establish new or changed services into production within the cost, quality, and time estimates

Establish new or modified management information systems and tools, technology and management architectures, service management processes, and measurement methods and metrics to meet requirements established during the Service Design stage of the service lifecycle

Ensure that all parties adopt the common framework of standard re-usable processes and supporting systems

Provide clear and comprehensive plans that enable customer and business change projects to align with these plans

Identify, manage, and control risks to minimize the chance of failure and disruption across transition activities

Monitor and improve the performance of the Service Transition stage of the Service Lifecycle"[2]

> **Key Point**
>
> An objective of transition planning and support is to plan and coordinate resources to ensure that the requirements of service strategy encoded in service design are effectively realized in service operation.

VALUE TO BUSINESS

Effective service transition is similar to the manufacturing arm of a product-based company. In manufacturing, the product that has been designed through the research and development (R&D) teams is realized and able to be introduced to the market. Effective manufacturing is required in order to be able to meet the needs of the overall organization. Through effective manufacturing, the company is able to respond to market needs quickly, and the manufacturing organization can provide a consistent response to new or changed designs.

Service transition needs to provide this same level of consistency in order for the IT service provider to meet the needs of their customers. Through transition planning and support, the underlying transition processes can be properly managed and supported by understanding the timeline of individual transitions and ensuring that they are properly planned for.

The overall scope of transition planning and support includes:

"Maintaining policies, standards, and models for service transition activities and processes

---

2   Quoted text is from Service Transition © Crown copyright 2011 Reproduced under license from the Cabinet Office

Guiding each major change or new service through all the service transition processes

Coordinating the efforts needed to enable multiple transitions to be managed at the same time

Prioritizing conflicting requirements for service transition resources

Planning the budget and resources needed to fulfill future requirements for service transition

Reviewing and improving the performance of transition planning and support activities

Ensuring that service transition is coordinated with program and project management, service design, and service development activities"[3]

ACTIVITIES

The activities in transition planning and support revolve around providing the proper support for not only individual transitions, but the organizational approach to service transition as a lifecycle stage.

Transition Strategy

The service transition strategy defines the overall approach to organizing service transition and allocating resources.

Service Transition Lifecycle Stages

The service design package should define the lifecycle stages for service transition and the criteria to move from one stage to the next. Typical stages in the life of a service transition may include:

"Acquire and test new configuration items and components

Build and test

Service release test

Service operational readiness test

---

[3]   Quoted text is from Service Transition © Crown copyright 2011 Reproduced under license from the Cabinet Office

Deployment

Early life support

Review and close service transition"[4]

Prepare for Service Transition

Preparing for service transition activities involve reviewing and accepting inputs from other service lifecycle stages and their deliverables (such as the SDP, service acceptance criteria, change proposals, and evaluation criteria). When inputs are reviewed, RFCs may be raised to address issues from service transition.

Preparation for service transition also ensures that the required configuration baselines are checked into the CMS prior to transition start as well as overall transition readiness.

Planning and Coordinating Service Transition

Planning and coordination addresses the planning for an individual transition into the overall transition workload and integrating these plans with other individual transition plans.

A best-practice approach is to leverage the capabilities of project and program management within an organization to track and manage the individual transitions and their relationships with other transitions. Common project management approaches and standards include Projects in a Controlled Environment version 2 (PRINCE2®) and Project Management Book of Knowledge (PMBOK®) based on the Project Management Institute (PMI®).

Planning and coordinating also includes reviewing the plans for individual transitions to ensure that lead times can be established to assemble the required capabilities and resources to enable these transitions to be completed. This includes scheduling resources, assessing costs and risks, performing compatibility checks with other configuration items, and ensuring the plans are understood and capabilities are available to meet the requirements of the transition.

Provide Transition Process Support

Providing transition process support includes providing overall advice and guidance to the stakeholders when preparing or performing a transition; administering individual transition work orders, risks, deviations and issues, tools, and processes; and monitoring for improvements to the process or transition activities.

---

4   Quoted text is from Service Transition © Crown copyright 2011 Reproduced under license from the Cabinet Office

CHANGE MANAGEMENT

OVERVIEW

Change requests can be generated from any place in the organization for a number of reasons. Some proactive reasons for a change request can be reduction of costs, productivity improvements, quality improvements, service improvements, and functionality improvements. Reactive reasons for change requests can be to resolve errors or to adapt to a changing environment.

> **Key Point**
>
> A request for change (RFC) is a mechanism to request a change to be made to a service.

The change management process activities are triggered by requests for change (RFCs). An RFC is a mechanism to request a change to be made to a service.

PURPOSE

> **Key Point**
>
> The purpose of change management is to control the lifecycle of all changes, enabling beneficial changes to be made with minimum disruption to IT services.

The purpose of change management is to "control the lifecycle of all changes, enabling beneficial changes to be made with minimum disruption to IT services."[5] Change management also ensures that all changes to service assets and configuration items are recorded in the configuration management system (CMS). All of these activities ensure that change management minimizes overall business risk.

Without an effective change management process in place, an organization cannot effectively control changes. This results in a low change success rate and unplanned outages. Without the ability to plan for changes, an organization will experience a high number of emergency changes. In effect, unauthorized changes become the norm. An effective change management process strives for no unauthorized changes in the environment but rather an environment where all changes are managed.

Change management ensures that any change to a service follows a well-defined, documented, measurable, and consistent process. This does not mean that all changes must follow the same path through the process but that the types of changes are understood and have paths through the process.

---

[5]   Quoted text is from Service Transition © Crown copyright 2011 Reproduced under license from the Cabinet Office

The most difficult part of change management is to understand the types of change that an organization implements on a regular basis. By classifying the types of change that an organization encounters, these changes can be modeled in a change management process in a way that all changes can be anticipated and supported.

Change management's objectives are to:

> "Respond to the customer's changing business requirements while maximizing value and reducing incidents, disruption and re-work

> Respond to the business and IT requests for change that will align the services with the business needs

> Ensure that changes are recorded and evaluated, and that authorized changes are prioritized, planned, tested, implemented, documented and reviewed in a controlled manner

> Ensure that all changes to configuration items are recorded in the configuration management system

> Optimize overall business risk – it is often correct to minimize business risk, but sometimes it is appropriate to knowingly accept a risk because of the potential benefit"[6]

VALUE TO BUSINESS

Changes are inherently risky. Proper change management balances the risk with the expected return of the change to ensure that the risk is worth the value associated with the change.

Change management provides value to the business by:

> "Protecting the business, and other services, while making required changes
> Implementing changes that meet the customers' agreed service requirements while optimizing costs
> Contributing to meet governance, legal, contractual and regulatory requirements by providing auditable evidence of change management activity
> Reducing failed changes and therefore service disruption, defects and re-work

6   Quoted text is from Service Transition © Crown copyright 2011 Reproduced under license from the Cabinet Office

Reducing the number of unauthorized changes, leading to reduced service disruption and reduced time to resolve change-related incidents

Delivering change promptly to meet business timescales

Tracking changes through the service lifecycle and to the assets of its customers

Contributing to better estimates of the quality, time and cost of change

Assessing the risks associated with the transition of services (introduction or disposal)

Improving productivity of staff by minimizing disruptions caused by high levels of unplanned or 'emergency' change and hence maximizing service availability

Reducing the mean time to restore service (MTRS), via quicker and more successful implementations of corrective changes

Liaising with the business change process to identify opportunities for business improvement"[7]

KEY CONCEPTS

Key Point

All changes must follow the Change Management process.

Regardless of the type or source of change, all changes must follow a process with specific procedures to ensure that all changes are recorded, evaluated, authorized, prioritized, planned, tested, implemented, and documented. A proper change management process ensures that these overriding objectives are met for every change.

7 Rs OF CHANGE MANAGEMENT

Every change must be evaluated to answer the following seven questions. The following seven questions reflect the 7 Rs of change management.

Who RAISED the change?

This identifies the person that requested the change. This person is often also a stakeholder for the change.

---

[7]   Quoted text is from Service Transition © Crown copyright 2011 Reproduced under license from the Cabinet Office

What is the REASON for the change?

> A business case should accompany the change to ensure that there is a valid business reason for performing this change.

What is the RETURN required from the change?

> This identifies what is expected from the change.

What are the RISKS involved in the change?

> Every change should involve a risk assessment to ensure that as many risks as possible are identified and managed to either reduce the likelihood of that risk occurring or mitigating the impact should the risk occur.

What RESOURCES are required to deliver the change?

> This identifies the resources required, such as funding, people, and technology.

Who is RESPONSIBLE for the build, test, and implementation of the change?

> This identifies the individuals who are expected to perform the activities involved in the change.

What is the RELATIONSHIP between this change and other changes?

> Changes often impact one another, particularly when implemented at the same time. This identifies these interrelationships to reduce the risk associated with the change.

> *Key Point*
>
> The 7 Rs of Change Management serve as a checklist for managing changes.

CHANGE PRIORITY

All changes are assigned a priority. The priority is based on the urgency and impact. The urgency refers to how long the implementation can afford to be delayed and is often a subjective measure based on the requestor's needs and/or wants.

The impact is the beneficial change to the business that will follow from a successful implementation or the degree of damage and cost to the business due to the error that the change will correct. Impact should be measured by disruption to the business-defined outcomes, such as revenue.

> *Key Point*
>
> The priority of a change is determined by the urgency and impact of the change.

Some organizations measure their impact by business desired outcomes other than revenue. For large city police departments, for example, communications failures are high impact. Other organizations may measure impact by loss of life or limb or threat to the populace.

These two things, urgency and impact, are evaluated to determine the priority of a change, incident, or problem.

TYPES OF CHANGE

> **Key Point**
>
> The three types of changes are standard changes, normal changes, and emergency changes.

Not all changes are created equal. Identifying change types helps to determine the level of scrutiny that these changes require in order to meet the requirements defined in the policies created by change management.

For example, adding memory to a user's desktop machine has far less impact, risk, and complexity of planning than adding memory to a server machine that supports critical business processes. Because of this disparity, these two changes should not be treated equally. Instead, these two changes should belong to different change types with differing levels of scrutiny.

Change types include standard changes, normal changes, and emergency changes.

Standard Changes

> **Key Point**
>
> Standard Changes are pre-approved changes that are well understood and common and have pre-established procedures and low risk.

Standard changes are pre-approved changes that are well understood and common and have pre-established procedures and low risk. These types of changes are usually operational in nature and include those changes that occur within IT. Examples of these changes include changing backup schedules, submitting a batch job, or applying patches to a server during a maintenance window.

Normal Change

> **Key Point**
>
> Normal changes are those changes that follow the full path through the process and are usually initiated through an RFC.

Normal changes are those changes that follow the full path through the process. This type of change undergo scrutiny and due diligence that are appropriate for the level of change. For a normal change, it must be assured that appropriate planning and testing have been performed to minimize the risk associated with the change. Normal changes are usually initiated through a request for change (RFC) and are evaluated by the change advisory board (CAB).

Emergency Change

Emergency changes are those that must be implemented in a time-critical manner in order to prevent unacceptable loss or impact to the business. Emergency changes are not to be used as a mechanism because somebody needs a change quickly, but must meet specific business-impact requirements to be considered. Emergency changes should have a path through the process and should be considered before they occur.

CHANGE ADVISORY BOARD

The change advisory board (CAB) is the name provided for the group of stakeholders that meets to evaluate high-impact requests for change. The CAB consists of representatives from IT and the business and includes customers, users, IT management, IT staff, consultants, and vendors, if necessary. The attendees of a CAB meeting depend on the specific change being considered.

Potential CAB members include:

> Change manager (chairs the CAB)
> Customers
> User managers
> User group representatives
> Applications developers/maintainers
> Specialists/technical consultants
> Services and operations staff
> Service desk
> Test management
> Facilities/office services staff for accommodation-based changes
> Contractors or third parties
> Others, as applicable

Attendees at the CAB meeting may depend on the changes being considered. CAB meetings should be very focused and not waste people's time. If the CAB meeting is considered to be unproductive, then the CAB attendees will stop coming. Therefore, the meetings should be short and very focused on the changes being considered.

To accommodate multiple changes for different attendees, the CAB meetings may involve different people even during the course of a single CAB meeting. One of my clients established a morning CAB meeting that lasted

> **Key Point**
>
> An Emergency Change is a change that is required to be implemented in a time-sensitive manner. Emergency changes prevent potential failure, lack or loss of functionality, or lack or loss of revenue.

> **Key Point**
>
> The change advisory board (CAB) is the name provided for the group of stakeholders that meets to evaluate high-impact requests for change.

for half an hour. This half hour meeting was sectioned into three ten-minute sessions. People knew when their specific changes were being discussed and would show up at the appointed time. This resulted in minimal impact to people's schedule and met the goals of the CAB meeting.

CAB meetings may involve suppliers, if useful. This is particularly true for a large supplier-oriented change, such as the rollout of new desktops. Other people involved in the CAB will include the service owner, the problem manager, and the service level manager.

The CAB agenda should be published in advance of all meetings to allow the CAB members to review the proposed changes prior to the meeting. At each CAB meeting, the following agenda should be considered.

> Failed, unauthorized, backed-out changes
>
> RFCs, in priority order
>
> Scheduling
>
> Change reviews
>
> Change management process
>
> Outstanding changes
>
> Advance notice of any expected RFCs

Emergency Changes

An emergency change is defined as *"a change that is required to be implemented in a time-sensitive manner."*[8] Emergency changes prevent potential failure, lack or loss of functionality, or lack or loss of revenue.

In a perfect world, there would be ample opportunity to ensure that all changes are evaluated, planned, and implemented with proper procedures being followed. However, this is not always possible, as emergencies occur that require immediate, or almost immediate, changes to be made. In such cases, emergency changes should have a path through the change management process and be anticipated in advance to ensure that change requirements can be met.

Authorization

Since emergency changes are part of the process, the process must consider these changes to provide an expedited path. Authority for emergency changes should be delegated and documented so it can be understood.

8   Quoted text is from Service Transition © Crown copyright 2011 Reproduced under license from the Cabinet Office

During an emergency change, it may be impossible or highly inconvenient to assemble a full CAB meeting to evaluate the change. In these cases, an emergency CAB (ECAB) may be convened. This ECAB is a subset of the CAB and is tasked with providing as much reasonable oversight as possible during an emergency.

Testing

During an emergency, testing may not always be possible. For example, if a router fails, it is highly unlikely that a spare router is available for testing due to the cost of the extra router. In these cases, testing should be performed to the extent possible and may be done during implementation. After implementation, full testing should be conducted to ensure that the change is operating as expected.

Documentation

Documentation during an emergency change may not always be possible to complete prior to the change occurring. However, even though it is an emergency change, the documentation must still be completed, but may be completed after the implementation.

Review

All emergency changes should be reviewed. These reviews are to determine if the change is indeed deemed to be an emergency and attempt to find ways to improve the process to reduce the number of emergency changes. Emergency changes are inherently risky, and steps to reduce the number of emergency changes should be determined.

CHANGE MODELS

For commonly occurring changes, change models that pre-define the steps required to conform to the change management process can be developed. These change models are developed to pre-define the workflow, management, authorization, escalation, and all other activities in change management for a particular type of change.

> **Key Point**
>
> Change Models are developed to pre-define the workflow, management, authorization, escalation, and all other activities in change management for a particular type of change.

189

REMEDIATION PLANNING

Most organizations do not plan for when changes fail. Since all change has inherent risk, planning for failure must be part of that change. A failed change refers not only to changes that cannot be implemented correctly, but also changes that fail to provide their expected benefit. Remediation planning accepts the fact that a change may fail and plans for that contingency.

Explicit plans must be made for all changes in the event of failure of the change. Some remediation options include back-out planning, ensuring recovery resources are available if needed (such as having people on-call to respond to failures), and in extreme circumstances, invoking the IT service continuity management plan.

Combined with change models, remediation planning only needs to be done once for each change model. By doing this, any change that conforms to that change model will have remediation planning already completed.

Note that remediation planning is not the same as a back-out plan. A back-out plan may be part of a remediation plan, but the remediation plan includes other possible actions such as escalation, communication and other actions to remediate a failed change.

CHANGE DOCUMENTATION

All changes must be properly documented. Some changes may require more documentation than others, based on the type of change and the change model being used. Not all of the documentation will be available during the submission of the RFC for the change. The change documentation is completed as the change is being performed and the knowledge required for the documentation is gained.

Not all change types will require the same amount of documentation. Standard changes require far less documentation than high-impact changes. It is important to ensure that the amount of documentation required for a change is consistent with the type of change. Otherwise, the process may be deemed too bureaucratic and will not be followed.

OVERALL ACTIVITIES

While the change management process has discrete activities, there are some overall activities that should be considered. These activities involve ensuring that a change is well planned, coordinated, and communicated. Communication is a key component of change management and involves ensuring that all stakeholders are aware of the changes before they occur and communicated with after the changes are completed.

Overall activities include:

> Planning and control of changes
>
> Change and release scheduling
>
> Communications
>
> Change decision making and change authorization
>
> Remediation planning
>
> Measurement and control
>
> Management reporting
>
> Impact assessment
>
> Continual improvement of the process

PROCESS ACTIVITIES

The change management process flow diagram shows the overall change management process. These activities are shown sequentially, but are often iterative. Additionally, not every type of change follows the same path through the change management process based on the type of change or the change model identified for that change.

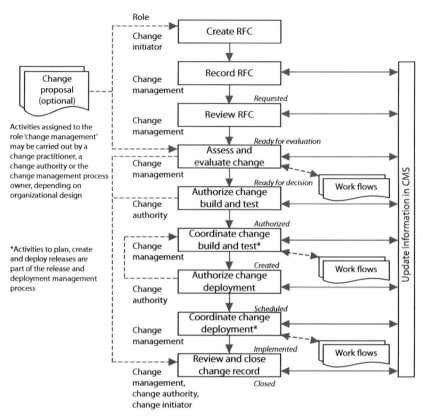

Figure - Change Management Process Flow

The individual activities for the change management process are discussed in the following pages.

Create and Record RFC

The first activity in change management is to ensure that the request for change (RFC) has been created and that the RFC accurately reflects the change that is being proposed. An RFC is more than just a request, but often serves as an artifact that the change has occurred. This RFC documents the details of the change, when it occurred, and what the outcome was and is a historical record of that change.

The service desk uses the record of the change after the change has been completed to identify a possible cause for incidents that have occurred.

Review RFC

When a change is submitted, it is reviewed to ensure that the change is correct and feasible. The correctness of the RFC assists in establishing the routing of the change to ensure that the change can be implemented in a timely manner. This is also an opportunity to reject changes that make little business sense or lack correct documentation.

Assess and Evaluate

The assess and evaluate activity establishes the appropriate level of change authority and ensures that the change has the appropriate level of oversight. The scope of a change is determined to identify the stakeholders of the change. These stakeholders are candidates for the change advisory board (CAB).

This activity also involves assessing and evaluating the business justification, impact, cost, benefits, and risk to ensure that the value of the change is worth the cost and effort. An independent evaluation of the change may be performed if required.

Service asset and configuration management is consulted during the assessment, as the configuration management system (CMS) contains details about the environment that assist with the assessment of impact and risk.

Authorize Change Build and Test

Change authorization ensures that the change is understood and properly documented and is approved by all stakeholders identified for this change. Some changes may require a change advisory board (CAB) meeting, while others may obtain approval from a single individual or may already be pre-approved according to the type of change or associated Change Model.

Coordinate Change Build and Test

Change management does not actually build a change but relies on release and deployment management to build and test the change as part of a release package. Change management provides overall coordination of the change to ensure that it is properly managed.

Some changes require more detailed planning than others, so the planning should be consistent with the scope and effort of the change. Planning and scheduling the change should consider the business schedule to ensure that there is no impact to the business during critical processing times.

Authorize Change Deployment

Once the change has been built and tested, change management authorizes the deployment of the change as part of a release package. This authorization is done once the change has been built and checked into the DML as appropriate.

Coordinate Change Deployment

While release and deployment management deploys the change through a release, change management coordinates the effort to provide overall management of the change.

Review and Close

Once the change has been completed, the change is reviewed for correctness and to ensure that the change met its objectives. It is also an opportunity to ensure that all documentation has been completed and saved to serve as a record of that change being performed.

A new baseline of the environment that considers the new change may be established. This baseline serves as a point to compare against the future state.

Change reviews should occur for both successful changes and failed changes, as deemed appropriate. In particular, a failed change is not an opportunity to "point fingers," but an opportunity to improve the change management process. Most failed changes are usually the result of a fault in the process or a failure to adhere to the process. This review provides an opportunity to understand where these improvements can be made.

Once all actions have been completed and the documentation reviewed, the change is formally closed.

Change management has dependencies on other processes and some optional activities. The following activities show these relationships and alternate additional activities depending on the complexity or scope of the change.

Change Proposal

Some changes may have significant complexity or cost associated with them to require a change proposal. A change proposal is submitted for those changes where the work to prepare the change or obtain funds for the change must be authorized and approved.

An example of a change proposal may be for a new service. If a new service has been proposed by service portfolio management, the change proposal will be evaluated by change management to determine the potential risk and impact of the new service on existing services.

Authorize Proposal

When a change proposal is required, the proposal is authorized or rejected. The proposal must be authorized in order for the resources to be expended to move the change forward. Once a proposal is authorized, it may result in a series of RFCs to implement the proposal.

Update CMS

Upon the implementation of the change, the configuration management system (CMS) is updated to ensure that the CMS reflects the new state of the environment.

Evaluation Report

Upon closure of a change, the change is evaluated for correctness. This evaluation consists of an audit to ensure that the process has been adhered to. Post implementation reviews (PIRs) may be conducted to evaluate complex changes and failed changes. Every emergency change should have a PIR to ensure that it has the appropriate oversight, even after the fact, and that it actually required an emergency change.

CHANGE MANAGEMENT PROCESS RELATIONSHIPS

Change management is the process of managing changes that may have been identified by other processes. All of the processes may be a source of RFCs. These processes may also review proposed changes to determine the impact that the change may have on services. Specific relationships with other processes include:

Service Asset and Configuration Management

Service asset and configuration management records the CIs as they move through the change process, as well as assists change management in the assessment of the impact and risk of changes.

Problem Management

Problem management removes errors from the environment through changes.

IT Service Continuity Management

IT service continuity management reviews changes for impact to the continuity plan.

Information Security Management

Information security management reviews changes for impact to information security, as well as submits RFCs to change management to improve security.

Availability Management and Capacity Management

Availability and capacity management review RFCs for impact to availability and capacity, as well as submit RFCs to improve availability and capacity.

SERVICE ASSET AND CONFIGURATION MANAGEMENT

OVERVIEW

Service asset and configuration management is the process that provides control to the infrastructure. Through the creation of a configuration model, the relationships between components are recorded to ensure that the environment is documented and well-understood. Through the documentation of the components and their relationships to each other to provide services, the service can be better supported.

The service asset and configuration management process provides the foundation for all other processes. All other processes rely on the configuration management system (CMS) as a repository of information regarding the environment in order to be as efficient and effective as possible.

> **Key Point**
>
> All other processes rely on the configuration management system (CMS) as a repository of information regarding the environment in order to be as efficient and effective as possible.

PURPOSE AND OBJECTIVES

The purpose of service asset and configuration management is to "ensure that the assets required to deliver services are properly controlled, and that accurate and reliable information about those assets is available when and where it is needed."[9] This is accomplished through a configuration management system (CMS) that stores relevant configuration and asset information, as well as relationships to each other.

The objectives os service asset and configuration management are to:

> "Ensure that assets under the control of the IT organization are identified, controlled and properly cared for throughout their life-cycle

> **Key Point**
>
> The purpose of service asset and configuration management is to "ensure that the assets required to deliver services are properly controlled, and that accurate and reliable information about those assets is available when and where it is needed

---

9   Quoted text is from Service Transition © Crown copyright 2011 Reproduced under license from the Cabinet Office

Identify, control, record, report, audit and verify services and other configuration items (CIs), including versions, baselines, constituent components, their attributes and relationships.

Account for, manage and protect the integrity of CIs through the service lifecycle by working with change management to ensure that only authorized components are used and only authorized changes are made.

Ensure the integrity of CIs and configurations required to control the services by establishing and maintaining an accurate and complete configuration management system

Maintain accurate configuration information on the historical, planned and current state of services and other CIs

Support efficient and effective service management processes by providing accurate configuration information to enable people to make decisions at the right time"[10]

Through this CMS, service asset and configuration management provides a central point for information to support all other service management processes, as well as other organizational processes, such as finance and procurement.

KEY CONCEPTS

CONFIGURATION MODEL

> **Key Point**
>
> The configuration model shows the services and how the individual components, systems, and applications are related to provide these services.

The service asset and configuration management process includes the concept of a configuration model in the CMS to provide a logical model of the services in the environment. The CMS records this model for use by the other processes. This model shows the services and how the individual components, systems, and applications are related to provide these services.

Service

Services are the top level of the configuration model and should be linked to the business service that the service supports. This service should also be related to a service in the service catalog.

---

10   Quoted text is from Service Transition © Crown copyright 2011 Reproduced under license from the Cabinet Office

Systems

The systems level represents the systems that provide the service and are decomposed into the applications and components that make up this system level to support the service.

Applications

Applications are not services themselves. A service may rely on more than one application, and an application may support more than one service.

Components

The component level represents the individual components, hardware, software, etc. used to provide the overall service.

Configuration models are used to model services and their underlying components within the CMS. The CMS and these configuration models are used by all other processes to provide information that make these processes more effective and efficient. Some examples of this include:

> To assess the impact and cause of incidents and problems
>
> To assess the impact of proposed changes
>
> To plan and design new or changed services
>
> To plan technology refreshes and software upgrades
>
> To plan release and deployment packages and migrate service assets to different locations and service centers
>
> To optimize asset utilization and costs

CONFIGURATION MANAGEMENT SYSTEM

The configuration management system (CMS) is a set of tools and databases that are used to store a service provider's configuration data. The CMS stores records of service and component details and their relationships to each other. This system is not a single database, but is a collection of databases and data sources that are accessed from one place. The records stored are called configuration items (CIs) that contain component details, as well as their relationships to each other. These CI records include:

> Relationships between CIs
>
> Related incidents
>
> Related problems
>
> Related Known Errors
>
> Related Change Records
>
> Release documentation

> **Key Point**
>
> The configuration management system (CMS) is a set of tools and databases that are used to store a service provider's configuration data.

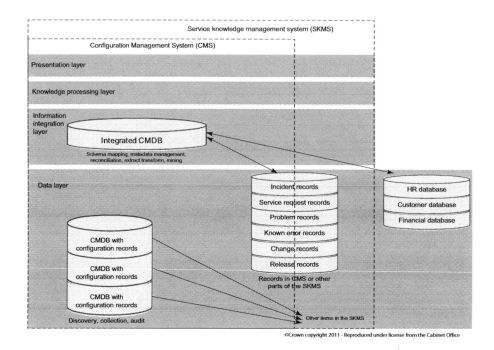

©Crown copyright 2011 - Reproduced under license from the Cabinet Office

Figure - Configuration Management System

The CMS is the repository for all information related to the infrastructure and the components that support the services. This information should be stored and related to enable quick access to it when it is needed.

CONFIGURATION ITEM

A Configuration Item (CI) is defined as *"any asset, service component, or other item that is, or will be, under the control of Configuration Management."*[11] These CIs are the individual components that make up a service. In order to be a CI, it must be needed to deliver a service, be uniquely identifiable, be subject to change, and can be managed. These CIs are categorized by type. Each CI also has attributes that describe information about the CI in the CMS.

---

11   Quoted text is from Service Transition © Crown copyright 2011 Reproduced under license from the Cabinet Office

Examples of CIs include hardware and software, applications, network infrastructure, contracts, and even people. Anything could potentially be a CI if it is required to provide a service.

Each CI has a set of attributes that holds characteristics about the CI, including but not limited to, the CI name, version, model number, status, and relationships. These relationships to other CIs may include relationships to other physical components, contracts, incidents, problems, changes, errors, and documentation, as well as other relevant links.

CIs have a lifecycle status that shows where they are in their individual lives. CIs start with a status of "on order" and move through the lifecycle (delivered, test, production, retired, etc.) until they are formally disposed.

Configuration Baselines

A configuration baseline is similar to a "master" image of a configuration. Configuration baselines are a formally reviewed and agreed upon configuration of a service, product, or infrastructure. Through these baselines, an organization can recover the infrastructure or component back to a specific baseline, mark a milestone in the development of a service, or perform a configuration audit. Configuration baselines are also very useful to other processes in order to prepare for disaster recovery, make changes to the infrastructure, or plan for improvements.

Roles

Configuration management involves several roles, often performed by different people, to ensure that the technology required to record the environment is well maintained, the process is effective, and the media is properly recorded. Other roles involve other processes to ensure that the relationships between asset and configuration management and these other processes are maintained.

A brief overview of the roles include:

Service Asset Manager

The service asset manager manages the asset management process to ensure conformance to the process and ensure that assets are identified, labeled, and tracked.

Configuration Manager

The configuration manager ensures the configuration management processes are adhered to and implements the configuration management policy and standards.

Configuration Analyst

The configuration analyst supports the configuration management plan by ensuring accuracy of information in the CMS, performing configuration audits, and providing information across the organization.

Configuration Administrator/Librarian

The configuration administrator/librarian controls the receipts, identification, storage, and withdrawal of all CIs in the CMS and definitive media library (DML) and provides information regarding these CIs. The configuration administrator/librarian also maintains the DML and the definitive spares (DS).

CMS/Tools Administrator

The CMS/tools administrator is responsible for evaluating and maintaining the tools used in service asset and configuration management. The CMS/tools administrator also monitors the capacity of the CMS and ensures the integrity and performance of the configuration management system.

RELEASE AND DEPLOYMENT MANAGEMENT

OVERVIEW

The transition of a service into operation is inherently risky. Many IT organizations fail to consider all of the aspects involved in the transition of a service into operation. Many times, the transition of a service involves only the installation of an application, after which the transition team considers the transition complete and disengages from the transition. This leaves the responsibility of the service entirely to the operational staff – often without the proper training, support from second-level IT, and little knowledge regarding the service.

Release and deployment management strives to minimize the risk associated with transitioning a service by considering all aspects of a service to ensure that the service meets the needs of the business and can be well supported. This transition involves assuring that high-quality services and components are released, as well as ensuring that all elements of the release - including training, knowledge, support processes, contracts, and other items - are included as part of the release.

Release and deployment management also ensures that the service is not "installed and forgotten." Through early life support, release and deployment management provides resources to ensure that the service's critical early life is well supported until operations staff can fully support the service.

> **Key Point**
>
> Through early life support, release and deployment management provides resources to ensure that the service's critical early life is well supported until operations staff can fully support the service.

PURPOSE AND OBJECTIVES

Release management's purpose is to "plan, schedule and control the build, test and deployment of releases, and to deliver new functionality required by the business while protecting the integrity of existing services."[12] A release is far more than just the technology being provided, but also the documentation, the supporting processes, and the knowledge to enable ongoing opera-

---

12   Quoted text is from Service Transition © Crown copyright 2011 Reproduced under license from the Cabinet Office

tion and continual improvement of the release after it is in operation.

The specific objectives of release and deployment management are to:

"Define and agree release and deployment management plans with customers and stakeholders

Create and test release packages that consist of related configuration items that are compatible with each other

Ensure that the integrity of a release package and its constituent components is maintained throughout the transition activities, and that all release packages are stored in a DML and recorded accurately in the CMS

Deploy release packages from the DML to the live environment following an agreed plan and schedule

Ensure that all release packages can be tracked, installed, tested, verified and/or uninstalled or backed out if appropriate

Ensure that organization and stakeholder change is managed during release and deployment activities

Ensure that a new or changed service and its enabling systems, technology and organization are capable of delivering the agreed utility and warranty

Record and manage deviations, risks and issues related to the new or changed service and take necessary corrective action

Ensure that there is knowledge transfer to enable the customers and users to optimize their use of the service to support their business activities

Ensure that skills and knowledge are transferred to service operation functions to enable them to effectively and efficiently deliver, support and maintain the service according to required warranties and service levels"[13]

KEY CONCEPTS

Releases are deployed through release packages. Release packages contain one or more release units. A release unit is defined as *"the portions of the IT infrastructure that are normally released together."*[14]

For example, Microsoft Office® is considered a release package. The Microsoft Office® package includes many release units, such as Microsoft Word®, Microsoft Excel®, and Microsoft PowerPoint®.

13   Quoted text is from Service Transition © Crown copyright 2011 Reproduced under license from the Cabinet Office

14   Quoted text is from Service Transition © Crown copyright 2011 Reproduced under license from the Cabinet Office.

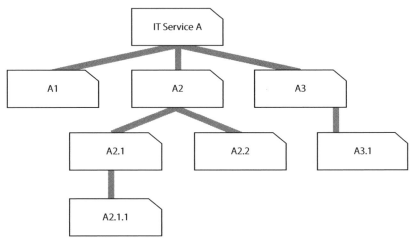

©Crown copyright 2011 - Reproduced under license from the Cabinet Office

Figure - Release Units and Release Packages

RELEASE OPTIONS AND CONSIDERATIONS

There are many considerations regarding releases and deployment of releases into the live environment. The three main considerations are big bang versus phased, push versus pull, and automated versus manual.

Big Bang versus Phased

A big bang approach to a release is when the entire service is released into the environment at the same time. A phased release is staging a release such that the release is introduced into the live environment in a series of stages, each stage building on the previous stage.

Push versus Pull

Pushing a release into service applies the release into the environment from a central location for all users, regardless of whether or not the users want the release at that time. A pull mechanism makes the release available for users and gives the users control of when they want to install the release on their systems. Popular Internet messaging software and music software follow the pull model. They inform you when a new release is available and provide you the mechanisms to install the release on your computer.

> **Key Point**
>
> Release options and considerations include:
>
> Big bang vs. phased
>
> Push vs. pull
>
> Automation vs. manual

Automation versus Manual

Automated releases apply the release through automation tools. These automation tools involve software distribution tools to install the release. Automation helps eliminate human error, makes the release repeatable, and ensures consistency. Manual releases apply the release by hand. Manual releases are usually quicker to deploy but are difficult to make repeatable and consistent.

COORDINATING RELEASE AND DEPLOYMENT

Release and deployment management activities work together to ensure that a release is properly built, packaged, and tested prior to being deployed in the production environment.

Once the service package or release has been acquired from the implementation team, it must be built and packaged in a manner that ensures consistency across the deployment environments. Once built and packaged, the release is deployed to a test environment to ensure that it can be deployed correctly. This may require that sub-components of the release are deployed first to support the full release.

Once the release has been deployment tested, it is deployed into the production environment(s), which may involve more than a single deployment. The deployment of multiple packages of a release may require careful coordination to ensure correctness and proper timing of the deployed release packages.

After deployment to the production environment, the release enters early life support and is supported by both service transition and service operation until service operation can fully support the release.

PHASES OF RELEASE

When deploying a release into production, there are multiple phases that the release progresses through. The release and deployment phases are authorized by change management to ensure the correctness and quality of the release.

RELEASE AND DEPLOYMENT PLANNING

The release and deployment planning phase involves creating plans for creating and deploying the release. Change management triggers this phase with an authorization to plan a release. This phase ends with change management authorization to create the release.

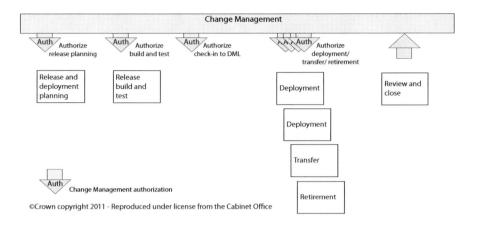

Figure - Phases of Release and Deployment

RELEASE BUILD AND TEST

The release build and test phase begins with change management authorization to build the release. During this phase the release package is built and checked into the DML once the release has been quality tested and is complete. Change management ends this phase with the authorization for the baselined release package to be checked in.

DEPLOYMENT

During the deployment phase, the release package that has been checked into the DML is deployed into the live environment. Change management begins this phase with an authorization to deploy the release package to the location(s) in the live environment.

Deployment will include the actual movement of the release package into the live environment but will also include the transfer of the release and its assets to operation. This is performed through early life support until the formal handoff to service operation has been performed.

Also included in the deployment phase is the retirement of service assets in the event that a new release and its components will replace existing components in the live environment. Deployment ensures that these service assets are recovered and re-tasked or retired as appropriate.

> **Key Point**
>
> The four phases of release and deployment are:
>
> Release and deployment planning
>
> Release build and test
>
> Deployment
>
> Review and close

Some deployments may be performed on behalf of another organization. In this case, the financial transfer of the deployed assets may be completed.

REVIEW AND CLOSE

In the review and close phase, the experiences of the release are captured, performance targets and achievements are reviewed, and lessons learned are analyzed.

ROLES

RELEASE AND DEPLOYMENT MANAGER

The release and deployment manager ensures the policies created for release and deployment are followed to ensure management of all aspects of the process end-to-end. The release and deployment manager ensures that the appropriate planning of releases is conducted, activities are communicated, and records updated in the CMS and SKMS.

RELEASE PACKAGING AND BUILD MANAGER

The release packaging and build manager is responsible for ensuring that a specific release is built and packaged correctly and finalizes the details of the release configuration to be deployed to the production environment. The release packaging and build manager is also responsible for reporting any outstanding known errors and workarounds to problem management for inclusion in the known error database.

DEPLOYMENT MANAGER

The deployment manager ensures that the release is deployed to the production environment effectively and correctly. The deployment manager also assumes the responsibility for early life support to ensure that the release is supported properly until service operation can fully assume the support responsibility for the release.

KNOWLEDGE MANAGEMENT

OVERVIEW

Knowledge management is the process that ensures that organizational knowledge is stored and retained for use throughout the service lifecycle. This organizational knowledge plays a key role in not only improving the stability and supportability of a service in service operation but also supporting the other service lifecycle stages.

PURPOSE AND OBJECTIVES

The purpose of Knowledge Management is to "share perspectives, ideas, experience and information; to ensure that these are available in the right place at the right time to enable informed decisions; and to improve efficiency by reducing the need to rediscover knowledge."[15]

The objectives of knowledge management are to:

> "Improve the quality of management decision-making by ensuring that reliable and secure knowledge, information and data is available throughout the service lifecycle
>
> Enable the service provider to be more efficient and improve quality of service, increase satisfaction and reduce the cost of service by reducing the need to rediscover knowledge
>
> Ensure that staff have a clear and common understanding of the value that their services provide to customers and the ways in which benefits are realized from the use of those services
>
> Maintain a service knowledge management system (SKMS) that provides controlled access to knowledge, information and data that is appropriate for each audience
>
> Gather, analyze, store, share, use and maintain knowledge, information and data throughout the service provider organization"[16]

| **Key Point** |
| The purpose of Knowledge Management is to share perspectives, ideas, experience and information; to ensure that these are available in the right place at the right time to enable informed decisions; and to improve efficiency by reducing the need to rediscover knowledge. |

15   Quoted text is from Service Transition © Crown copyright 2011 Reproduced under license from the Cabinet Office

16   Quoted text is from Service Transition © Crown copyright 2011 Reproduced under license from the Cabinet Office.

KEY CONCEPTS

Knowledge management is about retaining knowledge. Organizational knowledge begins as data. Data is discrete facts about events. Data is converted to information when we analyze the data in some context. Information with experiences, ideas, insights, values, and judgment of people is called knowledge. This knowledge, along with discernment of the material and having the application and contextual awareness, is wisdom.

KNOWLEDGE SPIRAL/D-I-K-W MODEL

> **Key Point**
>
> The D-I-K-W model is the data, information, knowledge, wisdom model.

Knowledge management strives to convert data to information to support knowledge which, in turn, can be wisely used. The intent of the knowledge spiral is to improve organizational knowledge by collecting data, distilling information from it, and obtaining knowledge from the information that facilitates wisdom. Data, information, knowledge and wisdom are not synonymous. The knowledge spiral is also known as the D-I-K-W Model.

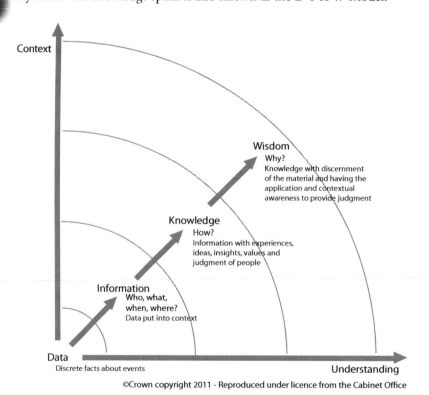

©Crown copyright 2011 - Reproduced under licence from the Cabinet Office

Figure - DIKW Model

Data is defined as *"numbers, characters, images, or other outputs from devices to convert physical quantities into symbols. Data is quantitative."*[17]

Information is defined as *"a message received and understood. Information is a collection of facts from which a conclusion can be drawn."*[18]

Knowledge is defined as *"information combined with experience, context, interpretation, and reflection."*[19]

Wisdom is defined as *"the ability to make correct judgments and decisions."*[20]

Data, information, and knowledge can be stored for later use in the service knowledge management system (SKMS). Wisdom however, cannot be retained, as wisdom is the ability to make correct decisions based on this knowledge.

SERVICE KNOWLEDGE MANAGEMENT SYSTEM

The service knowledge management system (SKMS) represents all of the knowledge that is present within IT. Many times, this knowledge is available in other systems, such as the CMS and its CMDBs, as well as the known error database, capacity management information system, availability management information system, and many other places. Each of these systems, databases, and repositories is a source of data and information to improve the overall knowledge of a service. Therefore, these systems, databases, and repositories are considered part of the SKMS.

> **Key Point**
>
> Data is defined as numbers, characters, images, or other outputs from devices to convert physical quantities into symbols. Data is quantitative.

> **Key Point**
>
> Information is defined as a message received and understood. Information is a collection of facts from which a conclusion can be drawn.

> **Key Point**
>
> Knowledge is defined as information combined with experience, context, interpretation, and reflection.

> **Key Point**
>
> Wisdom is defined as the ability to make correct judgments and decisions.

---

17   Quoted text is from Service Transition © Crown copyright 2011 Reproduced under license from the Cabinet Office

18   Quoted text is from Service Transition © Crown copyright 2011 Reproduced under license from the Cabinet Office.

19   Quoted text is from Service Transition © Crown copyright 2011 Reproduced under license from the Cabinet Office.

20   Quoted text is from Service Transition © Crown copyright 2011 Reproduced under license from the Cabinet Office.

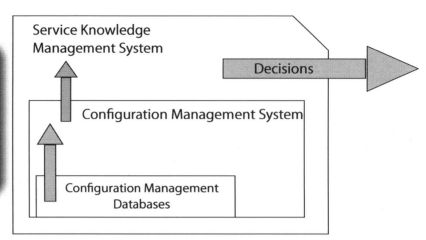

(c) Crown copyright 2011. Reproduced under licence from the Cabinet Office

Figure - Service Knowledge Management System

Key Point

The service knowledge management system (SKMS) represents all of the knowledge that is present within IT.

Key Point

The CMS and its CMDB(s) are a part of the SKMS.

ACTIVITIES

The activities in knowledge management are focused on understanding the sources of knowledge and developing techniques to retain this knowledge. These activities include:

Knowledge Management Strategy

Developing a knowledge management strategy involves understanding what knowledge to capture, deciding where and when the knowledge will be captured, and who will capture the knowledge. This strategy should consider all stages of the service lifecycle, as critical knowledge is inherent within all stages.

Knowledge Transfer

Knowledge transfer involves sharing knowledge between parts of the organization. When developing processes, particularly those that involve transfer of responsibilities for services, the knowledge should be focused on, as well. Specific points in the process when knowledge will be transferred from one part of the organization to another should be determined.

Data and Information Management

This activity involves development and maintenance of the service knowledge management system (SKMS). The SKMS is a system in which organizational knowledge is captured, maintained, and available for use by others in the organization.

Using the SKMS

Using the SKMS involves understanding what knowledge is useful, how it will be used, and how it will be accessed. This activity involves understanding the consumers of the knowledge to develop a system that will be useful and accessible and contain pertinent information.

TERMS & DEFINITIONS

Request for change (RFC)

Standard change

Normal change

Emergency change

Change advisory board (CAB)

Change models

Configuration management system (CMS)

Configuration Item (CI)

Release unit

Release package

DIKW model

Data

Information

Knowledge

Wisdom

Service knowledge management system (SKMS)

IMPORTANT POINTS

The processes within service transition are:

> Transition planning and support
> Change management
> Service asset and configuration management
> Release and deployment management
> Knowledge management

The purpose of transition planning and support is to provide overall planning for service transitions and to coordinate the resources that they require.

An objective of transition planning and support is to plan and coordinate resources to ensure that the requirements of service strategy encoded in service design are effectively realized in service operation.

The purpose of change management is to ensure that standardized methods and procedures are used for efficient and prompt handling of all changes.

The three types of changes are standard changes, normal changes, and emergency changes.

The purpose of service asset and configuration management is to provide a logical model of the IT infrastructure.

The configuration model shows the relationships between components, systems, applications, and services.

The purpose of release and deployment management is to take a holistic view of a set of changes to a service and ensure that all aspects of a release, both technical and non-technical, are considered, planned, and prepared for that release.

The release options and considerations are big bang vs. phased, push vs. pull, and automation vs. manual.

The four phases of release and deployment are:

> Release and deployment planning
> Release build and test
> Deployment
> Review and close

The purpose of knowledge management is to ensure that the right information is delivered to the appropriate place or competent person at the right time to enable an informed decision.

The configuration management system (CMS) forms part of the service knowledge management system (SKMS).

SECTION REVIEW

1. Which process ensures that standardized methods and procedures are used for efficient and prompt handling of all changes?

   A. Change management

   B. Release and deployment management

   C. Knowledge management

   D. Service asset and configuration management

2. All changes should be treated the same, regardless of complexity, scope, or risk.

   A. True

   B. False

3. What is the term used for the explicit plans that are made for all changes in the event of a change failure?

   A. IT service continuity management

   B. Remediation planning

   C. Backout planning

   D. Post implementation review

4. The CAB is responsible for what?

   A. Evaluating high-impact requests for change

   B. Performing a post implementation review of all changes

   C. Evaluating all requests for change

   D. Informing the business of impending outages to implement changes

5. Emergency changes have no place in change management.

   A. True

   B. False

6. Before an emergency change is implemented, the CAB must be convened.

   A. True

   B. False

7. What is the name of the process that provides a logical model of the IT infrastructure and holds its data in the CMS?

   A. Service modeling

   B. Service asset and configuration management

   C. Release and deployment management

   D. Demand management

8. What is the name given for the place where definitive versions of software are stored?

   A. Federated database

   B. Definitive media library

   C. Definitive software library

   D. Software catalog

9. What is a release unit?

   A. A tested unit of code

   B. All of the hardware and software that make up a service

   C. A set of packages that is installed to support a service

   D. The portions of the IT infrastructure that are normally released together

10. Which of the following cannot be stored in a database or management system?

   A. Knowledge

   B. Wisdom

   C. Data

   D. Information

11. What is the order of the knowledge spiral (DIKW Model)?

   A. Collection->correlation->normalization->analysis

   B. Data->knowledge->wisdom->information

   C. Data->knowledge->information->wisdom

   D. Data->information->knowledge->wisdom

Comprehension

1. Discuss how the CMS may be used by other processes throughout the service lifecycle. Would this be useful in your organization? Why?

2. Describe the different types of change in change management. Why should an organization determine the types of change and why is this important?

3. Describe how release and deployment management works with change management. Why are these processes separate?

8

SERVICE OPERATION OVERVIEW

OVERVIEW

Service operation is where value is delivered to the customer and the strategy of the organization is executed. Think about an automobile manufacturer. The manufacturer develops a strategy for the market, designs an automobile to meet customer requirements, builds the car, and delivers it for sale through an automobile dealership. Up to this point, there has been a lot of work put into the manufacture of that car, but it isn't until the car is sold and the new owner drives the car off the lot that the value of the vehicle is realized.

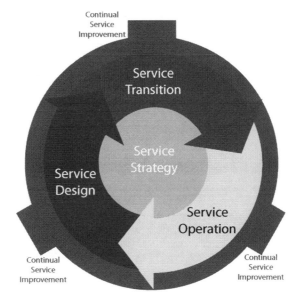

(c) Crown copyright 2011. Reproduced under license from the Cabinet Office.

Figure - Service Lifecycle

Service operation delivers this value by supporting the solutions that the customer requires. Service operation does this through assuring the service is well supported and available to the customer.

This chapter introduces the basic concepts of service operation, including its purpose, objectives, and value to business.

PURPOSE

The purpose of service operation is to "coordinate and carry out the activities and processes required to deliver and manage services at agreed levels to business users and customers. Service operation is also responsible for the ongoing management of the technology that is used to deliver and support services."[1]

The objectives of service operation are to:

"Maintain business satisfaction and confidence in IT through effective and efficient delivery and support of agreed IT services

Minimize the impact of service outages on day-to-day business activities

Ensure that access to agreed IT services is only provided to those authorized to receive those services"[2]

Service operation receives the deployed service through early life support as input, which includes the service solution, architectures, processes, service management tools, and methods for metrics and measurement. The main output of service operation is value to the customers and the service operation reports to continual service improvement. These service operation reports are used to identify improvements to services and are the main input to continual service improvement.

KEY CONCEPTS

Value to the business is realized through service operation. However, service operation has some specific challenges. Once the service is delivered, it is service operation's responsibility. Many times the scoping and funding of the service fails to include the operational costs of the service, only the design,

> **Key Point**
>
> Service operation is where value is delivered to the customer and the strategy of the organization is executed.

> **Key Point**
>
> The purpose of service operation is to coordinate and carry out the activities and processes required to deliver and manage services at agreed levels to business users and customers.

> **Key Point**
>
> The main input to service operation is the deployed service through early life support. The main output is service performance reports to continual service improvement.

1   Quoted text is from Service Operation © Crown copyright 2011 Reproduced under license from the Cabinet Office

2   Quoted text is from Service Operation © Crown copyright 2011 Reproduced under license from the Cabinet Office

development, and rollout of the service. Service operation is then forced to support a service without the appropriate funding. This is exacerbated when the service has flaws in it and there is no funding to address these flaws.

Once a service has been introduced to the customer and users, the service is taken for granted. It is assumed that the new service is part of the standard within IT, even though the financial and support aspects have not been considered. Service design and service transition attempt to remedy this issue by ensuring that all aspects of a service are considered so that it can be supported effectively and efficiently as a continuing concern in service operation.

COMMUNICATION IN SERVICE OPERATION

Good communication is needed with other IT teams and departments, with users and internal customers, and between the service operation teams. Issues can often be prevented or mitigated with appropriate communication.

Examples of communication in service operation include:

> "Routine operational communication
>
> Communication between shifts
>
> Reporting
>
> Communication related to changes, exceptions and emergencies
>
> Training on new or customized processes and service designs
>
> Communication of strategy and design to service operation"[3]

SERVICE OPERATION BALANCE

Service operation is constantly striving to balance the continuous demands IT faces. Changes in business, changes in technology, and legislative changes can produce conflict in IT. Service operation's challenge is to provide standard levels of service despite these conflicts.

Internal View vs. External View

One area of balance to be achieved is an internal versus external view of IT. Internal views of IT focus on the components, technology and systems that are used to deliver service. IT with an internal view usually consists of "silos" or multiple departments that focus on their individual areas without a view

---

3   Quoted text is from Service Operation © Crown copyright 2011 Reproduced under license from the Cabinet Office

of the overall service. Organizations that are too internally focused fail to understand the service being provided and risk the danger of failing to meet business requirements.

An organization with an extreme external view focuses on the end-result to the business with little understanding or concern about the technical detail of the service. An organization that is too externally focused tends to under-deliver on the promises made to the business.

Both views must be balanced in order to achieve the desired business outcomes while still being able to support the technology that provides the service.

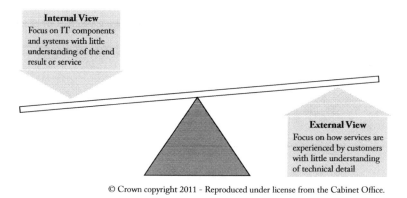

Internal View
Focus on IT components and systems with little understanding of the end result or service

External View
Focus on how services are experienced by customers with little understanding of technical detail

© Crown copyright 2011 - Reproduced under license from the Cabinet Office.

Figure - Service Operation Balance - Internal vs. External

Stability vs. Responsiveness

Another challenge that IT faces is to provide a stable environment for the business while still responding to changing business needs. IT organizations that are too responsive excel in meeting the needs of the business but tend to overspend on changes. Organizations that are too focused on stability provide a status quo for the business but fail to meet business requirements and their changing needs.

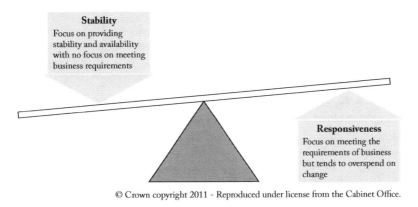

© Crown copyright 2011 - Reproduced under license from the Cabinet Office.

Figure - Service Operation Balance - Stability vs. Responsiveness

Quality vs. Cost

Quality versus cost is another common conflict. While business demands high quality, this quality comes at a higher cost as the quality requirements rise. The cost of quality is not directly proportional to the quality required. The majority of quality can be provided at a lower cost, but as incremental improvements in quality are required, the added costs increase.

Organizations that are too quality-focused provide great service but tend to overspend on the costs of those services. Organizations that are too cost-focused are in danger of losing quality because of cost cutting. However, IT constantly struggles with the demand to improve quality while still cutting costs.

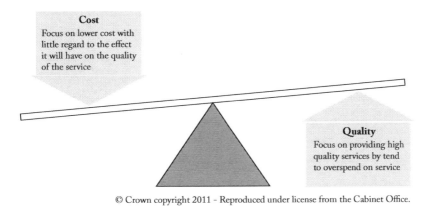

© Crown copyright 2011 - Reproduced under license from the Cabinet Office.

Figure - Service Operation Balance - Quality vs. Cost

Reactive vs. Proactive

IT organizations must also balance being reactive versus being proactive. Reactive organizations do not act until they are triggered to perform some action. Over time, all work is reactive with little opportunity to be proactive. The more reactive an IT organization becomes, the less likely it is able to effectively support the business strategy.

Proactive organizations are always looking for ways to improve their services. When IT organizations are too proactive, services that are not broken are trying to be fixed or improved. This results in services being overly expensive.

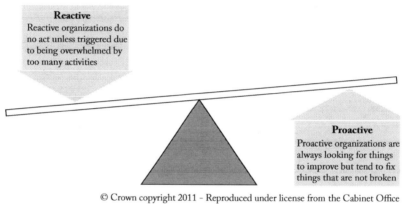

Reactive
Reactive organizations do no act unless triggered due to being overwhelmed by too many activities

Proactive
Proactive organizations are always looking for things to improve but tend to fix things that are not broken

Figure - Service Operation Balance - Proactive vs. Reactive

IMPORTANT POINTS

The main input to service operation is the deployed service through early life support from service transition.

The main output of service operation is the service performance reports to continual service improvement.

Service operation is where the value is delivered to the customer and the strategy of the organization is executed.

The purpose of service operation is to coordinate and carry out the activities and processes required to deliver and manage services at agreed levels to business users and customers.

Communication is vital in service operation.

SECTION REVIEW

1. Service operation is where the _____ is delivered to the customer and the _____ of the organization is executed.

    A. Service, coordination

    B. value, strategy

    C. Application, availability

    D. Service transition package (STP), service level package (SLP)

2. The main input to service operation is what?

    A. Service performance reports

    B. Deployed service

    C. Service package (SP)

    D. Service level package (SLP)

3. The main output of service operation is what?

    A. Service performance reports

    B. Service transition package (STP)

    C. Service package (SP)

    D. Service level package (SLP)

4. The purpose of service operation is what?

    A. To coordinate and carry out the activities and processes required to deliver and manage services at agreed levels.

    B. Restore service as quickly as possible

    C. Be the single point of contact between IT and users

    D. Ensure services are constantly aligned and realigned to the needs of the business

5. What types of communication might be useful in service operation?

    A. Routine operational communication

    B. Reporting

    C. Communication relating to changes, exceptions and emergencies

    D. All of the above

6. In addition to the balance between responsiveness and stability, from the following list, which is NOT one of the other balance factors?

    A. Cost and quality

    B. Internal view and external view

    C. Communication and reporting

    D. Reactive and proactive

COMPREHENSION

1. Describe the inputs and outputs of service operation

2. Describe why communication is important in service operation. What are some examples of communication from other service lifecycle stages into service operation?

9

SERVICE OPERATION PROCESSES

OVERVIEW

Service operation is the stage of the service lifecycle where the value is delivered to the customer and it is where the strategy of the organization is executed. Within service operation are the processes to ensure that this value can be provided effectively and efficiently. In this section, these processes are discussed.

The processes in service operation are:

> Event management
> Incident management
> Request fulfillment
> Problem management
> Access management

These processes should work closely together to ensure that the service is well supported and any requests regarding the service can be fulfilled.

EVENT MANAGEMENT

GEPPETTO GARCIA'S

Within Geppetto Garcia's infrastructure, events are flowing on a regular basis. Events communicate things that occur in their environment such as submission of a meal order, a customer payment transaction has occurred, someone logged into a server, a batch job has started, etc. These events occur all the time and in such frequency that there is no potential way that a human can discern what these events mean.

Some events are benign, while other events suggest something out of the ordinary. Combinations of events, such as someone attempting to log into a server multiple times with the wrong password, may be indicative of something out of the ordinary. To detect these events and determine if any action should be taken, Geppetto Garcia's has employed the use of an event management tool to detect these events, correlate the events, and take the appropriate control action.

Many times, this event management tool has detected issues in the environment before the user was impacted. On one occasion, it was detected that the drive capacity on a key database server was about to fill up. If this database server had been impacted, Geppetto Garcia's inventory control service may have been disrupted. If the inventory control service is disrupted, then food and supplies may not be ordered in time for individual restaurants, resulting in meals not being available for diners.

By the quick detection of this event, the event management tool automatically cleaned the drive to get rid of temporary files and compressed the databases. This automated action, as well as notification of the event, prevented an outage and provided important information to capacity management to analyze the capacity requirements for this server.

OVERVIEW

In today's IT organization, events occur on a regular basis. Many of these events are used as a mechanism for communication between devices to perform actions such as start scripts, creating user accounts, and many other activities. Some of these events, however, require some form of action or intervention such as incidents. Other events cause triggers for certain service management processes to initiate some action.

PURPOSE AND OBJECTIVES

The purpose of event management is to "manage events throughout their lifecycle."[1] This includes activities to detect events, make sense of them, and determine that the appropriate control action is provided. Event management is the basis for operational management and control and is used for automating operations management activities.

The objectives of event management are to:

> "Detect all changes of state that have significance for the management of a CI or IT service
>
> Determine the appropriate control action for events and ensure these are communicated to the appropriate functions
>
> Provide the trigger, or entry point, for the execution of many service operation processes and operations management activities
>
> Provide the means to compare actual operating performance and behavior against design standards and SLAs
>
> Provide a basis for service assurance and reporting; and service improvement"[2]

Key Point

The purpose of Event Management is to detect events, make sense of them, and determine that the appropriate control action is provided.

---

1   Quoted text is from Service Operation © Crown copyright 2011 Reproduced under license from the Cabinet Office

2   Quoted text is from Service Operation © Crown copyright 2011 Reproduced under license from the Cabinet Office.

KEY CONCEPTS

An event is defined as *a "change of state which has significance for the management of a configuration item or IT service."*[3] Note that an event is significant to the service, not necessarily to us. Events might include notification of batch jobs starting and stopping, someone logging into a server, a transaction occurred, among others. It is up to Event Management to determine when these are significant to us and let us know. Event Management notifies appropriate resources through alerts. An alert is defined as *"a warning that a threshold has been reached, something has changed, or a failure has occurred."*[4]

EVENT TYPES

There can be many types of events. Some events reflect a normal situation or initiate some action, such as starting a batch job, while others signify an abnormal situation, such as an outage or a batch job failing to run.

Informational Events

Events occur in the environment all the time. Most applications, computers, and network devices are instrumented with events that inform other components of activities. These types of events, called informational events, signify regular operation, such as a user logging on to a computer or a batch job that has been completed.

Warning Events

Warning events are types of events that signify unusual but not exceptional activities. For example, a batch job may be taking longer than normal, or a threshold has almost been violated.

Exception events

Exception events are those that signify something out of the ordinary occurring. For example, when a user attempts a login with an invalid password, a threshold on a computer has been violated, or a PC scan reveals unauthorized software, an exception event may be generated.

Many times these events may generate an alert. An alert is a form of communication that brings this event to the attention of someone or something to consider taking action.

3   Quoted text is from Service Operation © Crown copyright 2011 Reproduced under license from the Cabinet Office.

4   Quoted text is from Service Operation © Crown copyright 2011 Reproduced under license from the Cabinet Office

ACTIVITIES

Events can come from a number of different sources. Hardware and software can be instrumented to communicate events. Most of these events are notifications or informal, but event management must try to make sense of the events and take action when it is required.

Understanding what all these events mean requires knowledge and involvement throughout the organization. This knowledge is used to design instrumentation to generate the events; design filtering criteria to understand what events are important; develop correlation rules that evaluate combinations of events and how they may be related; and develop automatic and human responses to events.

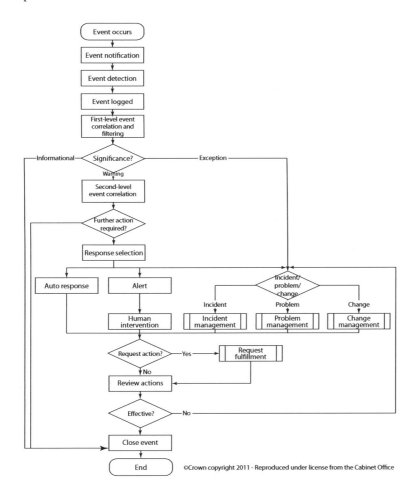

©Crown copyright 2011 - Reproduced under license from the Cabinet Office

Figure - Event Management Process Flow

Event Notification

Events may occur from any device such as routers, servers, databases and applications. The notification of the event will depend on the device. Some events may be transmitted across the network while others may be written to log files.

Event Detection

When events are initiated, they are useless unless they are detected. Detection depends largely on the technology being utilized to monitor these events. Detection may occur by monitoring log files to detecting an event broadcast on the network.

Event Logging

All events must be logged. Even informational events that denote normal operation should be logged for later trend analysis for demand patterns or reporting of operational activity.

Event Filtering

Once detected, the events are filtered to determine the significance. Not all events require action, so the filtering activity suppresses these events to prevent the event management process from being overwhelmed with events. This filtering determines the significance of the event.

Significance

The significance of the event is determined by the categorization of the event. Event levels are then applied to events to determine what actions to take based on the event.

Second-Level Event Correlation

Events can come from a variety of sources, and a determination is required to see if these events may be related in some way. Event correlation uses correlation rules to make the determination if events are related. If events are related, then a new event may be created to make event management aware of this relationship. Correlation may also modify a specific event based on its correlation rules. For example, if the same event occurs multiple times in a short time period, the correlation may determine that the series of events is more significant than if only one event were to occur in that same time period.

If the event is significant, as determined through correlation, the event may result in an Incident, Problem, or Change. Other event responses may also apply depending on your process.

Response Selection

When determining a response to an event, there are several options available. These options include:

Automatic Response

Some events have automatic actions designed into the event management system. An example of an automatic response may be that if a disk full event has been detected, then temporary files, cache files, and core files may be automatically deleted to reclaim disk space.

Problem management assists in determining these automatic responses, as well as service design establishing automatic responses during the design of the service.

Alerts and Human Intervention

When events require a specific action, an alert is generated to trigger this action. This action may require human intervention.

Incident

When opening an incident, any existing diagnostic information should be included to speed incident resolution.

Problem

Multiple incidents may require opening a problem record for evaluation.

Change

Changes may be opened based on an alert signifying that a threshold has been violated. The correlation engine specifies the conditions for which the change should be opened.

Not all events require handling of this nature. For example, when a redundant CI has failed, notification of the event should be performed, but it doesn't require an immediate response.

Review Actions

If actions are required for an event, the actions are reviewed prior to closure. This review helps to improve event management by evaluating the activities performed based on the event and determine improvements to the response to events.

Close Event

Most events do not have a status like incidents or problems, but they simply exist. The closure of an event is linked to the incident, problem, or change that is created as a result of an event.

INCIDENT MANAGEMENT

GEPPETTO GARCIA'S

Geppetto Garcia's, just like any other publicly-traded company, is required to report to the Security and Exchange Commission (SEC) each quarter by a certain date. They must submit the proper financial statements to the SEC or risk being in violation of regulatory requirements. The financial information that needs to be submitted includes their income statement, cash flow statement and balance sheet.

Andrea Dawson, a financial analyst, is preparing the forms for submission to the SEC. Andrea realizes that the printer on which she is trying to print the reports is not working and won't print her reports. Andrea calls the service desk to report the issue.

The service desk, upon getting Andrea's call, asks her some questions about what it is she is trying to do. They are determining what her business desired outcomes are. Printing itself is not a critical service, but an enabling service. By referring to the service catalog, they quickly realize that the service being impacted is the Financial Reporting Service. According to the SLAs that the service desk has access to, the Financial Reporting Service is critical during this time frame to prevent violations of regulatory reporting requirements.

The service desk attempts to print to the printer and finds that they cannot print to the printer either. Seeing that this printer has had issues in the past, they look up the issue in the known error database and perform a documented workaround to map Andrea's computer to a printer further down the hall.

Andrea tests the printer and finds that printing of her reports has been fixed. Andrea prints her financial reports, gets the Chief Operating Officer's signature, and then gets them sent to the SEC, where they arrive on time.

The service desk, after ensuring that Andrea's issue has been resolved, closes this incident.

Many people that I teach have issues with this scenario. Their main issue is the question "What about the printer?" In incident management, the printer is irrelevant. Incident management is not about fixing the underlying problem, such as the printer, but about restoring service as quickly as possible through whatever reasonable means necessary. We will get back to the printer in the problem management process.

OVERVIEW

Incident management supports the business by restoring normal service as quickly as possible to prevent the impact to the user. After all, if your cable service were to fail at the end of a football game, you don't care why it failed. You just want it back up and running. To achieve this objective, incident management does not focus on fixing the underlying problem. Instead, incident management employs the use of workarounds and solutions to restore service as quickly as possible. This rapid restoration of service minimizes the adverse impact to business and improves customer and user satisfaction.

Incident management is guided by the service level agreements. The SLAs document the expected levels of service for response targets for incident management. Incident management may also use the information in the SLAs to determine relative priorities of incidents.

The service desk initiates the incident management process based on calls received. For incidents that the service desk can resolve, the service desk handles the incident from recording to closure. For incidents that are beyond the technical ability of the service desk or that are too complex, other resources are utilized. Through the relationship with the service desk, incident management helps to ensure that resources are utilized in an optimal manner by using specialized staff for the incidents that cannot be resolved by the service desk.

The incident management process records every incident that occurs in the environment. These incidents are tracked to ensure that no incident is lost, forgotten, or ignored. These incidents are also managed to ensure that they are responded to and resolved according to the service level agreements.

> **Key Point**
>
> The purpose of incident management is to restore normal service operation as quickly as possible and minimize the adverse impact on business operations, thus ensuring that agreed levels of service quality are maintained.

PURPOSE AND OBJECTIVES

The purpose of incident management is "to restore normal service operation as quickly as possible and minimize the adverse impact on business operations, thus ensuring that agreed levels of service quality are maintained."[5] Incident management coordinates the activities of everyone involved in restoring service to ensure that the service is restored according to the SLAs. Incident management also ensures that no incident is lost, forgotten, or ignored.

---

5   Quoted text is from Service Operation © Crown copyright 2011 Reproduced under license from the Cabinet Office

The objectives of incident management are to:

"Ensure that standardized methods and procedures are used for efficient and prompt response, analysis, documentation, ongoing management and reporting of incidents

Increase visibility and communication of incidents to business and IT support staff

Enhance business perception of IT through use of a professional approach in quickly resolving and communicating incidents when they occur

Align incident management activities and priorities with those of the business

Maintain user satisfaction with the quality of IT services"[6]

BUSINESS VALUE

Incident management is one of the most visible processes to the business. Business values the incident management process through the ability to detect and resolve incidents, which results in reduced downtime to the business which, in turn, means higher availability of the service. While the business may not notice that a service is operating better than expected, it definitely notices when the service is unavailable. Incident management strives to reduce downtime for the benefit of the business.

Proper prioritization of incidents can provide alignment between IT and real-time business priorities. This requires that the incident management process has knowledge about the business processes and any changes to those processes. Much of this information is conveyed in the service level agreements.

---

6   Quoted text is from Service Operation © Crown copyright 2011 Reproduced under license from the Cabinet Office

KEY CONCEPTS

INCIDENT

An incident is defined as *"an unplanned interruption to an IT service or reduction in the quality of an IT service or a failure of a CI that has not yet impacted an IT service."*[7] Incident management is responsible for managing these incidents to minimize impact of an incident. Incident management is defined as the process for dealing with all incidents reported by the users, by technical staff, or automatically detected and reported by event-monitoring tools. In essence, an incident can be reported from any source – users, technicians, monitoring tools, etc. Regardless of the source of an incident, an incident is an incident. Just because a technician reports something to the service desk does not make it a problem, but an incident.

TIMESCALES

To best support the expectations of business, the incident management process should be well-documented with predefined timescales of each stage of the process. These timescales may be driven by the service level agreements and may differ based on priority of the incident. All support groups must be made aware of these timescales to ensure that they can meet the requirements for responding to incidents.

INCIDENT MODELS

Most of the incidents that occur in an environment are not unique. Many organizations report that 80% or more of their incident volumes are incidents that they have seen before and have experience with. In these cases, incident models can be used to pre-define the steps required, responsibilities, timescales, escalation procedures, and resolutions for commonly occurring incidents. Incident models can reduce the response time greatly by documenting the incident and the steps required to resolve these commonly occurring incidents in anticipation of the incident re-occurring.

---

7   Quoted text is from Service Operation © Crown copyright 2011 Reproduced under license from the Cabinet Office

MAJOR INCIDENTS

Major incidents are those incidents with a high level of disruption to the business. While IT service management strives to eliminate major incidents, they should be anticipated. Managed by the incident manager, major incidents should have a pre-defined procedure with an expedited path through the process for quick resolution. Major incidents have the highest priority for resolution so when possible, these resolutions steps should be expedited.

> **Key Point**
>
> Major Incidents are those incidents with a high level of disruption to the business.

ESCALATION

At times, the service desk, or anyone who is investigating an incident, may not have the ability to determine how to resolve the incident. This may require the incident to be escalated to a person or group with more specialized knowledge of that service or component. This is known as functional escalation.

> **Key Point**
>
> Functional Escalation is forwarding the details of an incident to a person or group with more specialized knowledge

An incident may also be escalated to a supervisor, manager, director, or higher in order to notify them of the incident and possible impact, as well as to obtain resources to resolve the incident. This is known as hierarchic escalation. Users can initiate hierarchic escalation to request more attention be provided for their incident.

Escalation, both functional and hierarchic, could also occur when SLA timeframes are about to expire. This escalation provides an additional mechanism to ensure that incidents can be resolved to meet the needs of the business.

> **Key Point**
>
> Hierarchic Escalation is forwarding the details of an incident to a supervisor in order to notify them of the incident and possible impact, as well as to obtain resources to resolve the incident.

ACTIVITIES

Incidents can come from anywhere in the environment. Users can call the service desk to report incidents, or incidents can originate from technical management, IT operations management, event-monitoring tools, or even vendors. While many of the incidents are initiated with the service desk, this is not required, as other sources of incidents, such as monitoring tools, automate submission to the incident management process.

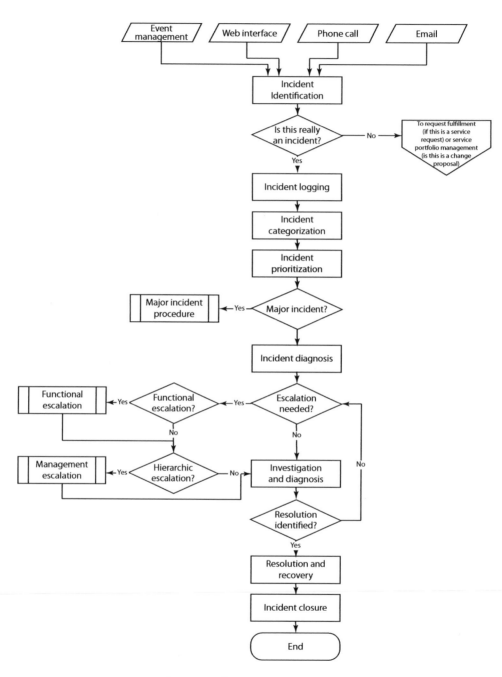

Figure - Incident Management Activities

Identification

When an incident occurs, it is not always readily identified as an incident. Even though a service may be impacted, the service desk may not be notified until much later. Monitoring tools assist with the identification of an incident to reduce the time it takes to begin taking corrective action.

Is it an Incident?

The incident management process may determine that the incident is actually a service request. Service requests are managed by the request fulfillment process. Service requests interact with incident management because the user contacts the service desk to report an incident or to obtain some service. The service desk begins the logging and categorization of the call to ensure that the information is recorded for all calls, not just incidents.

Logging

Every incident must be logged. Logging an incident involves ensuring that all relevant documentation regarding an incident is recorded to reduce unnecessary communication. This documentation may be updated as required as more information becomes available regarding the incident.

The resulting incident records are vital to identifying trends in service and identify areas for improvement, as well as to provide information that can be used later to resolve other similar incidents. Logged incidents will be used in incident matching to look up similar incidents and their resolutions when future incidents occur. Incident matching is vastly improved if prior incidents were logged effectively.

Categorization

Once logged, an incident is categorized according to the type of incident and what it affects. Categorization is used for correct escalation to specialist groups, reporting, and incident matching. Incident matching involves researching previous incidents to see if there is a similar incident for which the resolution can be leveraged to resolve the current incident.

Prioritization

Incidents are prioritized based on urgency and impact. When multiple incidents occur at once, they must be prioritized in order to resolve the most important incidents before less important incidents. Urgency is defined as *"the time within which the incident must be resolved in order to meet business deadlines."*[8] This is usually determined by the user and is a subjective measure. Impact, however, is a more objective measure and is defined as *"the likely effect that the incident will have on the business service being disrupted."*[9] The priority may change over time as urgency or impact or both change.

> ### Key Point
>
> The priority of an incident is based on both urgency and impact.

Major incidents, as discussed previously, have the highest priority, and they should be handled through the pre-defined major incident procedure.

Initial Diagnosis

The service desk provides the initial diagnosis of an incident based on its knowledge, diagnostic scripts, known errors, or other information it may have. Over time, the service desk's ability to perform an initial diagnosis will improve as staff become more able to recognize the incident.

Investigation and Diagnosis

Investigation and diagnosis includes understanding the true nature of the incident. In this activity, the incident is analyzed to understand what has occurred and what events led up to the failure. The impact will be confirmed, which may result in updating the priority of the incident. The possible causes for the incident will be reviewed to determine the approach for resolving the incident. Note that while incident management is not necessarily determining the root cause of the failure, the root cause may still be uncovered. Incident management's objective is to restore the service, not to determine the root cause. However, the root cause may still be determined and the error removed if this is the quickest path to resolution.

In this activity, incidents previous to the current one are researched to determine if this incident has occurred in the past. Called incident matching, any matches to incidents are reviewed to leverage any knowledge that exists from past incidents. Through proper documentation of incidents, historical incidents can be leveraged to provide swift resolution should those incidents occur again.

Resolution and Recovery

Resolution is performed when the most appropriate action is determined. The potential resolution is tested either by the resolution implementer, the

---

8   Quoted text is from Service Operation © Crown copyright 2011 Reproduced under license from the Cabinet Office

9   Quoted text is from Service Operation © Crown copyright 2011 Reproduced under license from the Cabinet Office

user, or both. Once the incident has been resolved, recovery may be necessary to restore the service to its operational state. This may involve recovering data or recovering transactions. Upon restoration and recovery, the incident is passed back to the service desk for formal closure.

The incident is closed when the service desk verifies that the resolution satisfied the user expectations and the service has been restored. This includes determining a closure code for the incident, ensuring the incident is correctly documented, and conducting a user satisfaction survey (probably through email or Web).

Closure

The service desk performs formal closure of the incident by verifying that the user is satisfied with the resolution. The service desk reviews the incident record to assign a closure category, ensure the documentation is completed, and conduct a user satisfaction survey. Based on the outcome of the incident, the service desk may consider opening a problem record for further action.

Once an incident is closed, it may be reopened if the incident has not been fully resolved. However, rules must be established to determine how an incident can be reopened and by whom.

> **Key Point**
>
> The incident management activities are:
>
> Identification
>
> Logging
>
> Categorization
>
> Prioritization
>
> Initial diagnosis
>
> Escalation
>
> Investigation and diagnosis
>
> Resolution and recovery
>
> Incident Closure

REQUEST FULFILLMENT

GEPPETTO GARCIA'S

In order to facilitate the needs of the business, Mark Renner recognized that not all calls into the service desk are incidents. Based upon historical records, Mark realized that more than half of the calls into the service desk are not regarding disruption to business. Instead, these calls are about requests for something to be done for the user.

Based on this information and the published service catalog, Mark established a request fulfillment process with the service desk. This request fulfillment process provides a mechanism for requests based on services documented in the service catalog to be fulfilled. Mark has integrated the service catalog with the service desk to provide a Web-based front end for many types of contact with the service desk.

The request fulfillment process has helped the service desk prioritize on what is important. Through analysis of the requests, many of the requests have now been automated, providing users access to self-help service desk capabilities. Based on the most common types of requests, the service desk found that the most common and labor-intensive request is installation of new-user software. As a result, the service desk implemented self-help capabilities that provide users access to software to be installed on demand. This access to back-end processes and reducing the interaction of service desk staff has resulted in the service desk being far more responsive to incidents and improving the productivity of the user community.

Key Point

A service request is defined as a request from a user for information or advice or for a standard change or access to an IT service.

OVERVIEW

A service request is defined as *"a request from a user for information or advice or for a standard change or access to an IT service."*[10] These requests occur on a regular basis, such as adding software to a computer, requesting toner for a printer, or requesting a cell phone or pager, along with many other types of requests. Most service requests are based on services that are documented in the service catalog.

---

10   Quoted text is from Service Operation © Crown copyright 2011 Reproduced under license from the Cabinet Office

PURPOSE AND OBJECTIVES

Request fulfillment is the process "responsible for managing the lifecycle of all service requests from the users."[11] Objectives of Request Fulfillment are to:

> "Maintain user and customer satisfaction through efficient and professional handling of all service requests
>
> Provide a channel for users to request and receive standard services for which a predefined authorization and qualification process exists
>
> Provide information to users and customers about the availability of services and the procedure for obtaining them
>
> Source and deliver the components of requested standard services such as licenses and media
>
> Assist with general information, complaints or comments"[12]

Key Point

The purpose of request fulfillment is to manage the lifecycle of all requests from users.

KEY CONCEPTS

Users regularly request many types of services. Most, if not all, service requests are initiated due to a product or service published in the service catalog. With an online service catalog, many service requests can be initiated from within the Service catalog, similar to an online shopping experience.

Requested services can be supplied through internal or external support teams. Adding software, for example, is usually provided through internal support teams through software distribution tools. A cell phone or pager request is also provided through internal support teams but uses external providers for equipment, service contracts, and fee schedules.

Requests are not always automatic. Some requests may require approval to ensure that the requestor is entitled to receive the service. Funding may also be required to obtain the components to fulfill the request. This funding may also require approval.

---

11   Quoted text is from Service Operation © Crown copyright 2011 Reproduced under license from the Cabinet Office

12   Quoted text is from Service Operation © Crown copyright 2011 Reproduced under license from the Cabinet Office.

REQUEST MODELS

Request models are similar to incident models. Request models are established to automate responses to commonly occurring requests. These models can automate the workflow in fulfilling the request, as well as document the fulfillment activities.

ROLES

A service request is handled similarly to an incident. The service desk has first line responsibility to respond to service requests. Service requests are handled using existing teams, such as the service desk and other functional teams. The procurement department may also be involved, particularly when a request involves purchasing new equipment.

A service request may involve other teams outside of IT. An example of this could be a request to onboard a new employee. To service this request, it would require the involvement of not only IT for computer equipment and networking, but also HR, office coordination, telephony services, and perhaps, other teams.

PROBLEM MANAGEMENT

GEPPETTO GARCIA'S

Mark Renner noticed that the IT organization was very reactive. It seemed that everyone in IT was responding to incidents in the environment. This caused IT to become overwhelmed, forcing the organization to work nights and weekends, and the quality and timeliness of projects were declining. Mark realized that he needed to find a way to reduce the reactive nature of the IT organization and make it more proactive. One way he found to do this was by reducing the number of incidents that occurred in the environment. To address this, Mark turned to problem management.

Mark began by analyzing the incident history. He quickly realized that there were incidents that were occurring on a regular basis and resulted in the bulk of calls to the service desk. Based on this information, he assembled teams to understand the problems that caused these incidents. The team's goal was to analyze these problems, determine the root cause, and once the error was known, eliminate it from the environment. Even if the error could not be eliminated, the team was to document a workaround for that error and communicate the workaround to the service desk. This workaround helps the service desk address any related incidents that are related to this, or similar, errors.

By realizing the value of problem management and approaching problems in a disciplined manner, Geppetto Garcia's IT organization moved from a reactive organization to a proactive organization. Through problem management, they established workarounds for commonly occurring incidents and managed their problems and errors through their lifecycle to resolution.

OVERVIEW

Problem management is the process responsible for eliminating errors from the environment and reducing the incident volumes experienced by the users. Problem management is also responsible for developing and publishing information that can assist in the rapid resolution of incidents. This information includes workarounds, publication of known errors, diagnostic scripts, and other information that can assist with the rapid resolution of incidents. This information becomes part of the service knowledge management system (SKMS).

PURPOSE AND OBJECTIVES

> **Key Point**
>
> The purpose of problem management is to manage the lifecycle of all problems from first identification through further investigation, documentation and eventual removal.

The purpose of problem management is to "manage the lifecycle of all problems from first identification through further investigation, documentation and eventual removal."[13] Problem management does this by removing errors from the environment, thus reducing future incidents. Problem management minimizes the impact of incidents that cannot be prevented through the creation of workarounds and documenting the workaround in the known error database (KEDB).

Problem Management performs the root cause analysis (RCA) of problems to determine where the error is. Problem management then converts this problem to a known error and manages the known error through resolution.

Problem management also has a strong relationship with knowledge management and provides documented workarounds for the service knowledge management system (SKMS). Problem management should utilize the same tools as the other related processes, such as incident management.

The objectives of problem management are to:

"Prevent problems and resulting incidents from happening

Eliminate recurring incidents

Minimize the impact of incidents that cannot be prevented"[14]

VALUE TO BUSINESS

Problem management is where the reduction in known errors in the environment occurs, resulting in improved availability and fewer incidents.

---

13   Quoted text is from Service Operation © Crown copyright 2011 Reproduced under license from the Cabinet Office

14   Quoted text is from Service Operation © Crown copyright 2011 Reproduced under license from the Cabinet Office.

Through this reduction in known errors, IT services have higher availability, users and IT staff increase productivity, and there is a reduction in the costs of resolving repeating incidents.

Problem management is also responsible for documenting workarounds to improve the resolution times of incidents. Proper problem management reduces the costs of these workarounds or fixes that do not work.

KEY CONCEPTS

PROBLEM

A problem is defined as *"the cause of one or more incidents."*[15] Problems, once diagnosed and the root cause is found, result in the documentation of a known error. A known error is defined as *"a fault in the infrastructure for which a permanent solution or temporary workaround has been found."*[16]

PROBLEM MODELS

Similar to models that have been discussed elsewhere, Problem models are established for the problems that commonly occur. Problem models pre-define the activities, timescales, escalations, documentation, and workflow for a problem.

KNOWN ERROR DATABASE

When the root cause of problems is determined, a known error is created and associated with its workaround or permanent fix. This information is stored in a known error database (KEDB) to be shared with the organization.

A workaround is a predefined technique for reducing or eliminating the impact of an incident or problem for which a full resolution is not yet available. Problem management plays a key role in documenting workarounds for incidents and problems.

---

15   Quoted text is from Service Operation © Crown copyright 2011 Reproduced under license from the Cabinet Office

16   Quoted text is from Service Operation © Crown copyright 2011 Reproduced under license from the Cabinet Office.

> **Key Point**
>
> A problem is defined as the cause of one or more incidents.

> **Key Point**
>
> Problem models are established for the problems that commonly occur.

> **Key Point**
>
> A known error is a problem that has a documented root cause and a workaround.

> **Key Point**
>
> The known error database (KEDB) contains documented errors and their associated workarounds.

> **Key Point**
>
> A workaround is a predefined technique for reducing or eliminating the impact of an incident or problem for which a full resolution is not yet available.

TOOLS AND TECHNIQUES

Problem management is a disciplined process that requires an analytical approach to determine the root cause of problems. Techniques are utilized by Problem Management to assist with the analysis of problems. These techniques include:

Chronological analysis

Documenting the order of events that took place to determine how events relate to the problem.

Pain value analysis

Analyzing the broad view of the impact of the problem to determine the overall pain associated with the impact.

Kepner and Tregoe

Kepner and Tregoe is a technique for formal problem investigation.

Brainstorming

Presenting ideas without regard to context and then applying the context.

Ishikawa diagrams

Typically combined with brainstorming, Ishikawa diagrams (also referred to as fishbone diagrams) analyze the cause and effect of events leading to a problem.

Pareto analysis

Charting the symptoms of a problem to determine the main pain points.

These techniques are used to determine the overall pain associated with problems, as well as to identify the value associated with removing problems from the environment. Some problems, however, may be too complex or too costly or not provide enough value for the pain associated to warrant the resources required to remove the underlying error. In these cases, workarounds are established to minimize the impact of the problem and underlying error.

ACTIVITIES

Problem management is an undervalued process in many organizations. However, the activities in this process are important to manage problems and known errors through resolution.

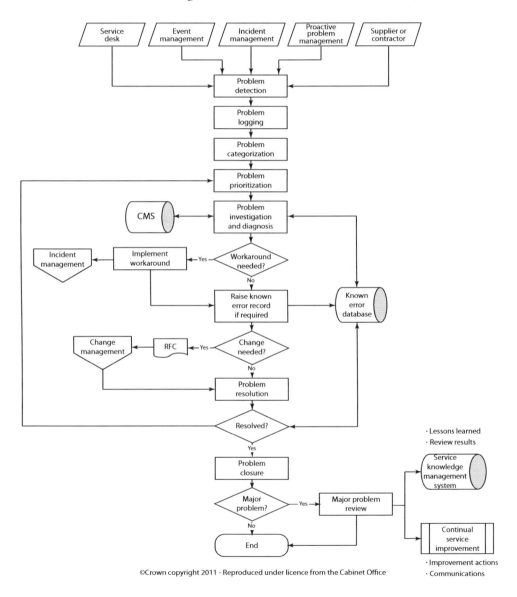

©Crown copyright 2011 - Reproduced under licence from the Cabinet Office

Figure - Problem Management Process Flow

Problem Detection

Detecting a problem could involve many tactics. Problem management analyzes incident records for trends. These trends may identify potential problems. Single incidents may also result in opening a problem record to trigger further action.

Problem Logging

Problems are logged to ensure that all information regarding the problem is recorded. This information is updated over time as more information is determined regarding this problem.

Problem Categorization

Similar to the categorization of incidents, problems are categorized to determine which support group to route the problem to. Categorizations may be done by service, technology, application, or many other categorizations. The categorization scheme for problems is usually identical to that of incidents.

Problem Prioritization

Prioritization of problems is similar to that in incident management and change management. Prioritization is based on the urgency, impact and other factors. Other factors that may assist with prioritization of problems include the complexity and cost of the problem, as well as available resources. If the problem stemmed from an incident, the priority may already be determined. However, as the problem matures or more information is discovered about the problem, the priority may change.

Problem Investigation and Diagnosis

Problem investigation and diagnosis is where the root cause of the problem is determined. Once the root cause is determined, a known error is created and linked to its associated workaround or fix.

Implement Workaround

Problem management determines the appropriate workarounds for the problems. These workarounds are documented and recorded in the known error database so they can be shared with the rest of the organization. The service desk, through incident management, leverages these workarounds to resolve incidents as quickly as possible.

Raising a Known Error Record

Once the known error is determined, it is recorded and documented to ensure that it is managed through resolution. The known error, and its workaround, are documented within the known error database (KEDB).

Problem Resolution

When the problem is resolved, the resolution is tested and verified with the user to make sure that it resolves the problem and the error is removed. If the problem resolution involved modifying the environment, an RFC is raised and the associated change is performed through change management.

Problem Closure

Similar to incidents, problems are formally closed to ensure that all associated documentation has been completed.

Major Problem Reviews

Some problems are large enough in scope that they may require reviews to determine and review both successes and failures. These reviews should be used as a way to improve the process.

Other Activities

Problem management includes other activities outside of this process flow to enable the management of problems throughout their lifecycle.

Recording Errors from Development

Development and introduction of new services are a major source of introduction of problems into the environment. Any outstanding errors in newly released software or services should be recorded in problem management to ensure they are managed through resolution. Problem management should work with release and deployment management to identify these errors in releases.

Monitoring and Tracking of Problems

Throughout the life of the problem, the problem is monitored and tracked through its lifecycle until it is resolved. This ensures that the problem obtains the appropriate attention that it needs.

ACCESS MANAGEMENT

OVERVIEW

The access management process has overall responsibility for maintaining the access of services through ensuring that access is granted to only the people who require access for legitimate business reasons. Access management does not decide who has access but instead carries out the policies developed regarding access during the service design stage of the service lifecycle.

PURPOSE AND OBJECTIVES

The purpose of Access Management is to "provide the right for users to be able to use a service or group of services. It is therefore the execution of policies and actions defined in information security management."[17] Access management executes the policies and actions defined in information security management and availability management. It is these other processes that determine what access should be provided and to whom it should be provided.

The objectives of access management are to:

> "Manage access to services based on policies and actions defined in information security management
>
> Efficiently respond to requests for granting access to services, changing access rights or restricting access, ensuring that the rights being provided or changed are properly granted
>
> Oversee access to services and ensure rights being provided are not improperly used"[18]

> **Key Point**
>
> The purpose of access management is to provide the right for users to be able to use a service or group of services.

---

17   Quoted text is from Service Operation © Crown copyright 2011 Reproduced under license from the Cabinet Office

18   Quoted text is from Service Operation © Crown copyright 2011 Reproduced under license from the Cabinet Office.

VALUE TO BUSINESS

Access management assists with the overall security of the environment and its information. The value to business is that the business can be assured that its information is secure and access is provided to those who require it. With proper access management, the business can be assured that access to confidential information is controlled, employees have the appropriate level of access, and that access can be audited if necessary. The business can also be assured that the organization is complying with regulatory requirements.

> **Key Point**
>
> Access is defined as the level and extent of a service's functionality or data that a user is entitled to.

KEY CONCEPTS

Access is defined as *"the level and extent of a service's functionality or data that a user is entitled to."*[19]

Service groups are defined as *"the concept of establishing sets of services that users or groups of users are entitled to, thus easing access management activities."*[20] Service groups identify users or services, or combinations of both, that are similar. Instead of providing access to a single individual for a single service, Service groups are used so when the user is added to the service group, the user is automatically granted the rights for all services within the service group.

> **Key Point**
>
> Identity is defined as the information about users that distinguishes them as individuals and which verifies their status within the organization.

Identity is defined as *"the information about users that distinguishes them as individuals and which verifies their status within the organization."*[21] Identity will be established by one or more pieces of information, such as an employee ID number, driver's license number, passport number, etc.

Directory services are defined as *"a specific type of tool that is used to manage access and rights."*[22]

> **Key Point**
>
> Directory services are defined as a specific type of tool that is used to manage access and rights.

Rights are defined as *"the actual setting whereby a user is provided access to a service or group of services."*

> **Key Point**
>
> Rights are defined as the actual setting whereby a user is provided access to a service or group of services.

---

19   Quoted text is from Service Operation © Crown copyright 2011 Reproduced under license from the Cabinet Office

20   Quoted text is from Service Operation © Crown copyright 2011 Reproduced under license from the Cabinet Office.

21   Quoted text is from Service Operation © Crown copyright 2011 Reproduced under license from the Cabinet Office.

22   Quoted text is from Service Operation © Crown copyright 2011 Reproduced under license from the Cabinet Office.

ACTIVITIES

The activities in access management involve not only managing access requests but also responding to organizational, individual, or service changes that may impact access to information for a service.

Access Requests

When access is requested, access management processes the request. These requests can come from a number of sources for a number of reasons, such as from Human Resources when an employee is hired, promoted, transferred or terminated. Requests for change may also result in access being requested for a service. Access requests may start as service requests through the service desk.

Verification

The verification activity involves determining who users are and confirming they are who they say they are. This establishes the identity of the user. Based on the identity of the user, a determination is made that the user has a legitimate need to access the service.

Providing Rights

Access is provided to the user based on the policies defined in service design through information security management.

Monitoring Identity Status

Access management monitors the status of individuals. An individual's status may change due to promotion, demotion, transfer, termination, retirement, disciplinary action, or many other reasons. Based on changes in a user's status, the rights may require changing. Access management adjusts the individual's rights based on such a change in status. Access management benefits from a relationship with Human Resources (HR) to submit an access request to modify access when the status of a user changes within the organization.

Logging and Tracking Access

Access to services is logged and tracked to ensure that an audit can be performed to determine who accesses which services. These logs may be required in the event of a security incident or other reason.

Removing or Restricting Rights

Access management may require removing or restricting rights based on access abuse or changes in service. Information security management may also change policies which result in requiring removal or restriction of rights.

ROLES

There is no specific access manager. Instead, the activities within access management are performed by the service operation functions.

Service Desk

Requests for access go through the service desk as a regular service request. The service desk fulfills the requests that it is able to and escalates requests that the service desk cannot fulfill to the appropriate team.

Technical and Application Management

The technical and application management functions may be responsible for some of the activities within access management. These functions fulfill the requests that the service desk is not able to fulfill. Technical management and application management functions are also responsible for creating mechanisms to simplify and control access management, as well as testing the service to ensure access can be granted, controlled, and prevented as designed.

IT Operations Management

The operational activities of access management may be delegated to IT operations management, including verifying users and granting access.

TERMS & DEFINITIONS

Event

Alert

Incident

Incident model

Major incident

Functional escalation

Hierarchic escalation

Service request

Request model

Problem

Known error

Known error database
(KEDB)

Workaround

Access

Identity

Rights

Directory services

IMPORTANT POINTS

The processes in service operation are:

Event management
Incident management
Request fulfillment
Problem management
Access management

The purpose of event management is to detect events, make sense of them, and determine the appropriate control action.

The three types of events in event management are informational events, warning events, and exception events.

The purpose of incident management is to ensure that service is restored as quickly as possible and to minimize the adverse impact to the business.

The incident management activities are:

Identification
Logging
Categorization
Prioritization
Investigation and diagnosis
Closure

The purpose of the request fulfillment process is to deal with requests from users.

The purpose of problem management is to prevent incidents from occurring as well as minimize the impact of incidents that cannot be prevented.

The purpose of access management is to provide access for services that users are entitled to while preventing access to users that are not entitled.

SECTION REVIEW

1. What is the primary purpose of incident management?

   A. Remove problems and errors from the infrastructure

   B. Be the first point of contact for all calls from users

   C. Restore normal operation as quickly as possible

   D. Ensure best possible levels of availability

2. Incident models help to ensure what?

   A. All incidents can be resolved quickly

   B. Problems can be removed from the environment

   C. Common incidents can be resolved through pre-defined steps

   D. Workarounds are available for all incidents

3. Urgency and impact determine what?

   A. Work order number

   B. Priority

   C. Escalation

   D. Resolution timescales

4. The term used when an incident is forwarded to a specialized team is called what?

   A. Functional referral

   B. Functional escalation

   C. Hierarchic escalation

   D. Workload balancing

5. The term used when an incident is forwarded to someone with more authority is called what?

   A. Functional referral

   B. Functional escalation

   C. Hierarchic escalation

   D. Workload balancing

6. The process responsible for handling requests from the user is known as:

   A. Change management

   B. Request management

   C. Incident management

   D. Request fulfillment

7. Which of the following is an example of a service request?

   A. A request to change the functionality of an application

   B. A request for a new application to be developed

   C. User requests the memory on his or her computer be upgraded

   D. A request for a memory upgrade on a server

8. The process that is responsible to identify and remove errors from the infrastructure is what?

   A. Problem management

   B. Error control

   C. Error management

   D. Incident management

SECTION REVIEW

9. Which group outside of IT would be useful for access management to have a relationship with?

   A. Finance

   B. Procurement

   C. Sales

   D. Human resources

10. A temporary resolution to resolve an incident is known as what?

   A. Change

   B. Workaround

   C. Problem model

   D. Fix

11. Service operation processes include incident management, event management and problem management. What processes are missing from this list?

   A. Access management and availability management

   B. Access management and request fulfillment

   C. Access management and capacity management

   D. Request management and user management

Comprehension

1. Describe how an incident may result in a problem and trace the flow through final resolution.

2. What are some reasons that a user's access to a service may require modification?

3. How might the known error database (KEDB) be used in the processes within service operation.

4. What determines what is a service request and what is not a service request? Why are some things service requests and others are not?

10

SERVICE OPERATION FUNCTIONS

OVERVIEW

Throughout this book, we have explored many processes with many activities in each one. The question that comes up often is, "Who does all this work?" The answer is the functions described within service operation. Until now, organizational structures within IT have been largely left out. In this section, the service operation functions are explored. It is these functions that perform a large number of the activities that we have discussed.

IT is supported by many organizations. These organizations are referred to as functions and have overall responsibility for ensuring the stability of the operational environment while responding to business needs. Remember that functions are defined as units of organizations specialized to perform certain types of work and responsible for specific outcomes. The functions within service operation include the service Desk, technical management, application management, and IT operations management.

Service Desk

The service desk provides a single point of contact between users and IT service management. The service desk manages all calls from users, including incidents, service requests, questions, and feedback (compliments and complaints).

Technical Management

Technical management includes the technical teams responsible for the infrastructure that are usually organized by areas of expertise.

IT Operations Management

IT operations management is responsible for the ongoing day-to-day activities of IT. This function has two sub-functions of IT operations control and facilities management. IT operations control is responsible for the daily activities within IT, including console management, job scheduling, backup, print, and output, etc. Facilities management is responsible for the physical environment of the data center and recovery sites.

Application Management

Application management involves the teams responsible for the specialty applications. Application management is usually organized by area of specialty, such as financial applications, manufacturing applications, etc.

The functions perform the activities in the processes from earlier chapters and rely on the processes for coordination across the functions.

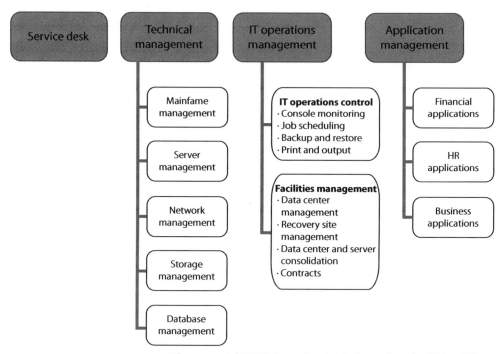

Figure - Service Operation Functions

SERVICE DESK

OVERVIEW

The service desk is the function that users of IT services interact with on a daily basis. From a user's perspective, this is the most critical function, as the service desk is the only function the typical user interacts with directly. The service desk serves as the single point of contact between the service provider and the users. A typical service desk manages incidents and service requests and also handles outward communication with users.

The business finds a high-performing service desk to be highly valued. The service desk provides this value through improving customer service, perception, and satisfaction. A well-run, customer-oriented service desk can make up for a lot of imperfections within IT. How failures are handled can dramatically impact perception of value.

The service desk increases accessibility of users to IT. By providing a single point of contact for any user issue, question, or request, IT becomes easier to work with from the user perspective. The service desk also improves communications with the users and business. By providing proactive status updates and informing users of additional services that may be of interest, the service desk becomes proactive in improving the productivity of the business. Through the service desk, it becomes apparent to the users and business that IT is there to help instead of hinder.

Productivity of the users is only part of the benefit of a well-run service desk. The service desk also improves the productivity of IT by handling all calls that it can and escalating only the ones that it cannot. When escalated, the service desk coordinates the work of IT support resources by ensuring that the calls are escalated to the proper resources.

The service desk also provides IT with an understanding of the daily issues that users are experiencing. The service desk has the "pulse" of the users and understands the types of issues that they experience on a daily basis. This perspective can be communicated to IT to assist with identifying opportunities for improvement.

> **Key Point**
>
> The service desk serves as the single point of contact between the service provider and users for all operational issues.

The objectives of the service desk include:

> "Logging all relevant incident/service request details, allocating categorization and prioritization codes
>
> Providing first-line investigation and diagnosis
>
> Resolving incidents/service requests when first contacted whenever possible
>
> Escalating incidents/service requests that they cannot resolve within agreed timescales
>
> Keeping users informed of progress
>
> Closing all resolved incidents, requests and other calls
>
> Conducting customer/user satisfaction call-backs/surveys as agreed
>
> Communication with users – keeping them informed of incident progress, notifying them of impending changes or agreed outages etc.
>
> Updating the CMS under the direction and approval of service asset and configuration management if so agreed"[1]

KEY CONCEPTS

SERVICE DESK STRUCTURES

There are many service desk structures. One of these is not necessarily better than the other. In fact, some organizations combine service desk structures and others provide multiple levels of service desks utilizing multiple structures.

Local Service Desk

The local service desk is structured so that IT resources are co-located with the business. Wherever the business is, there is an IT organization in the same location. The local service desk only supports that local business unit.

---

1   Quoted text is from Service Operation © Crown copyright 2011 Reproduced under license from the Cabinet Office

This results in a greater ability to satisfy user requests, but it can become very expensive, as the IT resources are spread throughout the organization. This approach can also result in the IT resources in these disparate locations not using the same processes or tools.

Central Service Desk

The central service desk is the opposite of the local service desk. The central service desk organizes all IT resources in one location, regardless of the location of the business units. This results in a single point of contact for all users to contact IT.

With a central service desk, all calls are routed to a single location. This results in providing less expensive support. However, this form of a service desk may not be able to provide support when local support resources are required. It may also leave users feeling isolated from support resources, and the language or culture may be different between users and support – particularly for multi-national organizations.

Virtual Service Desk

The virtual service desk is a service desk that utilizes technology to make it irrelevant where IT resources are located. With a virtual service desk, IT resources can be located anywhere and still provide that central point of contact for their users.

With the proper tool support, the virtual service desk ensures that the same processes are being used regardless of the location. A virtual service desk can also optimize operational costs.

With a virtual service desk, it is important to ensure that the tools used can support this service desk structure. The virtual service desk may also result in not having the right staff in the right place when needed. A common language must be decided when recording information within organizations with different cultures and languages.

Follow the Sun

Many organizations use a "follow the sun" technique by transitioning call ownership to service desk facilities around the world based on times of day. For example, as the day ends in New York, the calls may be transitioned to Los Angeles for handling and resolution. When the day ends in Los Angeles, the calls may be transitioned to Asia. This transitioning continues based on time of day in an effort to support the business 24 hours per day.

> ### Key Point
>
> The four service desk structures include:
>
> Local service desk
>
> Central service desk
>
> Virtual service desk
>
> Follow the sun

SERVICE DESK CONSIDERATIONS

The service desk is a critical element in the delivery of consistent IT services. As such, there are many things to be considered. Each of these considerations is dependent on your unique IT environment.

Specialized Groups

Some services, particularly newly released services, require specialized knowledge. The service desk may opt to provide a specialized team to support these services. The specialized group may be staffed by other IT groups until the service desk has the knowledge to effectively support the service on its own.

Specialized groups are commonly used as part of early life support when a large transition is taking place. Suppose that a new time-management service is being transitioned and replacing the older time-management service. Until the operations staff and the users have adjusted to the new service, a specialized group that focuses on this service may be established to ease the transition to the new service.

Building a Single Point of Contact

The service desk should be well publicized. Without knowledge of how to access the service desk, the users may not be able to benefit from the service desk. Adding the service desk contact information to Web sites increases the user's awareness of the service desk. Other publicizing techniques include adding stickers on the phone and organizational newsletters.

Staffing

Demand for the service desk may be highly volatile. There may be certain times of the day, week, month, or year when demand is greater than others. To determine when this demand occurs, the call rates should be analyzed to determine when demand is highest. To satisfy demand, the service desk should consider part-time workers, home workers, or virtual workers.

Service Desk Training

The service desk requires a unique combination of skills and abilities in order to be most effective. Not only does the service desk require technical expertise to resolve incidents, but more importantly, requires customer-service skills to be able to communicate effectively with the users.

SIDEBAR - SERVICE DESK STAFFING

Many years ago, a popular microprocessor manufacturer that I worked for was found to have a flaw in the floating point arithmetic in one of their chips.

They satisfied their customers by offering to replace these chips with fault-free chips free of charge. As expected, the call volumes from customers rose substantially.

The company supplemented their service desk by rotating non-service desk employees onto the phones to meet this increased volume. This is an example of addressing volatile service desk demand through temporary, specialized resources.

The service desk should also have knowledge of the business. This knowledge helps the service desk communicate better with the users by being able to communicate with them on their terms. The service desk should understand what the users are tasked with accomplishing so they can support these tasks more effectively.

Training at the service desk can involve mentoring or shadowing. A person working on the service desk may be mentored by someone more senior to pass along the knowledge obtained. Shadowing is another technique in which service desk staff shadow other organizations to understand better what activities are involved within IT that the service desk supports.

Staff Retention

Losing service desk staff can be very costly and disruptive to the effectiveness of the service desk. It is important to understand the value of the service desk and the importance of the people who staff the service desk. The service desk is often a stepping stone to other roles, and staff retention can be improved by preparing the individuals for new roles. Even though an individual may leave the service desk to assume a new role in the organization, it serves as a greater motivator to others than if the person were to leave the company.

Super Users

In some organizations, there are users who may be leveraged to provide support above and beyond what the service desk provides. These super users may have knowledge of specific applications, business functions, or business processes. These super users may be utilized to train service desk staff and can also be considered to be an extension of the service desk.

These super users can be a conduit for communications both into the service desk and from the service desk. As such, incident "storms" can be avoided by streamlining communications when a failure occurs. However, an incident, regardless of how it is communicated to the service desk, must still be logged.

Service Desk Environment

The service desk can be a high-stress and often thankless job. The environment that the service desk staff operates in should be conducive to lowering these stresses as much as possible. Providing an area that is well-lit and quiet and with adequate space and break areas can play a large role in service desk staff satisfaction.

SERVICE DESK STAFFING CONSIDERATIONS

Staffing the service desk can be problematic. There are times when there may be too many people and times when there may not be enough. To better staff the service desk, the following factors should be considered:

Customer Service Expectations

Response times are an important consideration in staffing levels. If there is a high requirement for responsiveness, staffing levels will be higher.

Business Requirements

The most important consideration for staffing is the business requirements. What the business expects from the service desk will impact the staffing levels. If the business is largely self-supporting, the staffing levels will be lower.

Customers and Users

The customers and users are an important consideration. Customers and users that are diverse have diverse support requirements. Language, culture, skill levels and abilities for self-support affect support-level requirements at the service desk.

Service Desk Abilities

The abilities of the service desk staff should be considered. Service desks with a high level of ability may not require high staffing levels. However, service desk staff with a low level of ability and who only serve as a pass-through for calls may require lower staffing levels. A balance between ability and staffing levels must be achieved.

Processes and procedures can assist with lowering staffing levels. If well-defined processes and procedures are in place, they can be followed routinely to increase responsiveness to calls.

Support Aspects

Considerations should be given for what type of support is required: telephone, email, in person, remote control, and video are only a few considerations. Different levels of support access have different staffing levels. In-person support, for example, requires someone to be in a particular place at a particular time. In contrast, remote control technologies remove this requirement.

Training can also be an important aspect – both for the support staff, as well as the users. Highly trained users do not require as high level of support. Additionally, constant turnover at the service desk requires a higher level of training for the service desk staff.

In any case, technology considerations should be made to determine how best to utilize technology to lessen staffing requirements. The proper use of technology can minimize staffing requirements.

ACTIVITIES

The service desk's main activity is to manage calls that come in. When we refer to calls, we refer to any form of contact with the service desk. These calls could be in the form of a telephone call, email, walk-up, pager, Web submission, or even fax. Your organization will determine the accepted forms of contact to the service desk.

Managing Calls

When a call comes in, the service desk ensures that it is logged and all relevant details are recorded. Based on the call, the service desk will allocate the proper categorization and prioritization. These calls can be one of four basic types. Types of calls include incidents, service requests, question and information, and feedback (complaints and compliments).

> ### *Key Point*
>
> The Service Desk manages all types of calls including:
>
> Incidents
>
> Service Requests
>
> Questions and information
>
> Feedback

269

Incidents

The user has been interrupted by some failure, or perceived failure, in the IT environment.

Service Requests

The user contacts the service desk for information, to provide feedback, or a service request.

Questions/Information

The user requires some information regarding an outstanding call or regarding some service.

Feedback

The user wants to provide feedback, either positive (compliments) or negative (complaints) regarding service.

Managing Incidents and Service Requests

When responding to an incident or service request, the service desk performs the following activities:

Provides first-line investigation and diagnosis

The service desk provides the initial investigation and diagnosis of an incident to determine where the true nature of that incident is.

Resolving incidents and Service Requests

The service desk resolves incidents and service requests which they can. Over time, the ability of the service desk will increase to resolve more and more incidents and service requests as the knowledge improves. The key to being able to resolve incidents and service requests is ensuring that the technical management and application management functions take the time to relay information on how to resolve incidents and service requests to the service desk.

Escalating incidents and Service Requests

Many incidents and service requests cannot be resolved by the service desk. While it is preferred that the service desk has the ability to resolve all incidents and service requests, it is highly unlikely that this will ever happen, as some of these incidents and service requests require detailed knowledge.

When the service desk cannot resolve an incident or service request, the service desk will escalate it to be resolved by someone with more technical expertise

Closing all resolved incidents, requests, and other calls

The service desk has the responsibility of ensuring that incidents and service requests are closed and the resolution meets the needs of the submitter.

This provides the ability to provide feedback to the user to ensure that the incident or service request is properly managed.

This activity ensures that no calls to the service desk are lost, forgotten, or ignored.

Communications

Communication with users is more than just waiting for a call to come in. The service desk also provides out-bound communication regarding interruptions to service, new services, or changed services. Examples of communications from the service desk include: informing users of progress of their calls: and conducting customer- and user-satisfaction callbacks and surveys

Updating the CMS

When the service desk receives a call, the service desk verifies that the information contained in the CMS represents what the user sees. These "mini-audits" are checking basic information to ensure that the CMS reflects the actual environment.

KEY PERFORMANCE INDICATORS

Service desk key performance indicators (KPIs), or metrics, are focused on calls to the service desk. These metrics are used to evaluate the health, maturity, efficiency, and effectiveness of the service desk, as well as to determine staffing requirements and areas of improvement.

These key performance indicators (KPIs) include:

First-line resolution rates

Refers to the resolutions provided by the service desk without relying on other staff.

First call resolution

The resolutions provided almost immediately upon the first call to the service desk.

Average time to resolve

This metric shows the average resolution time from initiation of the call to closure.

Average time to escalate

This metric shows the average time each call stays at the service desk before it is escalated to other support staff.

Average cost of handling

The average cost of calls, incidents, questions, and feedback should be determined and recorded by type of call.

This can be calculated a number of ways, such as the total cost of the service desk divided by the number of calls to the service desk. This calculates the cost per call. Another way to calculate this metric is to take the total cost of the service desk divided by the total time the calls are in progress. This calculates the cost per minute or other time unit.

Average time to review and close a call

Once a call is resolved, it should be reviewed and formally closed. This metric shows the average time it takes for a review and formal closure.

Calls by time of day, week, etc.

Determining call volumes by day, time of day, week, etc., provides information regarding call patterns and when additional staffing may be required.

CRITICAL SUCCESS FACTORS

The service desk is critical in performing the activities in the incident management process. In many organizations, but not all, the service desk is the owner of the incident management process. In some organizations, particularly large, global organizations, there may be an owner for the incident management process other than the service desk. Regardless of whether or not the service desk owns the incident management process itself, the service desk owns all of the incidents to ensure that they are effectively managed and no incident is lost, forgotten, or ignored.

To be most effective, the service desk must have access to information and people who understand the services being supported. Some of the information, such as incident record history, is the responsibility of the service desk. However, other information is provided to the service desk from outside. Information that should be available to the service desk includes:

Configuration management system (CMS)

Problem records

Known errors

Change schedule

Alerts from monitoring tools

Service catalog

SLAs

Service knowledge management system (SKMS)

The service desk should also have access to the configuration management system (CMS). When responding to incidents, the service desk uses the CMS to better understand the nature of the incident and also updates the CMS when necessary should any configuration errors be discovered.

Service level agreements are also provided to the service desk to ensure that the service desk understands the levels of service that have been agreed to. Without the SLAs, the service desk cannot prioritize incidents effectively. This is particularly true when incidents occur for services that have variable priorities. An example of this type of service is financial reporting. Financial reporting is typically most important at the end of the quarter and particularly at the end of the year, when financial reports must be completed within a specific time period to meet regulatory requirements.

The service desk should publish response times and possibly resolution times for calls made to the service desk. However, the service desk is not solely responsible for the services that the users call about. The rest of IT is readily involved in providing ongoing support of these services.

In order for the service desk to accurately publish response and resolution times, the service desk must be supported by agreements and contracts from the rest of the organization. Operational level agreements (OLAs) are agreements between IT organizations that specify how the organizations support each other, as well as expectations for that support. OLAs are critical between the service desk and the organizations that provide support for the service desk.

Services are also supported by external vendors through contracts. These contracts should be communicated to the service desk to enable the service desk to publish response times accordingly.

> ### Key Point
>
> The service desk needs access to information to be most effective. The types of information the service desk needs includes:
>
> Configuration management system (CMS)
>
> Problem records
>
> Known errors
>
> Change schedule
>
> Alerts from monitoring tools
>
> Service catalog
>
> SLAs
>
> Service knowledge management system (SKMS)

273

As can be realized from the above sources of information and support for the service desk, an effective service desk is not the responsibility of the service desk alone. The service desk must be supported by all parts of IT in order to be most effective and efficient.

TECHNICAL MANAGEMENT

OVERVIEW

Technical management is the function responsible for providing technical skills in support of IT services and management of the IT infrastructure. The technical management function involves the various teams required in order to design, deliver, support, and continually improve IT services. These teams are typically organized by specialty, such as the database team, the server administration team, the desktop support team and others.

OBJECTIVES

The objective of the technical management function is to help plan, implement and maintain a stable technical infrastructure through designing a highly resilient, cost effective and technical topology, the use of adequate technical skills to maintain the technical infrastructure in optimum condition, and the swift use of technical skills to diagnose and resolve technical failures that occur. The technical management function has responsibilities for activities through the entire service lifecycle, not just service operation.

DUAL ROLE

Technical management has a dual role within IT. While technical management provides stability to an organization, technical management must also be responsive to the business needs. The technical management function's responsibilities are to provide resources to support services through the service lifecycle. In addition, the teams are called upon to provide knowledge

> **Key Point**
>
> Technical management is the function responsible for providing technical skills in support of IT services and management of the IT infrastructure.

> **Key Point**
>
> The objective of the technical management function is to help plan, implement, and maintain a stable technical infrastructure and the swift use of technical skills to diagnose and resolve technical failures that occur.

and information regarding the services and the components that make up the services.

The technical management function is called upon in every process to perform the numerous activities in these processes. The activities involve every aspect of the service lifecycle to develop strategy (particularly providing input to the service portfolio and service catalog), design the service, transition the service into operation, support the service through its operation, and continually improve the service over time.

ORGANIZATIONAL CONSIDERATIONS

Within the technical management function, considerations must be made in order to best optimize staffing levels. In an ideal world, the most specialized resources would be hired to provide support for IT services. However, these specialized resources can be very expensive, so a balance must be achieved between the specialization and skill levels of resources, as well as the costs associated with those resources.

As a result, technical management staffing is often taken from pools of technical resources. In particular, teams of specialists are assembled for project-related work and also to resolve problems.

Highly specialized work may involve the use of contractors or specialized external staff. While external staff can be quite expensive, it is likely that the work can be done quicker through the knowledge and specialized skills of such staff.

APPLICATION MANAGEMENT

OVERVIEW

The application management function is the function responsible for managing applications through their lifecycle. This responsibility includes applications within the infrastructure, regardless of whether they are developed in-house or externally procured. Most of the time, this includes the highly specialized, core application sets that are critical to business processing, such as the ERP system or other highly specialized, complex applications.

OBJECTIVES

Application management works with technical management to identify functional and manageability requirements for application software to support the business processes, assist in the design and deployment of applications, and assist in the ongoing support and improvement of applications.

To accomplish these objectives, the applications must be well designed, resilient, and cost effective. Through application rollout, the required functionality must be available to achieve the required business outcome. Also, application management must ensure it maintains adequate technical skills to operate applications in optimum condition and to swiftly diagnose and resolve any technical failures.

The major decision that must be made with application support is whether to build versus buy an application. Different organizations will approach this decision differently based on strategy, culture, capabilities, and other considerations.

A common misconception is that an application is a service. While an application may play a critical role in providing a service, the service involves far more than an application. It also includes the people, processes, underlying technology, and partners required to deliver and support the business-desired outcomes provided, in part, by the application.

> ### Key Point
>
> The objective of the application management function is to help plan, implement, and maintain applications and the swift use of technical skills to diagnose and resolve any failures that occur.

DUAL ROLE

Application management has a dual role within IT. While application management provides stability to an organization, application management must also be responsive to the business needs. The application management function's responsibilities are to provide resources to support services through the service lifecycle. In addition, the teams are called upon to provide knowledge and information regarding the services and the components that make up the services.

The application management function is called upon in every process to perform the numerous activities in these processes. The activities involve every aspect of the service lifecycle to develop strategy (particularly providing input to the service portfolio and service catalog), design the service, transition the service into operation, support the service through its operation, and continually improve the service over time.

ORGANIZATIONAL CONSIDERATIONS

Application management guides IT operations in how best to manage applications in the service operation stage of the service lifecycle, and it also designs management of the applications in the service design stage. Therefore, application management should be integrated into the entire IT service management lifecycle to ensure that the application lifecycle is understood and is integrated into specific points in the service lifecycle.

Application management is a separate responsibility from application development. Application management assists application development in determining the requirements, application design, application testing, rollout, and operation of the application. Application development has the responsibility of developing the application.

IT OPERATIONS MANAGEMENT

OVERVIEW

The IT operations management is the function within an IT service provider which performs the daily activities needed to manage IT services and the supporting IT infrastructure. IT operations management accomplishes this by maintaining the status quo to achieve stability of the organization's day-to-day activities and processes. This requires regular scrutiny and improvements to achieve improved service at reduced cost.

IT operations management must also utilize swift application of operational skills to diagnose and resolve any IT operations failures that may occur. Driven by procedures, IT operations management records this knowledge to provide operational workflow that improves the speed of resolution.

IT operations management must balance the requirement for infrastructure stability with the requirement to change according to business needs. To achieve balance between these roles, it requires an understanding of how technology is used to provide IT service, as well as an understanding of the relative impacts of services on the business. The value of IT operations management should be based on return on investment (ROI), not cost. By communicating the ROI of the function, the value of the IT operations management can more easily be discerned.

> **Key Point**
>
> The IT operations management is the function within an IT service provider which performs the daily activities needed to manage IT services and the supporting IT infrastructure.

CHARACTERISTICS

The IT operations management function differs from the technical management and application management functions in that it focuses on operational activities directly in line with specific business processes, such as manufacturing or product distribution. The IT operations management function provides specific activities that are well defined and repeatable to support these business activities. These activities include ensuring that a device, system, or process is running or working as expected.

IT operations management focuses on shorter-term activities and improving those activities, not projects. Using specialized technical staff, IT operations management performs these daily activities to build repeatable, consistent action to ensure success.

This function is where the value of the organization is delivered and measured. To provide this value, IT operations management requires an investment in equipment, people, or both.

OPERATIONS CONTROL AND FACILITIES MANAGEMENT

The IT operations management function includes two sub-functions: operations control and facilities management. Operations control is also known as the network operation center (NOC) or operations bridge. Operations control is primarily responsible for ensuring that business processes are running to support the business. This is usually accomplished through monitoring via event management and is very involved in operational event management.

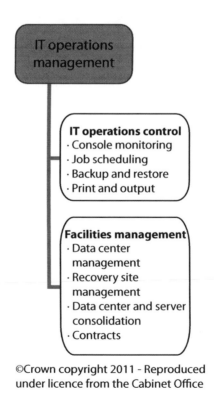

©Crown copyright 2011 - Reproduced under licence from the Cabinet Office

Figure - IT Operations Management

Operations control's responsibilities include performing specific tasks, such as console management, job scheduling, backup and restore, print and output management, as well as maintenance activities. These responsibilities are activity-based as opposed to project-based. Operations control focuses exclusively on individual activities and improving these activities. Project-based activities are the responsibility of other functions.

The facilities management sub-function of IT operations management is responsible for maintenance of the physical environment. Specific examples include the data center, recovery sites, power, and other environmental controls such as heating, ventilation and air conditioning (HVAC).

Facilities management, unlike operations control, is involved in some project-based activities. Typical project-based activities that facilities management would be involved with include server consolidation efforts and datacenter consolidation efforts. Projects related to recovery sites would also involve facilities management

> **Key Point**
>
> IT operations management function includes two sub-functions:
>
> Operations control
>
> Facilities management

ORGANIZATIONAL OVERLAP

While it is easy to visualize application management, technical management, and IT operations management as separate functions, often they are not. These functions may not be clearly delineated from one function to another. Therefore, an organizational overlap occurs where these lines of demarcation are not clear. An organization may combine the responsibilities of these functions into a single organization.

> **Key Point**
>
> Organizational overlap may exist between technical management, application management, and IT operations management.

TERMS & DEFINITIONS

Local service desk

Central service desk

Virtual service desk

Follow-the-sun service desk

Super users

Operations control

Facilities management

IMPORTANT POINTS

The service operation functions are the service desk, technical management, IT operations management, and application management.

The service desk serves as the single point of contact between the service provider and the users for all operational issues. The service desk minimizes disruptions to the business by managing incidents, as well as managing service requests from users.

The four service desk structures are local service desk, central service desk, virtual service desk, and follow-the-sun service desk.

The service desk manages incidents and service requests.

The service desk must be supported by other processes to be most efficient and effective.

Technical management is the function responsible for providing technical skills in support of IT services and management of the infrastructure.

Technical management is the custodian of technical knowledge and expertise pertaining to the infrastructure and provides resources to support the activities within the service lifecycle.

Application management is the custodian of technical knowledge and expertise pertaining to the applications and provides resources to support the activities within the service lifecycle

Application management helps identify functional and manageability requirements, assists in the design and deployment of applications and assists in the ongoing support and improvement of applications. Application management is not responsible for the coding of applications.

IT operations management performs the daily activities needed to manage IT services and the supporting infrastructure.

IT operations management consists of two sub-functions. The sub-functions are operations control and facilities management.

Operations control performs the day-to-day activities related to the infrastructure. IT operations management is also referred to as a network operations center (NOC) or operations bridge.

Facilities management is responsible for the management of the physical environment, such as the data center and the recovery site.

SECTION REVIEW

1. Which of the following is a function within service operation?

   A. Service desk

   B. Vendor management

   C. Request fulfillment

   D. Capacity management

2. The applications management function includes the teams that are responsible for applications development.

   A. True

   B. False

3. The function that is responsible to be the single point of contact between the service provider and the users is called what?

   A. IT operations management

   B. Service desk

   C. Technical management

   D. Applications management

4. The function that is responsible for managing incidents and calls is called what?

   A. IT operations management

   B. Service desk

   C. Technical management

   D. Applications management

5. Which of the following is not a service desk structure?

   A. Local service desk

   B. Central service desk

   C. Virtual service desk

   D. Help desk

6. What is the term used for users with exceptional knowledge of a service that may assist the service desk with service-related issues?

   A. Trained users

   B. Super users

   C. Special users

   D. Application developers

7. What things must the service desk have access to in order to be most efficient and effective?

   A. All incident records

   B. Known errors

   C. CMS

   D. All of the above

8. The function that is responsible for providing technical skills in support of IT services and management of the IT infrastructure is called what?

   A. Service desk

   B. Applications management

   C. Technical management

   D. IT operations management

9. The function that is responsible for managing applications throughout their lifecycle is called what?

   A. Applications management

   B. Technical management

   C. IT operations management

   D. Service desk

SECTION REVIEW

10. IT operations management includes what other two functions?

   A. Job scheduling and batch management

   B. Operations control and facilities management

   C. Capacity management and availability management

   D. Service desk and request fulfillment

Comprehension

1. The service desk structures may be combined for some organizations. Describe an example of an organization that may combine service desk structures.

2. Describe how technical management and application management support the activities within the service lifecycle.

11

CONTINUAL SERVICE IMPROVEMENT

OVERVIEW

The continual service improvement (CSI) stage of the service lifecycle focuses on ensuring that services, and all elements that make up the service, are aligned and continually realigned to ensure they meet business needs and can be improved. Drawing an analogy to a popular television show, CSI is aptly named because it focuses on the forensics of the service to ensure that it is properly measured. There is nothing out of scope for CSI as it strives to provide measurements not only for the service itself, but also the processes that support it: the design processes, the transition processes, the strategy, and the organization.

In this chapter, you will be introduced to continual service improvement, its key concepts, overall activities, purpose, objectives, scope, and value to business.

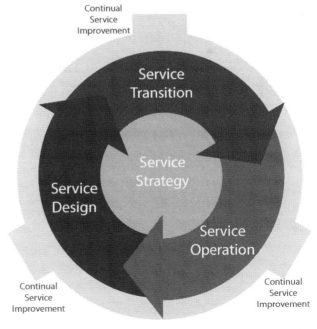

(c) Crown copyright 2011. Reproduced under licence from the Cabinet Office.

Figure - Service Lifecycle

PURPOSE

Key Point

The purpose of CSI is to ensure that services are continually aligned and realigned to the needs of the business.

CSI ensures that services are continually aligned and realigned to the needs of the business. There is little that is out of scope for CSI in that anything that can be improved is a candidate for CSI. However, continual service improvement focuses on three key areas: the overall health of IT service management as a formal discipline, ensuring that services are constantly aligned with the service portfolio, and the maturing of the enabling IT processes for each stage in the service lifecycle.

VALUE TO BUSINESS

Key Point

The scope of CSI includes:

The overall health of IT service management as a discipline

The continual alignment of the portfolio of IT services with the current and future needs of the business

The maturity of enabling IT processes

The value of CSI is obvious, but commonly overlooked. CSI strives to improve quality of services, return on investment (ROI), and value of investment (VOI). ROI is improved by identifying opportunities to lower costs. VOI is improved by identifying opportunities to provide increased value for the cost. VOI includes the intangible benefits including:

"Increased organizational competency

Improved integration between people and processes

Reduced redundancy, increasing business throughput

Minimized lost opportunities

Assured regulatory compliance that will minimize costs and reduce risk

Improved ability to rapidly react to change"[1]

Improvements are defined as "*outcomes that, when compared to the before state, show a measurable increase in a desirable metric or decrease in an undesirable metric.*"[2]

Benefits are defined as "*achievements through realization of improvements usually, but not always, expressed in monetary terms.*"[3]

---

[1]   Quoted text is from Continual Service Improvement © Crown copyright 2011 Reproduced under license from the Cabinet Office

[2]   Quoted text is from Continual Service Improvement © Crown copyright 2011 Reproduced under license from the Cabinet Office.

[3]   Quoted text is from Continual Service Improvement © Crown copyright 2011 Reproduced under license from the Cabinet Office.

Return on Investment (ROI) is defined as *"the difference between the benefit achieved and the amount expended to achieve that benefit expressed as a percentage."*[4]

Value of Investment (VOI) is defined as *"the extra value created by establishment of the benefits that include non-monetary or long-term outcomes."*[5]

GOVERNANCE AND CSI

CSI supports the concept of governance by ensuring that processes are documented and being performed correctly. Governance is a broad topic that addresses different areas. Overall, governance helps ensure fairness and transparency for an organization.

Governance can be broken down into different areas. Enterprise governance describes a framework that covers both the corporate governance and business management aspects of the organization. Corporate governance is concerned with promoting corporate fairness, transparency and accountability.

IT governance addresses the responsibility of the board of directors and executive management to ensure that value is being created and resources are appropriately utilized.

> **Key Point**
>
> Governance promotes fairness and transparency.

©Crown copyright 2011 - Reproduced under license from the Cabinet Office

Figure - Governance

---

4   Quoted text is from Continual Service Improvement © Crown copyright 2011 Reproduced under license from the Cabinet Office.

5   Quoted text is from Continual Service Improvement © Crown copyright 2011 Reproduced under license from the Cabinet Office.

PDCA/DEMING CYCLE

CSI is based on the principles of continuous quality control first published by Edwards Deming in the 1940s. In the 1940s, Mr. Deming developed his philosophy of improvement through his 14 points of attention to managers. Mr. Deming developed a process-led approach that underpins the concepts within continual service improvement.

Mr. Deming's Plan-Do-Check-Act cycle is a continuous process to identify opportunities for improvement. Taken as basic common sense today, the Plan-Do-Check-Act cycle was a novel approach to manufacturing in the 1940s. It essentially says that you should plan what you are going to do, do what was planned, check to see if you obtained the desired outcome according to the plan, and act to improve the plan before you act again. Each iteration of this cycle will improve the base level of quality.

Deming's improvement cycle is the basis for most, if not all, quality standards in existence today, such as 6-Sigma, TQM, and others.

> **Key Point**
>
> The Plan-Do-Check-Act cycle is a continuous process to identify opportunities for improvement.

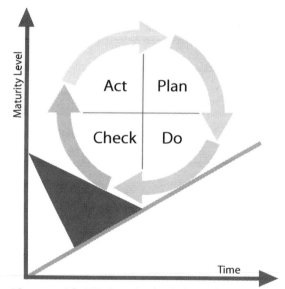

©Crown copyright 2011 - Reproduced under licence from the Cabinet Office

Figure - The Deming Cycle

OVERALL CSI ACTIVITIES

The activities around CSI are focused on the continued audit of services, processes, procedures, and organization to identify opportunities for improvement. All other service lifecycle stages provide input into the activities of CSI. CSI's activities include:

> "Reviewing management information and trends
>
> Periodically conducting maturity assessments to identify areas of improvement
>
> Periodically conducting internal audits to verify process compliance
>
> Reviewing existing deliverables for relevance to ensure deliverables are still needed
>
> Making improvement recommendations for approval
>
> Conducting customer satisfaction surveys
>
> Conducting external and internal service reviews to identify opportunities for improvement"[6]

All of these activities must be planned and are not automatic. Many of these activities take place in other service lifecycle stages and the processes within each stage.

CSI APPROACH

The CSI approach identifies six questions that have associated actions to determine the answers. This approach helps ensure that improvements are objective and measurable and meet the business strategy.

---

6   Quoted text is from Continual Service Improvement © Crown copyright 2011 Reproduced under license from the Cabinet Office

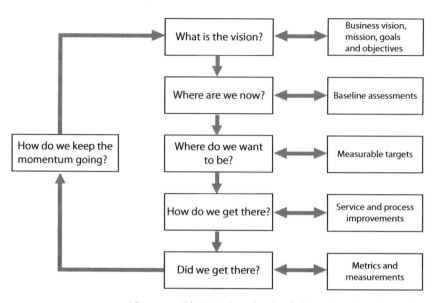

Figure - CSI Approach

What is the vision?

The "What is the vision?" question is answered by identifying the business vision, mission, goals, and objectives that need to be addressed.

Where are we now?

The "Where are we now?" question is answered through performing baseline assessments that obtain an accurate, unbiased snapshot of where the organization is. These assessments measure the organization in an objective manner to provide a basis for comparison later.

Where do we want to be?

The "Where do we want to be?" question is answered through identification of measurable targets that detail the CSI plan to achieve higher-quality service provision. These measurable targets should be objective and readily accepted by everyone. While it is easy to identify a measurable target, it should be an objective target to ensure that the target achieves the desired objective and accurately reflects the desired state.

How do we get there?

The "How do we get there?" question is answered through service and process improvements developed based on the principles defined in the vision. This is where the process improvement or re-engineering work takes place.

Did we get there?

The "Did we get there?" question is answered through metrics and measurements that ensure milestones were achieved, process compliance is high, and business objectives and priorities were met. This is where measurements are compared against the baseline that was established through the "Where are we now?" question.

How do we keep the momentum going?

The "How do we keep the momentum going?" question ensures that the improvements made are established and become part of the organization. Based on these improvements, the organization can establish new baselines for continued improvement.

SERVICE MEASUREMENT

Service measurement measures the services and processes to identify opportunities for continual improvement. When measuring, the following questions need to be answered regarding these measurements:

Why are we monitoring and measuring?

This question ensures that we know the reason for the monitoring and measuring, and our efforts are aligned to those reasons. Many IT organizations measure things without understanding the reason for the measurement only to become overwhelmed with data.

When do we stop?

This question acknowledges that measurements should not go on forever and that the effort expended to collect the measurements is valued.

Is anyone using the data?

This question ensures that the data is actually being used. It is quite common for organizations to begin collecting metrics and creating reports, only to deliver these reports to no one. This question must be asked periodically to ensure that more work is not created which does not add value.

Do we still need this?

Periodically, this question should be asked to ensure that metrics are being collected only for the things that are needed and extra effort is not being expended which does not add value.

Key Point

The CSI approach steps include:

What is the vision?

Where are we now?

Where do we want to be?

How do we get there?

Did we get there?

How do we keep the momentum going?

Key Point

Questions to ask regarding measurements include:

Why are we measuring?

When do we stop?

Is anyone using the data?

Do we still need this?

REASONS FOR MEASUREMENT

There are four reasons for service measurement. These reasons are:

To validate

> Measurements validate that previous decisions and actions were the correct decisions and actions.

To direct

> Measurements provide data that is used to make decisions and provide direction.

To justify

> Measurements provide proof that justify particular actions.

To intervene

> Measurements are used to intervene and provide changes in direction.

BASELINES

A baseline is a metric measured at a particular point in time in order to compare to a later measured metric. A baseline comparison can assist in determining if the process is improving or show general direction of trends. Baselines are the important starting point for later comparison. Therefore, in order to be recognized and accepted throughout the organization, baselines must be objective, documented, and agreed upon.

The CSI approach uses assessments to determine where an organization is at a certain point in time. These assessments document baselines that are referred to later as a point of comparison to see if the desired improvements have been made.

TYPES OF METRICS

There are three basic types of metrics that can be collected and used by CSI. Technology metrics are most common and are often collected today. Technology metrics are associated with the actual components and applications that make up a service.

Process metrics are intended to measure the performance of a process in an effort to improve process efficiency and effectiveness. These metrics take the form of critical success factors (CSFs), key performance indicators (KPIs), and activity metrics within the process.

Service metrics measure the overall ability of a service to achieve its goal. Service metrics measure end-to-end performance and often include individual technology metrics that correlate with each other to provide a view into the overall service performance.

> **Key Point**
>
> The three types of metrics include:
>
> Technology metrics
>
> Process metrics
>
> Service metrics

CSI Register

As multiple initiatives for improvement are identified, it is recommended to record these initiatives or opportunities in a CSI register under the ownership of the CSI manager.

The CSI register records opportunites for improvement and includes important information such as the category of the undertaking (small, medium, or large), time frame of the initiative (short-, medium-, or long-term) ,and overall priority.

> **Key Point**
>
> The CSI manager is responsible for the CSI register.

TERMS & DEFINITIONS

Benefits

Improvements

Value on investment (VOI)

Return on investment (ROI)

Governance

Baselines

CSI register

IMPORTANT POINTS

The major input to continual service improvement (CSI) is the service performance reports from service operation.

The major output of CSI is the service improvement plan (SIP) to service strategy.

The purpose of CSI is to ensure that services are continually aligned to meet changing business needs.

The scope of CSI includes the overall health of IT service management as a discipline, the continual alignment of the portfolio of IT services with the business needs, and the maturity of the enabling IT processes for each stage in the service lifecycle.

Governance helps to ensure fairness and transparency.

The PDCA cycle steps are Plan, Do, Check, Act.

The CSI approach steps are:

> What is the vision?
>
> Where are we now?
>
> Where do we want to be?
>
> How do we get there?
>
> Did we get there?
>
> How do we keep the momentum going?

The reasons to measure are to validate, to justify, to direct, and to intervene.

Metrics can be qualitative or quantitative.

CSI metrics include technology, process, and service metrics.

The CSI register maintains information about identified improvement initiatives.

The CSI manager is responsible for the CSI register.

SECTION REVIEW

1. These are used to establish a basis for later comparison:

   A. Baselines

   B. Snapshots

   C. Artifacts

   D. Trend Analysis

2. Which of the following is not a type of metric defined within CSI?

   A. Process metrics

   B. Service metrics

   C. Technology metrics

   D. Component metrics

3. The difference between the benefit achieved and the amount expended to achieve the benefit, expressed as a percentage, is called what?

   A. Improvement

   B. Value of investment (VOI)

   C. Benefit

   D. Return on investment (ROI)

4. Gains achieved through realization of improvements, usually, but not always, expressed in monetary terms is called what?

   A. Value of investment (VOI)

   B. Benefit

   C. Return on investment (ROI)

   D. Improvement

5. Activities for continual service improvement come naturally and do not have to be deliberately planned in the service lifecycle.

   A. True

   B. False

6. Which of the following is not a reason to measure?

   A. Intervention

   B. Justification

   C. Direction

   D. Financial

7. What are the steps in order of the Deming Cycle?

   A. Plan, Check, Do, Act

   B. Plan, Do, Act, Check

   C. Plan, Do, Check, Act

   D. Plan, Act, Check, Do

8. Which of the following is not within the scope of continual service improvement?

   A. Continual collection of requirements to improve services

   B. Maturity of the enabling of IT processes for each service in the service lifecycle

   C. Overall health of ITSM as a discipline

   D. Continual alignment of the portfolio of IT services with the business needs

9. The value to business of continual service improvement includes what?

   A. Lowering costs

   B. Improving value on investment (VOI)

   C. Improving service, quality and satisfaction

   D. All of the above

10. Metrics as defined within continual service improvement can be qualitative but not quantitative.

   A. True

   B. False

Comprehension

1. CSI metrics can be both qualitative and quantitative. Provide an example of both qualitative and quantitative metrics for a service or a process.

2. List the steps of the CSI approach and provide a brief description of each.

12

CONTINUAL SERVICE IMPROVEMENT PROCESS

OVERVIEW

Continual service improvement (CSI) is the stage of the service lifecycle that provides guidance in measuring and improving services including the processes, knowledge, capabilities, organization, and all other areas that support services. CSI ensures that an organization engages in disciplined practices to measure services, report on services, and identify opportunities for improvement.

The process within CSI is the 7-step improvement process. This process provides an approach for measuring services, including technologies and processes that support services; analyzing the data from measurement; developing useful information from the data; and presenting the knowledge to make better decisions regarding services.

7-STEP IMPROVEMENT PROCESS

OVERVIEW

The 7-step improvement process provides a disciplined approach to correlating data from a wide variety of measurements within a process or service. Through the 7-step improvement process, guidance is provided to ensure that the data collected is aligned to the need to collect data, and once collected, the data is properly analyzed to provide the knowledge and information needed to identify improvement opportunities.

PURPOSE

The purpose of the 7-step improvement process is to "define and manage the steps needed to identify, define, gather, process, analyze, present and implement improvements."[1]

The objectives of the 7-step improvement process are to:

"Identify opportunities for improving services, processes, tools, etc.

Reduce the cost of providing services and ensure that IT services enable the required business outcomes to be achieved

Identify what needs to be measured, analyzed, and reported to establish improvement opportunities

Continually review service achievements to ensure they remain matched to business requirements

Continually align and re-align services provided with the needs of the business

Understand what to measure, why it is being measured, and carefully define the successful outcome"[2]

---

1   Quoted text is from Continual Service Improvement © Crown copyright 2011 Reproduced under license from the Cabinet Office

2   Quoted text is from Continual Service Improvement © Crown copyright 2011 Reproduced under license from the Cabinet Office.

KEY CONCEPTS

There is nothing out of scope for the 7-step improvement process in that anything that is used to deliver services can be improved. The process includes analysis of the performance and capabilities of services, processes, partners and technology throughout the entire service lifecycle. The 7-step improvement process includes the continual alignment of the portfolio of IT services with the current and future business needs as well as the maturity of enabling IT processes for each service.

The 7-step improvement process ensures that an organization is making the best use of the technology that the organization has and strives to exploit new technology as it becomes available, provided there is a justifiable business case.

Also within scope of the 7-step improvement process is the organizational structure, the capabilities and skills of the people within the organization, and the roles and responsibilities needed to provide and support services.

ACTIVITIES

The 7-step improvement process fits into Deming's Plan-Do-Check-Act cycle discussed earlier. The Deming cycle provides steady, ongoing improvement and identification of these ongoing improvements is provided through appropriate measurements. The 7-step improvement process provides a structured approach to these measurements.

Another area that the 7-step improvement process fits into is the data-information-knowledge-wisdom (D-I-K-W) model discussed within knowledge management. Through the 7-step improvement process, the data collected is put into context to create information. This information is combined with our judgments and experience to provide knowledge, and the resultant improvements made from knowledge shows wisdom.

> **Key Point**
>
> The 7-Step improvement process fits within the Plan-Do-Check-Act cycle.

> **Key Point**
>
> The 7-Step Improvement Process fits within the D-I-K-W cycle

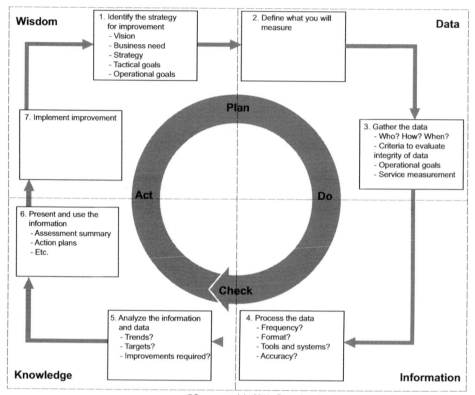

Figure - 7-step Improvement Process

Step 1 - Identify the strategy for improvement

In this step, the overall vision, business need, strategy, tactical and/ or operational goals are defined based on the scope of the process. This is where it is determined what should be measured to meet the overall vision, goal, and/or objective.

Step 2 - Define what you will measure

While service strategy and service design should have define this information early in the lifecycle of the service, CSI may approach this to determine how we operate today through the "Where are we now" question.

Step 3 - Gather the data

Data is gathered from the appropriate sources based on the goals and objectives identified. At this point the data is raw and no conclusions are drawn.

Step 4 - Process the data

In this step the data is processed in alignment with the critical success factors (CSFs) and key performance indicators (KPIs) specified. The goal of this step is to process data from multiple disparate sources to give it context within which it can be compared.

Step 5 - Analyze the information and data

As the data is brought more and more into context, it evolves from raw data into information from which answers can be provided regarding who, what, when, where and how as well as trends and the impact on the business. The analysis step is often overlooked in the urge to present data to management.

Step 6 - Present and use the information

In this step, the information is formatted in a way that it can be communicated to the various stakeholders to provide an accurate picture of the results of the improvement efforts. Knowledge is presented to the business in a form and manner that reflects their needs and assists them in determining the next steps.

Step 7 - Implement improvement

Knowledge gained is used to optimize, improve, and correct services and processes. From the issues identified, solutions are presented and wisdom is applied to the knowledge presented. The improvements that need to be taken are communicated to the organization. Following this step, a new baseline is established and the cycle begins again.

Key Point

The activities in the 7-Step Improvement Process are:

1. Identify the strategy for improvement

2. Define what you will measure

3. Gather the data

4. Process the data

5. Analyze the information and data

6. Present and use the information

7. Implement improvement

TERMS & DEFINITIONS

7-step improvement
process

IMPORTANT POINTS

The process in continual service improvement is the 7-step improvement process.

The 7-step improvement process fits within the overall plan-do-check-act (PDCA) cycle.

The 7-step improvement process fits within the data-information-knowledge-wisdom (D-I-K-W) model.

The steps in the 7-step improvement process are:

1. Identify the strategy for improvement
2. Define what you will measure
3. Gather the data
4. Process the data
5. Analyze the information and data
6. Present and use the information
7. Implement improvement

Once the last step in the 7-step improvement process is complete, a new baseline is established and the cycle begins again.

SECTION REVIEW

1. The 7-step improvement process fits within which model?

   A. Service model

   B. D-I-K-W model

   C. Incident model

   D. None of the above

2. How many steps are in the 7-step improvement process?

   A. 6

   B. 8

   C. 3

   D. 7

3. Which step of the 7-step improvement process is commonly overlooked?

   A. Gather the data

   B. Analyze the information and data

   C. Process the data

   D. Implement improvement

4. Which step is after the step of "implement improvement" in the 7-step improvement process

   A. None, the process is complete

   B. Identify the strategy for improvement

   C. The process starts again with gathering the data

   D. Optimization of services

5. Which step follows "gather the data" in the 7-step improvement process?

   A. Identify the strategy for improvement

   B. Analyze the information and data

   C. Process the data

   D. Present and use the information

13

TOOL AND TECHNOLOGY CONSIDERATIONS

OVERVIEW

Throughout this book, we have focused on processes. Processes, however, require the effective use of technology to support them and provide automation of the workflow within the process. In this chapter, some of the tools and technology considerations to support these processes are explored.

While ITIL® promotes a structured, disciplined, and process-oriented approach to IT service management, it is apparent that this cannot be accomplished without the use of tools and technology to assist. However, tools cannot implement these processes for an organization. The tools are only as good as the processes that they support.

Technology exists that assist greatly in automating good processes. This technology also assists in automating bad processes. The important consideration here is to ensure that the technology supports the processes, not defines the processes.

There are many reasons for turning to technology to assist with processes. People have a limited capacity for dealing with the inherent complexities of socio-technical systems. IT service management and its services are socio-technical systems. We cannot process as much information as a tool can to distill the information into what is truly important. Additionally, tools can assist with determining how the sub-systems affect each other.

SERVICE AUTOMATION

Service automation applies technology to automate routine activities and procedures. Through the use of service automation, the utility and warranty of services are improved. Service automation also assists with critical decision making during design and operation of services, including automating and documenting workflow, adjusting capacity, balancing workload, and optimizing the scheduling, routing and allocation of services and the resources they consume. Service automation also helps document the activities in a service, as well as capture knowledge of a service.

> **Key Point**
>
> Service automation improves the utility and warranty of services.

Many of the concepts that have been explored in this book are candidates for service automation. Some of these include:

Design and modeling of services

The service catalog

Pattern recognition and analysis (such as trend analysis)

Classification, prioritization, and routing of incidents, problems, Service requests, and changes

Detection and monitoring

Service optimization

Think about how banking, getting gas for your car, or traveling has changed over the last two decades. All of these industries are now assisted by service automation technology such as ATM machines, self-serve pumping machines and airline check-in kiosks that provide us the instant service we have come to expect.

SERVICE STRATEGY TOOLS

Part of service strategy is to understand how tools and technology can assist as a compensating factor for deficiencies in a service. Tools and technology can compensate for poor design, poor processes, and inadequate knowledge. While service strategy should work to improve design, processes, and knowledge, it cannot be done without the use of technology.

Service strategy benefits from simulation tools to evaluate the consequences of decisions prior to implementing them. Analytical models are used to evaluate the allocation of resources, as well as analyze demand patterns. Other tools used by service strategy include decision trees, queuing and work-flow models, forecasting models, and analysis of the variance of demand and resources.

SERVICE DESIGN TOOLS

Service design tools involve the use of tools to enable better design. These tools can speed up design, provide a higher-quality design, provide analysis of design options, as well as ensure that the design meets the requirements of the business. Tools used in service design can also ensure that standards and conventions are followed.

Modeling and prototyping are common types of tools used in service design to assist with optimizing the design of services and conducting "what if" analysis. These tools also ensure that interfaces and dependencies have been considered and validate the design of services to ensure they meet business requirements.

Some of the areas that design tools assist with include:

Hardware and software design

Environmental design

Process design

Data design

Service Transition Tools

Service transition tools can be classified into two types: enterprise tools and targeted transition tools. Enterprise tools include the tools that address the larger issue of IT service management. These tools are usually well integrated to provide a holistic approach to IT service management. At the core of many of these tools is the configuration management database that implements the CMS. Also, these tools usually include many types of support for network management, topology mapping, incident handling, service requests, change management, and many other areas.

Targeted service transition tools can be of many types to support the various activities of service transition. These tools are not limited to service transition activities, but may also provide support for other stages, as well.

Specifically, these tools include the following types:

Knowledge Management Tools

Knowledge management tools retain and propagate organizational knowledge. These tools assist with the management of documents, records, and content.

COLLABORATION TOOLS

Collaboration tools provide focused support for groups or teams that provide facilities for communication. Examples of collaboration tools include shared calendars, instant messaging, and email.

WORKFLOW MANAGEMENT

Workflow management tools assist with the automation of workflow, procedures or processes, as well as assist with workflow design, object routing, and event services.

CONFIGURATION MANAGEMENT SYSTEM (CMS)

The CMS contains details about the attributes and history of each CI and details important relationship between CIs. The definitive media library (DML) may be included.

SERVICE OPERATION TOOLS

The service operation stage of the service lifecycle is where value is delivered to the business. The processes in this stage involve communication, organization, and reporting. Tools and technology are required within this stage to facilitate this communication, organization, and reporting. Since the processes in this stage - incident management, problem management, request fulfillment, and event management - are so closely intertwined, it is expected that the tools for this stage of the service lifecycle support these processes in an integrated manner. These tools should also include integration to service asset and configuration management's CMS, change management and service level management.

The use of tools should also promote user self-help. A self-help solution available to the users provides knowledge of the services and assists with communication between IT and the users. This can reduce the staffing requirements at the service desk. The service desk can also benefit from tools through the use of an integrated approach to requests, problems, incidents, and any models or pre-defined workflows that can be developed within these tools. These tools can also provide direct access to the back-end automated processes, such as downloading new software to the desktop.

Discovery tools also can be leveraged to automate many of the activities involved in ensuring the environment is well-controlled and unauthorized changes are detected. These tools can also support the service operation stage of the service lifecycle through software distribution and license management.

Other tools can be leveraged to provide remote-control facilities that provide the ability to take over a user's computer remotely. Other diagnostic utilities should be considered as appropriate to better understand and resolve errors.

Reporting is a critical component of service operation to report how IT is meeting the needs of the business. Reporting tools should be considered to improve and automate reporting requirements. Part of the reporting may be provided through dashboards that show at a glance the overall operation of IT. As the IT organization matures and reporting is improved, integration to the business will show how technology relates to the business and how IT supports the business-desired outcomes. This is called business service management.

IMPORTANT POINTS

Tools and technology are important to assist with IT service management processes. However, tools should be considered only after the process has been designed. Tools support processes, not define processes.

Service automation improves the utility and warranty of services. Through Service automation, capacity and availability can be more easily adjusted.

Examples of service strategy tools include decision trees, queueing analysis tools, and forecasting tools.

Service design tools assist with the design of hardware, software, environment, processes, and data. Service design tools help ensure that standards and conventions are followed.

Service transition tools include the change management system, the CMS and CMDB, release and deployment tools such as software distribution tools, and the DML, as well as knowledge management tools to support the SKMS.

When considering service operation tools, an integrated suite of IT service management technology should be considered. The integrated suite should include considerations for self-help, workflow or process engines, an integrated CMDB, discovery and licensing technology, remote control, support for diagnostic utilities, reporting and dashboards, and BSM integration.

Section Review

1. When should tools be implemented to support IT service management processes?

   A. As soon as possible

   B. During the design of the supporting processes

   C. Once the process has been designed and the purpose of the tools to support the process is well understood

   D. IT service management does not require any support from underlying tools or technology

2. Which of the following is not an example of service strategy tools?

   A. Software distribution tools

   B. Queueing tools

   C. Decision trees

   D. Forecasting tools

3. Service automation assists with which of the following?

   A. Speeding up all processes to support services

   B. Improving the utility and warranty of a service

   C. Automating all processes to support a service

   D. Reducing the dependency of users to support the processes

4. Service design tools help to do what?

   A. Ensure standards and conventions are followed

   B. Implement applications more quickly

   C. Monitor services

   D. Respond to incidents effectively

5. Tools in service design assist with the design of what?

   A. Environment

   B. Data

   C. Hardware and software

   D. All of the above

6. Which of the following is not an example of a service transition tool?

   A. Tools to automate workflow

   B. Software distribution tools

   C. Content management System

   D. Event monitoring tools

7. When considering tools for service operation, considerations should be made to find the best tools in the market and integrate them all together after the CMDB has been selected and installed.

   A. True

   B. False

SECTION REVIEW ANSWERS

INTRODUCTION

1. _____ create value, remove risk of ownership from customers, facilitate outcomes customers want to achieve, and reduce the effects of constraints

   A. Resources

   B. Services

   C. Systems

   D. Processes

2. _____ is a set of specialized organizational capabilities for providing value to customers in the form of services

   A. Service management

   B. Information technology

   C. Technology management

   D. Service

3. Why might an organization want to use ITIL®?

   A. ITIL® is published good practice

   B. ITIL® is a validated framework

   C. ITIL® provides a basis on which to improve

   D. All of the above

4. ITIL® is a stand-alone, totally inclusive framework that eliminates the need to consider any other standard.

   A. True

   B. False

5. The ITIL® core volumes include service strategy, service design, continual service improvement and what other volumes?

   1. Service optimization
   2. Service operation
   3. Service release
   4. Service yransition

   A. 1 and 3

   B. 2 and 4

   C. 1 and 4

   D. 4 only

6. There are times when it is feasible to have more than one person accountable for an activity within a process.

   A. True

   B. False

7. Which of the following is NOT a characteristic of a process?

   A. Responds to a specific event (trigger)

   B. It is timely

   C. It is measurable and therefore performance driven

   D. It provides a specific output to a customer

8. What is the term defined by "units of organization specialized to perform certain types of work and responsible for specific outcomes?"

   A. Processes

   B. Functions

   C. Services

   D. Service management

9. The RACI Model is NOT used to identify which of the following roles?

    A. Who is responsible

    B. Who is accountable

    C. Who is consulted

    D. Who is charged

10. What is the term defined by "structured set of activities designed to accomplish a specific set of objectives?"

    A. Function

    B. Service

    C. Process

    D. Resource

SERVICE STRATEGY OVERVIEW

1. What is the major output of service strategy?

    A. Service lists

    B. Service level package (SLP)

    C. Service level agreement (SLA)

    D. Operational services

2. What is the purpose of service strategy?

    A. To provide the ability to think and act in a strategic manner

    B. To determine how to pay for services

    C. To justify ITIL® throughout the organization

    D. To ensure accountability of actions to an organization's shareholders

3. Service assets can best be described as what?

    A. The organization's capital purchases

    B. The ability to provide service to external customers

    C. A set of organizational capabilities for providing value to customers in the form of services

    D. Any capability or resources of a service provider.

4. Which of the following statements about value is most correct?

    A. The service provider determines the value of services

    B. The value of a service is determined by the customer

    C. Value of a service cannot be determined

    D. The customer's view of value is irrelevant

5. Service assets consist of what?

   A. Processes and functions

   B. Utility and warranty

   C. Capabilities and resources

   D. Financial capital, infrastructure, applications and information.

6. Which of the following statements is correct?

   A. Capabilities are intangible and resources are tangible.

   B. Capabilities are tangible and resources are intangible.

   C. Capabilities and resources are both tangible.

   D. Capabilities and resources are both intangible.

7. The value of a service is described in terms of what?

   A. Form and function

   B. Capabilities and resources

   C. Utility and warranty

   D. Applications and systems

8. Utility is best described as what?

   A. A promise or guarantee that a product or service will meet its requirements

   B. The functionality offered of a product or service.

   C. The added value that a service delivers to customers.

   D. None of the above.

9. A service works exactly as described but fails often due to lack of capacity. This is an example of what?

   A. High utility and high warranty

   B. High utility and low warranty

   C. Low utility and high warranty

   D. Low utility and low warranty

10. A service that delivers the basic outcomes desired by one or more customers is what?

   A. Supporting service

   B. Enabling service

   C. Enhancing service

   D. Core service

SERVICE STRATEGY PROCESSES

1. Which of the following is NOT a processes within service strategy?

   A. Service portfolio management

   B. Service catalog management

   C. Demand management

   D. Financial management

2. What is the purpose of service portfolio management (SPM)?

   A. Manage the service portfolio

   B. Maximize return at an acceptable risk

   C. Ensure proper governance of IT resources

   D. Match IT capabilities with demand for services

3. Which of the following is NOT a question answered by the service portfolio?

   A. How should our resources and capabilities be allocated?

   B. What is the availability of these services?

   C. What are the pricing or charge back models?

   D. Why should a customer buy these services?

4. The service pipeline is

   A. The list of services being considered as well as services in operation

   B. The list of services being considered before they go into operation

   C. The pipeline of requirements that should be considered for a new service

   D. The demand for application development resources

5. Which of the following is NOT a part of the service portfolio?

   A. Service specifications

   B. Service pipeline

   C. Service catalog

   D. Retired services

6. Which demand management focus involves the use of patterns of business activity and user profiles?

   A. Current

   B. Tactical

   C. Strategic

   D. Operational

7. Which demand management focus involves the use of differential charging to encourage customers to use IT services at less busy times?

   A. Tactical

   B. Strategic

   C. Current

   D. Operational

8. What are some possible sources of demand?

    A. People

    B. Processes

    C. Applications

    D. All of the above

9. The service portfolio documents services in terms of

    A. Outcomes

    B. Demand

    C. Value

    D. Capabilities

10. Which service strategy process has determining PBAs as an activity?

    A. Demand management

    B. Financial management

    C. Strategy management

    D. Service portfolio management

SERVICE DESIGN OVERVIEW

1. What is the major input to service design?

    A. Service design package (SDP)

    B. Service transition package (STP)

    C. Service level package (SLP)

    D. Service package (SP)

2. What is the major output from service design to service transition?

    A. Service design package (SDP)

    B. Service transition package (STP)

    C. Service level package (SLP)

    D. Service package (SP)

3. The purpose of service design is best described as what?

    A. To ensure value through the proper implementation of the functionality of a service

    B. The design of new or changed services for introduction into the live environment

    C. To ensure that cost-justifiable availability and capacity exist for current and future services

    D. To provide a logical model of the IT infrastructure and the relationships between components, applications, systems and services

4. The 4 Ps of service design include people, products, partners, and what other item?

   A. Vendors

   B. Positions

   C. Technology

   D. Processes

5. Ensuring that an entire service can be implemented, transitioned, and operated efficiently and effectively describes what?

   A. Five aspects of design

   B. 4 Ps of service design

   C. Functional specifications

   D. None of the above

6. The five aspects of design include which of the following?

   1. People

   2. Service solution

   3. Service management systems and tools

   4. Processes

   5. Technology and architectures

   6. Requirements and specifications

   7. Measurements and metrics

   A. 1, 3, 4, 5, 6

   B. 2, 3, 4, 5, 6

   C. 1, 3, 4, 6, 7

   D. 2, 3, 4, 5, 7

7. The service design package (SDP) is best described as what?

   A. A description of the 4 Ps of service design

   B. A set of documents defining all aspects of an IT service and its requirements though each stage of its lifecycle

   C. Everything necessary for the build, test, implementation and deployment of a service

   D. The business requirements for a new or changed service.

8. The service design package includes the service functional requirements, service design and topology, and what else?

   A. Service level requirements

   B. Service and operational management requirements

   C. Both A and B

   D. Neither A nor B

9. As an aspect of design, service management systems and tools might include what?

   A. Service portfolio

   B. Management requirements

   C. Processes

   D. People

SERVICE DESIGN PROCESSES

1. Service level management (SLM) represents IT as a service provider and

   A. Represents business interests to IT

   B. Manages the service desk

   C. Guarantees delivery of capabilities to the customer

   D. Improves all processes based on a continual improvement focus

2. Service level agreements should be consistent throughout the organization for all customers for all services.

   A. True

   B. False

3. The two views into the service catalog include:

   A. Vendor catalog and user catalog

   B. Business service catalog and technical service catalog

   C. User service catalog and business service catalog

   D. Technical service catalog and vendor catalog

4. Availability efforts are always reactive.

   A. True

   B. False

5. The term given for the business critical elements of a business process is called what?

   A. Business priority

   B. Critical business activity

   C. Critical business function

   D. Vital business function

6. What is the name given for the system that holds availability management reports, the availability plan, availability design criteria, and the availability testing schedule?

   A. Configuration management system (CMS)

   B. Availability management information system (AMIS)

   C. Capacity management information system (CMIS)

   D. Availability support system

7. What is the term used for the ability of a service, component, or CI to perform its agreed function when required?

   A. Availability

   B. Reliability

   C. Maintainability

   D. Serviceability

8. What process provides a point of focus and management for all capacity and performance-related issues, relating to both services and resources?

   A. Demand management

   B. Capacity management

   C. Availability management

   D. Service level management

9. What is the name given for the system that holds forecasts, the xapacity plan and capacity and performance reports, and data?

   A. Capacity management information system (CMIS)

   B. Configuration management system (CMS)

   C. Availability support system

   D. Availability management information system (AMIS)

10. What is the name of the process that aligns IT security with business security to ensure information security is effectively managed?

    A. Access management

    B. Information security management

    C. Availability management

    D. Network security management

11. What is the name of the process that is responsible for maintaining the ongoing recovery capability within the IT services and their supporting components?

    A. IT service continuity management

    B. IT service risk management

    C. Disaster management

    D. Risk management

SERVICE TRANSITION OVERVIEW

1. The main input to service transition is what?

   A. Service transition package (STP)

   B. Service level package (SLP)

   C. Service package (SP)

   D. Service design package (SDP)

2. The main output from service transition is what?

   A. Deployed service through early life support (ELS)

   B. Service level package (SLP)

   C. Service package (SP)

   D. Service design package (SDP)

3. The purpose of service transition is what?

   A. To manage the transition for a new, changed or retired service into production

   B. To ensure that all changes follow standardized processes and procedures

   C. To ensure that a new service can be properly supported until service operation can support the service on its own

   D. To ensure that services can be deployed into operation with minimal risk

4. What is described by the overlap between service transition and service operation to ensure that a service is adequately supported until service operation can support the service on its own?

   A. Organizational overlap

   B. Early life support
   C. Deployment

   D. Release considerations

5. What would NOT be stored in the definitive media library (DML)

   A. Definitive versions of electronic media

   B. Master copies of software

   C. Master copies of software documentation

   D. Backups of application data

6. The DML includes which of the following?

   A. A physical store only

   B. An electronic store only

   C. Both a physical and electronic store

   D. Neither a physical nor an electronic store

7. Which of the following is NOT an objective of service transition?

   A. To ensure there is minimal unpredictable impact on the production services, operations, and support organization

   B. To increase proper use of the services, underlying applications, and technology solutions

   C. Create a logic model of the IT infrastructure relating components, applications, systems, and services

   D. Provide clear and comprehensive plans that enable the customer and business change projects to align their activities with the service transition plans.

SERVICE TRANSITION PROCESSES

1. Which process ensures that standardized methods and procedures are used for efficient and prompt handling of all changes?

   **A. *Change management*
   B. Release and deployment management
   C. Knowledge management
   D. Service asset and configuration management

2. All changes should be treated the same, regardless of complexity, scope, or risk.

   A. True
   **B. *False*

3. What is the term used for the explicit plans that are made for all changes in the event of a change failure?

   A. IT service continuity management
   **B. *Remediation planning*
   C. Back out planning
   D. Post implementation review

4. The CAB is responsible for what?

   **A. *Evaluating high-impact requests for change*
   B. Performing a post implementation review of all changes
   C. Evaluating all requests for change
   D. Informing the business of impending outages to implement changes

5. Emergency changes have no place in change management.

   A. True
   **B. *False*

6. Before an emergency change is implemented, the CAB must be convened.

   A. True
   **B. *False*

7. What is the name of the process that provides a logical model of the IT infrastructure and holds its data in the CMS?

   A. Service modeling
   **B. *Service asset and configuration management*
   C. Release and deployment management
   D. Demand management

8. What is the name given for the place where definitive versions of software and other media are stored?

   A. Federated database
   **B. *Definitive media library*
   C. Definitive software library
   D. Software catalog

9. What is a release unit?

   A. A tested unit of code
   B. All of the hardware and software that make up a service
   C. A set of packages that is installed to support a service
   **D. *The portions of the IT infrastructure that are normally released together*

10. Which of the following cannot be stored in a database or management system?

    A. Knowledge

    B. Wisdom

    C. Data

    D. Information

11. What is the order of the knowledge spiral (DIKW model)?

    A. Collection->correlation->normalization->analysis

    B. Data->knowledge->wisdom->information

    C. Data->knowledge->information->wisdom

    D. Data->information->knowledge->wisdom

SERVICE OPERATION OVERVIEW

1. Service operation is where the _____ is delivered to the customer and the _____ of the organization is executed.

    A. service, coordination

    B. value, strategy

    C. application, availability

    D. Service transition package (STP), service level package (SLP)

2. The main input to service operation is what?

    A. Service performance reports

    B. Deployed service

    C. Service package (SP)

    D. Service level package (SLP)

3. The main output of service operation is what?

    A. Service performance teports

    B. Service transition package (STP)

    C. Service package (SP)

    D. Service level package (SLP)

4. The purpose of service operation is what?

    A. To coordinate and carry out the activities and processes required to deliver and manage services at agreed levels.

    B. Restore service as quickly as possible

    C. Be the single point of contact between IT and users

    D. Ensure services are constantly aligned and realigned to the needs of the business

5. What types of communication might be useful in service operation?

    A. Routine operational communication

    B. Reporting

    C. Communication relating to changes, exceptions and emergencies

    D. All of the above

6. In addition to the balance between responsiveness and stability, from the following list, which is NOT one of the other balance factors?

    A. Cost and quality

    B. Internal view and external view

    C. Communication and reporting

    D. Reactive and proactive

SERVICE OPERATION PROCESSES

1. What is the primary purpose of incident management?

    A. Remove problems and errors from the infrastructure

    B. Be the first point of contact for all calls from users

    C. Restore normal operation as quickly as possible

    D. Ensure best possible levels of availability

2. Incident models help to ensure what?

    A. All incidents can be resolved quickly

    B. Problems can be removed from the environment

    C. Common incidents can be resolved through pre-defined steps

    D. Workarounds are available for all incidents

3. Urgency and impact determine what?

    A. Work order number

    B. Priority

    C. Escalation

    D. Resolution timescales

4. The term used when an incident is forwarded to a specialized team is called what?

    A. Functional referral

    B. Functional escalation

    C. Hierarchic escalation

    D. Workload balancing

5. The term used when an incident is forwarded to someone with more authority is called what?

   A. Functional referral

   B. Functional escalation

   C. Hierarchic escalation

   D. Workload balancing

6. The process responsible for handling requests from the user is known as:

   A. Change management

   B. Request management

   C. Incident management

   D. Request fulfillment

7. Which of the following is an example of a service request?

   A. A request to change the functionality of an application

   B. A request for a new application to be developed

   C. User requests the memory on his or her computer be upgraded

   D. A request for a memory upgrade on a server

8. The process that is responsible to identify and remove errors from the infrastructure is what?

   A. Problem management

   B. Error control

   C. Error management

   D. Incident management

9. Which group outside of IT would be useful for access management to have a relationship with?

   A. Finance

   B. Procurement

   C. Sales

   D. Human resources

10. A temporary resolution to resolve an incident is known as what?

    A. Change

    B. Workaround

    C. Problem model

    D. Fix

11. Service operation processes include incident management, event management and problem management. What processes are missing from this list?

    A. Access management and availability management

    B. Access management and request fulfillment

    C. Access management and capacity management

    D. Request management and user management

SERVICE OPERATION FUNCTIONS

1. Which of the following is a function within service operation?

   A. Service desk
   B. Vendor management
   C. Request fulfillment
   D. Capacity management

2. The applications management function includes the teams that are responsible for applications development.

   A. True
   B. False

3. The function that is responsible to be the single point of contact between the service provider and the users is called what?

   A. IT operations management
   B. Service desk
   C. Technical management
   D. Applications management

4. The function that is responsible for managing incidents and calls is called what?

   A. IT operations management
   B. Service desk
   C. Technical management
   D. Applications management

5. Which of the following is not a service desk structure?

   A. Local service desk
   B. Central service desk
   C. Virtual service desk
   D. Help desk

6. What is the term used for users with exceptional knowledge of a service that may assist the service desk with service-related issues?

   A. Trained users
   B. Super users
   C. Special users
   D. Application developers

7. What things must the service desk have access to in order to be most efficient and effective?

   A. All incident records
   B. Known errors
   C. CMS
   D. All of the above

8. The function that is responsible for providing technical skills in support of IT services and management of the IT infrastructure is called what?

   A. Service desk
   B. Applications management
   C. Technical management
   D. IT operations management

9. The function that is responsible for managing applications throughout their lifecycle is called what?

   A. Applications management

   B. Technical management

   C. IT Operations management

   D. Service desk

10. IT operations management includes what other two functions?

    A. Job scheduling and batch management

    B. Operations control and facilities management

    C. Capacity management and availability management

    D. Service desk and request fulfillment

CONTINUAL SERVICE IMPROVEMENT

1. These are used to establish a basis for later comparison:

   A. Baselines

   B. Snapshots

   C. Artifacts

   D. Trend analysis

2. Which of the following is not a type of metric defined within CSI?

   A. Process metrics

   B. Service metrics

   C. Technology metrics

   D. Component metrics

3. The difference between the benefit achieved and the amount expended to achieve the benefit, expressed as a percentage, is called what?

   A. Improvement

   B. Value of investment (VOI)

   C. Benefit

   D. Return on investment (ROI)

4. Gains achieved through realization of improvements, usually, but not always, expressed in monetary terms is called what?

   A. Value of investment (VOI)

   B. Benefit

   C. Return on investment (ROI)

   D. Improvement

5. Activities for continual service improvement come naturally and do not have to be deliberately planned in the service lifecycle.

    A. True

    B. False

6. Which of the following is not a reason to measure?

    A. Intervention

    B. Justification

    C. Direction

    D. Financial

7. What are the steps in order of the Deming cycle?

    A. Plan, check, do, act

    B. Plan, do, act, check

    C. Plan, do, check, act

    D. Plan, act, check, do

8. Which of the following is not within the scope of continual service improvement?

    A. Continual collection of requirements to improve services

    B. Maturity of the enabling of IT processes for each service in the service lifecycle

    C. Overall health of ITSM as a discipline

    D. Continual alignment of the portfolio of IT services with the business needs

9. The value to business of continual service improvement includes what?

    A. Lowering costs

    B. Improving value on investment (VOI)

    C. Improving service, quality and satisfaction

    D. All of the above

10. Metrics as defined within continual service improvement can be qualitative but not quantitative.

    A. True

    B. False

CONTINUAL SERVICE IMPROVEMENT PROCESS

1. The 7-step improvement process fits within which model?

   A. Service model

   B. D-I-K-W model

   C. Incident model

   D. None of the above

2. How many steps are in the 7-step improvement process?

   A. 6

   B. 8

   C. 3

   D. 7

3. Which step of the 7-step improvement process is commonly overlooked?

   A. Gather the data

   B. Analyze the information and data

   C. Process the data

   D. Implement improvement

4. Which step is after the step of "implement improvement" in the 7-step improvement process

   A. None, the process is complete

   B. Identify the strategy for improvement

   C. The process starts again with gathering the data

   D. Optimization of services

5. Which step follows "gather the data" in the 7-step improvement process?

   A. Identify the strategy for improvement

   B. Analyze the information and data

   C. Process the data

   D. Present and use the information

TOOL AND TECHNOLOGY CONSIDERATIONS

1. When should tools be implemented to support IT service management processes?

    A. As soon as possible

    B. During the design of the supporting processes

    C. Once the process has been designed and the purpose of the tools to support the process is well understood

    D. IT service management does not require any support from underlying tools or technology

2. Which of the following is not an example of service strategy tools?

    A. Software distribution tools

    B. Queueing tools

    C. Decision trees

    D. Forecasting tools

3. Service automation assists with which of the following?

    A. Speeding up all processes to support services

    B. Improving the utility and warranty of a service

    C. Automating all processes to support a service

    D. Reducing the dependency of users to support the processes

4. Service design tools help to do what?

    A. Ensure standards and conventions are followed

    B. Implement applications more quickly

    C. Monitor services

    D. Respond to incidents effectively

5. Tools in service design assist with the design of what?

    A. Environment

    B. Data

    C. Hardware and software

    D. All of the above

6. Which of the following is not an example of a service transition tool?

    A. Tools to automate workflow

    B. Software distribution tools

    C. Content management system

    D. Event monitoring tools

7. When considering tools for service operation, considerations should be made to find the best tools in the market and integrate them all together after the CMDB has been selected and installed.

    A. True

    B. False

COMPREHENSION SAMPLE ANSWERS

INTRODUCTION

1. Describe the roles of the service owner and process owner.

   ### Sample Answer

   The service owner is accountable for the individual services and ensures that the processes that support that service are engaged with that service. Process owners are accountable for individual processes that support services. Process owners ensure that the processes are engaged with the services that they support.

2. Discuss briefly why an organization could benefit from the concepts of service management instead of technology management?

   ### Sample Answer

   Your answer may vary, but providing technology only answers part of the business needs. The business needs solutions, not technology. IT as a service provider provides these solutions through services that are better aligned to the business desired outcomes. Through services, IT can better understand the true needs of the business and can provide the services required to deliver value to the business.

SERVICE STRATEGY OVERVIEW

1. List the types and examples of service assets. Which are tangible and which are intangible?

   ### Sample Answer

   Service assets are any capability or resource of a service provider.

   The capabilities of a service provider are intangible and include the knowledge and skills of the organization, the processes, procedures and organization.

   The resources of a service provider are tangible and include the financial capital, infrastructure, applications and information.

   People are both capabilities and resources.

2. Most households subscribe to cable or satellite television. What are the core and supporting services for this service? Which are enabling services and which are enhancing services?

   ### Sample Answer

   The core service for cable television depends on what the customer's desired outcomes are. For most people, the desired outcome is to get a clear picture for the shows they want to watch. This would be a core service.

   Supporting services are those things that come with cable television that are in addition to our desired outcomes. Some supporting services enhance our experience with cable television. These services are the enhancing service. Other services enable the cable television service.

We usually do not have direct interaction with these enabling services. These are the enabling services.

Examples of enhancing services might include:

>   Video on demand
>
>   Universal remote
>
>   Movie packages
>
>   Sports packages
>
>   The ability to record programs through a DVR

Examples of enabling services might include:

>   Cable network infrastructure
>
>   Satellite services
>
>   Billing services

The combination of the core service, enhancing services and enabling services are bundled together. This bundling is the service package that the customer receives.

SERVICE STRATEGY PROCESSES

1. List, and provide a brief overview of the processes within the service strategy stage of the service lifecycle.

   ### Sample Answer

   The processes within service strategy include service portfolio management, demand management and financial management.

   Service portfolio management is a dynamic method for governing investments in service management across the enterprise and managing them for value.

   Demand management is a set of activities that understand and influence customer demand for services and the provision of capacity to meet these demands.

   Financial management provides financial input and output to other processes to enable more qualified and higher quality financial decision making.

2. In your organization, how does financial management play a role? Additionally, how could financial management support the processes throughout the service lifecycle?

   ### Sample Answer

   You specific answer will vary dependent upon your organization.

   Generally, financial management plays a role throughout the service lifecycle. In service strategy, financial management assists with the business case for investments in services as well as the approach not only to specific services, but the service strategy overall.

In service design, financial management assists all processes in determining what the most cost-effective approach would be in selection of technology to support the service as well as processes to support the service. Financial management assists with the evaluation of the availability (availability management) and capacity (capacity management) of a service, the approach to continuity (IT service continuity management) and security (information security management) as well as selection of suppliers and the specifics within the contracts (supplier management). Financial management plays a key role in service catalog management and service level management by providing financial information to better communicate with users and customers.

In service transition, financial costs of CIs will be collected and stored in service asset and configuration management. Financial management assists with decision making regarding the approach to provide changes (change management), deploy services (release and deployment management) and collect and maintain information and knowledge (knowledge management).

In service operation, financial management helps with decision making regarding the cost of restoring service (incident management), addressing the resolution of underlying errors (problem management), detecting events and determining the appropriate control action (event management) and optimizing the fulfillment of requests in a cost effective manner (request fulfillment).

Continual service improvement is, in part, driven by financial optimization in determining which services to improve and evaluating the options to improve them.

SERVICE DESIGN OVERVIEW

1. The service design package (SDP) is an important output of service design. What are some of the examples of what the service design package includes?

Sample Answer

The service design package includes everything necessary for the build, test, deployment and operation of a service. Some of the things included in an SDP includes:

Requirements

Functional requirements

Operational requirements

Transition requirements

Measurement plans

Technical architecture designs

Solution designs

Process designs

Service management tools requirements and designs

SERVICE DESIGN PROCESSES

1. Which processes within service design include activities that occur in other service lifecycle stages? What are some of the process activities?

Sample Answer

All of the processes with service design have activities in other service lifecycle stages. Every process is concerned with ongoing improvement of the process as well as the services the process supports.

Service level management assists in the design of services as well as reviews services within service operation and seeks to improve services as part of a continual service improvement effort.

Supplier management assess the need for suppliers in service design, and ensures that the suppliers are part of the transition of the service as appropriate. In service operation, supplier management actively manages the supplier to ensure that the suppliers are meeting the terms of their contracts.

Availability management designs availability of services in service design as well as designs availability standards. In service transition, availability management tests availability of services. In service operation, availability management monitors availability and provides availability reports.

Capacity management designs capacity of services in service design. In service transition, capacity management tests the performance of services through load testing of services. In service operation, capacity management monitors capacity and provides capacity reports.

Service catalog management prepares the service definition for inclusion into the service catalog during service design. In service operation, service catalog management manages the service catalog including any systems that support the service catalog if the service catalog is automated.

IT service continuity management develops an overall strategy for continuity, designs continuity in service design, tests continuity in service transition and ensures that an organization is prepared in the event of a disaster within service operation. As part of continual service improvement, IT service continuity management strives to improve the continuity plan throughout the service lifecycle.

Information security management develops an overall strategy for security, designs security in service design, tests security in service transition and ensures the security of information in service operation through the evaluation of security-related incidents and problems.

2. Before committing to a specific level of service within a service level agreement (SLA), service level management must consider all other service design processes. Why?

Sample Answer

All other processes assist in the design, transition, operation and improvement of a service. Service level management must understand the capabilities of these processes prior to committing to a specific level of service with the customer. Once a specific level of service has been committed, it is the responsibility of all processes to meet that level of service.

SERVICE TRANSITION OVERVIEW

1. Describe early life support. Why is early life support important when transitioning a new service into production?

   ### Sample Answer

   Early life support (ELS) is the overlap between service transition and service operation. While it would be desired that services, once delivered, operate exactly as expected, this is often not true. ELS helps to ensure that during the critical early operation of a service, that any modifications to a service can be made in a timely manner in order to increase the value delivered to customers.

SERVICE TRANSITION PROCESSES

1. Discuss how the CMS may be used by other processes throughout the service lifecycle. Would this be useful in your organization? Why?

   ### Sample Answer

   Your answer will vary but the CMS is used to underpin every other process. All processes use the CMS to be efficient and effective. Some examples include:

   Incident management uses the CMS to perform initial diagnosis.

   Problem management uses the CMS for root cause analysis.

   Financial management stores financial data regarding asset within the CMS.

   Availability and capacity management use the CMS to improve availability and capacity.

2. Describe the different types of change in change management. Why should an organization determine the types of change and why is this important?

   ### Sample Answer

   IT deals with many different types of change of varying scope, cost and complexity. Categorizing changes into change types assists an organization with developing a process that is applicable to the types of change they experience. This results in being able to respond to changes in an appropriate manner instead of lumping all changes together.

   The specific types of change documented in ITIL® include:

Standard changes are the operational, pre-approved changes that occur on a regular basis. These types of changes are low-risk, common, recurrent, well understood and usually associated with a well-defined change model. Some service request can be standard changes.

Emergency changes are types of changes that must be performed to prevent loss or disruption to the business. Emergency changes should be reserved for changes that are truly emergencies and not as a mechanism to force a change through the process. Emergency changes inherently involve risk due to the usually extreme time constraints and must be performed carefully.

Normal changes are changes that do not fall under other change types. These types of changes are usually more complex than standard changes, are higher risk or higher impact, and are usually reviewed by the change advisory board.

3. Describe how release and deployment management works with change management. Why are these processes separate?

Sample Answer

Release and deployment is the process of actually moving changes into production through well-defined processes. Change management manages the changes when they are submitted through the life of that change.

The processes are separate to ensure that changes can be properly managed while also assuring that processes and procedures are put in place to evaluate the set of changes going into production and ensuring that they are deployed correctly.

SERVICE OPERATION OVERVIEW

1. Describe the inputs and outputs of service operation

Sample Answer

The input to service operation is the service transition package (STP). The STP identifies everything about that service through the development of the strategy, design, build, test, implementation and deployment of that service. In order to be most effective and efficient, service operation needs as much information as possible about a service to ensure that the service can be properly supported.

The major output of service operation is the service performance reports to CSI. Through these reports of operational services, CSI can identify opportunities for improvement and include these improvement opportunities when conducting service reviews with the business.

2. Describe why communication is important in service operation. What are some examples of communication from other service lifecycle stages into service operation?

Sample Answer

Service operation needs communication with other service lifecycle stages to ensure that they are well-informed of future services and changes to services. Throughout the service lifecycle, service operations must be involved to ensure that service operation is properly prepared in terms of operational management, skills, resources, abilities and funding to support these future services.

SERVICE OPERATION PROCESSES

1. Describe how an incident may result in a problem and trace the flow through final resolution.

   ### Sample Answer

   Incidents can have a short life span (measured in minutes) to a long life span (measured in months). Ideally, most incidents will be resolved at the service desk through pre-defined resolutions or workarounds.

   Some incidents will result in a problem record being created. Problem management will evaluate this problem and perform root cause analysis to determine where the error is that caused the problem and the resulting incident(s). Once the error is found, problem management will determine the appropriate resolution. A resolution to remove the error may include submitting a request for change (RFC) to change management.

   Change management will evaluate this RFC and manage the change through its life. Once the change has been approved, release and deployment management will build the change and deploy it into production.

   Once the change has been made in the production environment, problem management will review the change to ensure that it resolves the problem. Upon closure of the problem, incident management may review any related incidents to provide feedback to users regarding the permanent resolution of their incidents. Incident management will also have additional knowledge available re-garding the original incident, any related problems and errors, and the change that was made to resolve the incident.

2. What are some reasons that a user's access to a service may require modification?

   ### Sample Answer

   Users do not stay in the same role forever. Users could retire, resign or pass away resulting in the need to revoke access to services. Users could also be promoted or be transferred to other departments or divisions resulting in their access being modified. This modification may be to revoke some access while enabling other access. Users may also be on temporary leave though extended vacations, leaves of absence or sabbaticals resulting in their access being suspended or restricted.

3. How might the known error database (KEDB) be used in the processes within service operation.

   ### Sample Answer

   The known error database (KEDB) contains information regarding any known errors in the environment and their workarounds. When an incident occurs, the service desk may consult the KEDB to identify the error that caused the incident. Once identified, the related workaround may be used to restore service.

   The KEDB may also be used within service operation to prioritize problems and errors in the environment and create a targeted action plan to resolve these problems and errors.

4. What determines what is a service request and what is not a service request? Why are

some things service requests and others are not?

Sample Answer

Service requests are requests from users. Keep in mind that IT staff may also be considered users. A service request is a call from someone that is not an incident. In other words, somebody needs something from IT but their service is not down. Service requests can be automated through tools. An example of an automated service request may be a software request that is submitted through an internal web site and fulfilled through automated software distribution tools.

Service requests may also include standard changes. An example of a service request that is also a standard change is a request to upgrade the memory in a user's laptop. This request is likely supported by a request model that predefines the steps necessary to fulfill that request including identifying the source for the upgrade, the steps to perform the upgrade, and any record keeping (such as updating the CMS) that may be required.

SERVICE OPERATION FUNCTIONS

1. The service desk structures may be combined for some organizations. Describe an example of an organization that may combine service desk structures.

Sample Answer

Organizations may structure themselves in many different ways. One example of the use of a combination of service desk structures is an organization that has a core infrastructure organization and a field services organization. The core infrastructure organization provides services that are common to all of their customers. These services are technical and infrastructure-related and are included in a service catalog. These services are supported by a central service desk that resides in a single location.

The field services groups provide business-related services to their customers. Their primary focus is on application development and support for the different business units located around the region. In this case, each of these field services units has their own set of services that are published in their service catalog. In this case, the field services units have established local service desks for their specific customers.

Note that there are multiple service catalog involved in this scenario. Service catalogs are focused on who the organizations customers are, not always dividing IT and business. In this case, the infrastructure IT group has field IT as their customer. Even though the infrastructure IT group's service catalog may be technical in nature, it is still considered a business service catalog because these services are focused on customer outcomes and these services are visible to customers.

2. Describe how technical management and application management support the activities within the service lifecycle.

Sample Answer

Technical management and application management are essentially all of the people within IT that are not at the service desk and not part of applications development. (This may be overly simplistic, but it makes the point) These are the people that perform many of the activities throughout the service lifecycle. They design availability and capacity of services, create availability and capacity reports, design and support continuity, support incident and problem management, create and document knowledge for the SKMS, define technical architectures and identify opportunities for improvement, among many other things.

CONTINUAL SERVICE IMPROVEMENT

1. CSI metrics can be both qualitative and quantitative. Provide an example of both qualitative and quantitative metrics for a service or a process.

Sample Answer

Your answer will vary. However, suppose that we support a corporate communications service that has been defined as including e-mail, electronic mailing lists, Internet chat and other forms of electronic communication. Qualitative metrics may include the rate of e-mail transfer and the response times for the instant messages. Other qualitative metrics may include user satisfaction survey ratings.

Quantitative metrics may include the number of e-mails sent, the number of instant messages sent and received as well as the number of users. Quantitative metrics may also include the number of incidents reported within a given time period.

2. List the steps of the CSI approach and provide a brief description of each.

Sample Answer

The CSI approach steps include the following:

1 - What is the Vision?

Identifying the business vision, mission, goals, and objectives that need to be addressed.

2 - Where are we now?

339

Performing baseline assessments that obtain an accurate, unbiased snapshot of where the organization is. These assessments measure the organization in a objective manner to provide a basis for comparison later.

3. Where do we want to be?

Identification of measurable targets that detail the CSI plan to achieve higher quality service provision. These measurable targets should be objective.

4 - How do we get there?

Performing service and process improvements developed based on the principles defined in the vision.

5 - Did we get there?

Monitoring metrics and measurements that ensure milestones were achieved, process compliance is high, and business objectives and priority are met.

6 - How do we keep the momentum going?

Identification of additional opportunities for improvement.

Index

Made in the USA
Middletown, DE
30 November 2017